CARE
OF
THE DOG

CARE OF THE DOG

by

CHARLES LEEDHAM

CHARLES SCRIBNER'S SONS

NEW YORK

For Brutus I and Brutus II

and Cato I

> *not Romans, but friends*

ACKNOWLEDGMENTS

Grateful acknowledgment is made to Mr. Warren Bushman, who took the photographs for this book; to Natalie and Monroe Stebbins for their help with the chapters on mating and whelping, and to the many other people who assisted with the manuscript.

The author is especially grateful to Dr. John Whitehead, Director of the Hospital and Clinic, ASPCA, New York City, for his invaluable assistance in checking the manuscript for technical accuracy.

FOREWORD

For many years there has been a need for a basic book on dog care for the average pet owner—one which would acquaint the reader with the facts of canine life and health, with what may go wrong and how to take the first steps in doing something about it, and with the proper care and feeding of the normal, healthy puppy or dog. "Care of the Dog" fills that need. It is both a primer and a manual of care and feeding, approached from the viewpoint of a reader who may know nothing at all of dogs when he first picks up the book.

While other books have been written on the subject, many of these have overlooked the basics needed by the average owner, and have placed considerable emphasis upon specific treatments for certain conditions, giving drug doses and methods of administration, and other technical procedures never intended for the pet owner. Such literature, in amateur hands, usually does more harm than good. Not only are disease conditions falsely diagnosed and thus improperly treated, but the time lost before professional aid is finally sought may well spell the difference between the life and death of a beloved pet.

Such is not the case in this refreshing new book presented by Charles Leedham. The author has followed the dog from birth to old age, and carefully covered the relevant points of care and health vital to the pet owner, but there has been no attempt to provide, between the covers of a book intended for the layman, a substitute for the veterinarian.

The important commonly occurring disease states are discussed simply, yet comprehensively, in a most orderly and helpful fashion—informing the dog owner of the nature and symptoms of the various diseases, conditions and injuries so that early recognition can be made and veterinary aid promptly secured when needed. In cases of injury or poisoning, first aid measures have been carefully outlined. General care and preventive medicine are fully and accurately covered through the book, as well as simple home treatments for minor situations not requiring the services of a veterinarian.

The necessity of getting the new puppy off to a proper start, with adequate diet, preventive vaccinations and worming, is laid out in clear terms. One entire section is devoted to the puppy's psychological development, based on recent research in animal behavior. This section alone would make the book worthwhile, as it points out the importance of owner-pet relationships during certain critical periods of the puppy's mental growth which will have a profound effect on the animal's ability to relate properly with people in later life.

The reader will find this book filled with useful information presented in an interesting and highly readable style. It presents the knowledge every dog owner should have, and is a book which can be freely recommended by veterinarians to their clients in the interest of better dog care.

John E. Whitehead, V.M.D.

New York, N.Y.

CONTENTS

Anatomical diagram of the dog, courtesy of
Gaines Research Center, New York

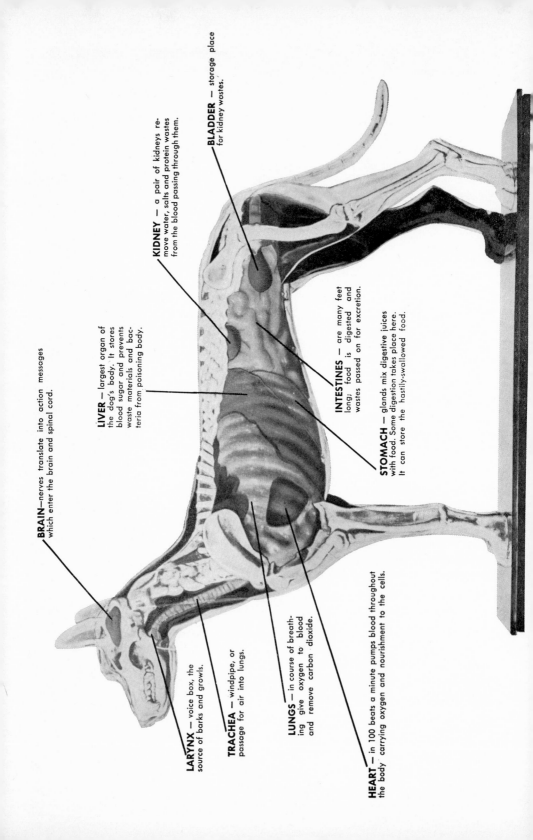

BRAIN—nerves translate into action messages which enter the brain and spinal cord.

LIVER — largest organ of the dog's body. It stores blood sugar and prevents waste materials and bacteria from poisoning body.

KIDNEY — a pair of kidneys remove water, salts and protein wastes from the blood passing through them.

BLADDER — storage place for kidney wastes.

INTESTINES — are many feet long; food is digested and wastes passed on for excretion.

STOMACH — glands mix digestive juices with food. Some digestion takes place here. It can store the hastily-swallowed food.

LARYNX — voice box, the source of barks and growls.

TRACHEA — windpipe, or passage for air into lungs.

LUNGS — in course of breathing give oxygen to blood and remove carbon dioxide.

HEART — in 100 beats a minute pumps blood throughout the body carrying oxygen and nourishment to the cells.

THE NATURE OF THE DOG

IF YOU know as much about your own body and how it works as the average person, then you know more about how a dog works than you probably imagined. Both being mammals, man and dog are built along strikingly similar lines, part for part and function for function. Each has a four-chambered heart for pumping blood, with arteries and veins to carry it. Each has a pair of lungs for breathing, and nearly identical systems for getting the air into the bloodstream. Each has stomach, pancreas, liver, kidneys, large intestine, small intestine, essentially the same bones in the same places (skull, jawbone, spinal column, ribs, shoulder blade, pelvic girdle, radius, ulna, tibia, fibula) with the obvious exception of the caudal or tail bones in the dog.

While the understanding of this comparison may be of little immediate use to you, it will stand you in good stead in the general consideration of your dog's health and well-being. Too many people have a tendency to think of a dog, however well-beloved, simply as an item that may get out of order and require repairs or adjustments—much as they think of their television set, and with as little conception of the inner workings.

This comparison of dog-to-human must not, however, be held to as a strict one-to-one identity, for there *are* differences, many of them not too obvious. There are certain drugs, for example, safely taken by humans, yet fatal to dogs in minute quantities. Thus the comparison should not be taken as license to dose a dog with the pills and nostrums designed for human ills.

There are diseases of dogs which do not affect humans. The same applies in reverse, but this number is rapidly dwindling as veterinarians find or suspect an increasing number of human ailments in their patients.

1

Dogs suffer, for example, from muscular dystrophy, tuberculosis, cancer, pneumonia, prostate troubles, and so on down an unpleasant list of ailments which most people would never associate with dogs. There are internal and external parasites afflicting dogs often and humans rarely, due less to physical differences than to cirmumstances and conditions of life.

Therefore, for the moment, and holding reservations, consider the dog as being astonishingly like a man, with a different posture, a smaller brain, and a tail. Having established this, the major part of the coming discussions will be concerned with the distinctions as they exist and as they may affect the health and functioning of your dog.

SKIN AND HAIR

The major external difference here is the obvious one, that the dog simply has more body hair than humans. Where humans have adopted clothes, the dog's own hair serves him as insulation against both cold and heat. Barring skin damage or infection, the dog's hair is replaced as it falls out or sheds, maintaining essentially the same coat from youth to extreme old age. Despite extensive knowledge of the structure of hairs, skin layers, hair follicles and secretions, little enough is known of the true mechanisms of hair growth and maintenance—why, for example, people grow bald with age and dogs don't.

The dog has considerably more—and more active—hair erector muscles, the tiny muscles that cause a dog's backhair to rise when he is angry or fearful. These muscles have little if any physical use, being only psychologically useful in times of stress. The mechanism is a simple one —the animal in a stress situation, one of anger or fear, is at an advantage if he appears to be larger in the eyes of an enemy. Being covered with hair, if the hair all stands up, he will appear larger. The hoped-for result, of course, is that the enemy will be impressed. While in cats the amount of body surface which can be involved in this activity is considerable, in dogs the area has been reduced to an irregular strip on the back, from the tail to the top of the head. In humans, the area has been further reduced to the back of the neck, the familiar prickling sensation in fear situations, when one's hair can quite literally "stand on end."

Although in general the dog's skin contains the same glands as the human's, the sweat glands are severely restricted in their function. Contrary to popular opinion, the dog does have sweat glands all over his body, but they function to regulate skin temperature far more than internal temperature. For purposes of comparison, although it may not be strictly accurate, the dog can safely be considered as not sweating. This is one of the reasons dogs are more prone to heat exhaustion than the average human—they are unable to cool themselves through the evaporation of a coating of perspiration. Dogs eliminate a great deal of their bodily heat through direct dry radiation (the warm feeling of the skin) and through breathing. Once these methods are operating at full heat-dispersal capacity, which is not as high as that of sweat-evaporation, a slight increase in atmospheric heat can seriously affect a dog.

The various skin parasites which plague dogs are largely the result of condition of life rather than special physiology. Fleas, lice, ticks and the like simply have a better chance with a dog, who lies unprotected on the ground, who has a thick coat to hide the beasts, and no good way to communicate the sensations of a beginning infestation to his owners and caretakers. If your dog lived in your identical circumstances—slept in bed, never ventured outside without his shoes on, bathed daily or nearly so, and had little hair except on the top of his head, he would have just about as little trouble with external parasites as you have.

One of the major apparent differences in the dog's skin is its ability to heal itself after cuts, gashes and scrapes. This is, at least partially, just that—apparent. It is true that the majority of dogs are hardier than humans, more resistant to infection, and this is in part because they are generally in better shape. Additionally, a dog's minor wounds are usually left open to the sun and air, two of the best healers known to man or dog. In human history, before the discovery of antiseptics and emmolients, people suffered and recovered from skin wounds, untreated, which would horrify modern citizens, and probably even modern dogs.

It is also a matter of attitude and communication, which are responsible for quite a number of misapprehensions about dogs. Tough though they are, millions of dogs have died over the years from infected skin abrasions, but one seldom hears much about it, dog mortality and pathology being of less interest than human.

THE SKELETON

The skeletal structure of the mammal is startlingly adaptable. From one end of the mammal group to the other, the bones, their positions and functions, remain much the same, though the bones vary in size from animal to animal. The giraffe, to quote an extreme example, has the same cervical (neck) vertebrae as a human, or a dog. They are simply fantastically elongated. The tiniest field-mouse has the same leg bones as an elephant, working in essentially the same way. Only the size is different.

If you stand a dog on his hind legs, or put a human in a dog-like position, the similarity becomes more striking. Put the human on his toe and finger tips, and even the seemingly dissimilar hands and arms, legs and feet assume almost an identity. This is the point at which most people think there must be a basic difference, for a dog's legs look quite different, especially the hind legs which appear to bend backwards at what would be the human knee. But the identity is there. Take the hind leg in comparison to the human leg:

Beginning at the top, there is the same ball-and-socket joining the upper leg bone (femur) to the hip girdle. Then there is the knee joint quite high up the leg, nearly hidden in the dog's heavy upper leg. The two lower leg bones follow (tibia and fibula) and end at the wrong-looking bend, which is in fact exactly analagous to the human heel. From the "heel," the lower part of the dog's leg is in actuality foot bones, the dog standing on what would be the ball of the human foot, the "shin" being the long bones of the human foot.

The position of the dog is considerably better in an engineering sense than the erect human posture. The various internal organs of the dog are suspended from the skeleton in quite an orderly manner, while in the human they are in effect piled one atop the other, causing all sorts of stresses and malfunctions foreign to the dog. As the human grows older, the organs tend to sag of their own weight, settling to the bottom like flour in a bag, causing the too-familiar "pot." Aging dogs, if they are overweight, are simply fat all over, and do not suffer from this type of organ displacement.

The really major structural difference, of course, is the dog's lack of an opposable thumb, the feature which truly distinguishes the erect human from the "all-fours" dog. The bones are there—if you will hold your forearm, hand and fingers in a vertical line over a table-top, you will see that your thumb is in just about the same position as the dewclaw of the dog's leg—but there is no functional control in the dog.

THE NERVOUS SYSTEM

While the basic nerves in dog and man are again similar, in distribution and functions of carrying sensations to the brain and commands away from it, the reflex nervous system is more highly organized in the dog. This is of little use in understanding a dog's health, but it is interesting to note, for it does explain some of the dog's actions. There are few human reflexes similar to those of a dog—the Babinski foot-toe reflex is one which may be familiar to parents. (If you scratch the sole of a baby's foot, he will involuntarily curl his toes—an action seemingly left over from the days when reflex grasping of a branch might mean life or death. People outgrow it but it may come to the surface in cases of brain damage when the higher brain centers are knocked out.)

Perhaps the best example in the dog is the scratching reflex. When a dog itches, it scratches. Simple enough, you say—so do humans. But in the dog the mechanism is different. If you itch, you feel the itch, direct your fingers to the spot, and attempt to get relief. The dog bypasses the middle steps, going straight from itch to scratch with essentially no brain direction in between—a reflex action. You can very easily see proof of the reflex nature of scratching if you happen to scratch a dog where he itches, and one of his legs starts swinging in a scratching motion which scratches nothing. Also, a dog may scratch quite efficiently by himself, but completely miss the itching spot—his nervous system, reacting to an itch, has directed the appropriate leg to scratch in the appropriate area, but not infrequently manages to miss the affected spot.

THE DIGESTIVE SYSTEM

The physical organization of the dog's digestive system is also closely similar. Beginning with the mouth, there follow the esophagus, stomach, pylorus (an essential valve which controls passage of food from the stomach), small intestine, large intestine and finally rectum. It is in the digestive chemistry that one of the major differences between dog and man exist.

Humans begin digesting food in the mouth. While the food is being chewed for easy passage to the stomach, certain secretions from mouth glands begin the digestive processes. In the stomach further action takes place. The dog, however, chews his food only enough to get it down, and the human parental admonition, "Don't bolt your food, dear," would be misapplied to dogs. They bolt their food because in days less removed than in humans, it was expedient to bolt as much food as quickly as possible and run before something bigger and nastier came along to bolt you. Thus digestion begins in the dog's stomach rather than in the mouth, and the stomach's secretions are of a ferocious nature. More digestion takes place in the small intestine, but here the process is very similar to that of humans.

Despite enduring legend, the dog *is* able to digest potatoes and other starches perfectly well, *does* require fat in his diet, and, in general, despite the mechanical differences in digestive processes, can and does use and profit from almost any food which humans eat. These factors will be taken up at considerably greater length in the next chapter, but for the present suffice it to say that chemically the dog's system is not noticeably different from the human's.

THE MOUTH AND TEETH

The dog's considerably longer jaws, one of the major skeletal differences, hold quite a few more teeth than humans have. There are 42 in total, 20 in the upper jaw and 22 in the lower. Dogs, or rather puppies, sprout baby teeth shortly after birth. These are soon replaced by larger permanent teeth and the puppies go through the same teething problems as human babies.

Hereditarily missing teeth (most usually premolars) are far more common in dogs than in humans, for reasons nobody much understands. It just seems to have begun somewhere in the dim history of dogs and has never been bred out, although professional breeders of show dogs avoid breeding either a male or a female who is lacking one or more teeth. This will be taken up in greater detail in the chapter on Puppy Care, but you might want to check your own dog for missing teeth at this point, just for curiosity. The normal complement is six incisors (the chisel-shaped front teeth) in each jaw; the two long canines next in each jaw; four premolars on each side, upper and lower behind the canines, and then two molars on each side in the upper jaw and three on each side in the lower. It is easier to count them by type and location like this than to try to reach a total of 42 while holding a squirming dog's mouth open, or trying to count gaps.

The muscles around the mouth are fairly limited as compared to human equipment. The major lack is an effective orbicularis oris, which is an impressive and euphonious name for the sphincter muscle of the mouth. This muscle, in humans, something like a controllable thick rubber band running all around the mouth, helps you purse your lips, open them in a circle, pucker them, and engage in a number of facial contortions. Try them for a moment, and you will be convinced they are considerable. Watch your dog and you will see that he is capable of very few of them.

About the only controlled muscular act a dog can perform with his mouth muscles is the familiar and fearsome lip-lifting which exposes a number of teeth as a warning and signal of displeasure. He is not able, for example, to open his lips while his teeth are closed (other than in the warning snarl), or his teeth while his lips are closed. There is only enough muscle tone around the dog's lips to retain liquids while they are in the mouth, and this only to a degree. This is more a dog character- istic than generally a mammalian one, for cows and horses, for example, can and do chew their food with lips closed and do have considerable mobility of the lips. But a dog can't and doesn't, and thus a dog cannot obey another standard human parental admonition, "Chew with your mouth closed, dear."

EYES, EARS AND NOSE—THE SENSES

In gross construction, the dog's eye is almost identical with the human's —lids, lens, iris, cornea, pupil, retina and optic nerve leading to the brain. One of the major physical differences is the presence of a half- operative nictitating membrane—a sort of "third eyelid"—which you may notice sliding back from the eye, towards the inner corner, when your dog just wakes up. This membrane is fully operative in such aquatic ani- mals as frogs, serving to protect the eye while open underwater (it is transparent or translucent), but it is nearly vestigial in dogs. A dog who sleeps with his eyes partly open, and with this membrane covering the open part, can be an unnerving sight, but it does not mean that there is anything wrong with the dog.

The major operating differences in a dog's eyes are that the retina totally lacks the cells which allow color perception, and the fovea which brings objects into sharp focus. Dogs are, despite numerous letters from indignant owners which appear in the dog magazines as regularly as the seasons, completely color blind. It is hard to convince a good many people of this, largely because they do not fully understand what color blindness is. Generally they assume that it means total lack of shade perception, quite another thing, and insist that if a dog can tell the difference between a white coat and a black one, he cannot be color blind. Nonetheless, he is.

So far as it is possible to tell, the dog goes through life seeing one long black-and-white movie. He does not miss color because he never has seen it. He can and does use his eyes to quite good effect, just as you could if you saw everything through some curious permanent glasses which took all the color out of the world and made it seem like a black-and-white picture. In a non-color snapshot or movie, you can easily tell the difference between a black and a white coat, and can distinguish a thousand shades of grey. So can a dog, and is no more handicapped by color-blindness than you are in watching a normal movie versus a Technicolor one.

The distinction between shades of grey is what sometimes gives owners the impression that their dog can actually see color. A dark red object and a light blue object will appear different in a black-and-white photograph, and appear different to dogs. But they simply don't see color. (As is pretty generally known now, neither do most other animals see color. The bull in the barnyard or bullring couldn't care less whether the shirt or cape you wave at him is red—it is the motion that he charges at, as bullfighters well know.)

A logical question at this point is how anybody really knows whether dogs see color, dogs being as uncommunicative as they are. The best answer is that although no one *really* knows, in the fullest sense of the word "really," dogs simply cannot be induced to respond in any way to different colors. In psychology laboratories they can be trained to respond to different intensities of light, different shapes painted on doors leading to food, and even to flashing light codes. But even the hungriest experimental dogs have never learned that the food is behind the red door rather than the blue one, always provided that the shades of red and blue are the same. About the only three conclusions possible from many repeated experiments of this sort are that dogs cannot see color, that they lose their appetites when they see differently colored doors, or that dogs are sly enough, and purposeful enough, to hoodwink experimental psychologists. Take your choice.

Dogs are also as a rule considerably near-sighted, this being the best term available to describe the lack of fine-detail focus in the dog's eye. There is one definite major, and one possible minor reason for this. First, the shape of the dog's eyeball causes the lens to focus light rays a slight distance in front of the retina, which is the standard cause of myopia, or near-sightedness. This is the major reason, definitely established, but it gives rise to the question: why, then, over tens of thousands of generations of dogs, hasn't it corrected itself by a minor turn of evolution?

There are two possible answers here. First, there is the fact that a dog, even in the wild state, has no real need for sharp focus and highly acute vision—some dogs known as "sight hounds" or "gaze hounds" have better vision than others and hunt by sight as much as by smell, but even they do not have "normal" human-type vision. Therefore a logical assumption can be made that lack of need is the reason nature never bothered to tune up the dog's vision beyond the point of near-sightedness. Another possible explanation is in the physical construction of the retina. In the human, there is a tiny spot called the fovea, directly in the center of another structure called the macula—on this area light rays are brought to fine focus, and this area is capable of perceiving tiny objects and focussing sharply on them, as would be required in reading small print. The fovea is missing in the dog's eye, and the macula is less well defined, and there is the possibility that even if the lens brought light rays to focus properly on this area of the retina, it would do little good because of the lack of the proper cells to realize the focus.

All of this leads into realms of discussion which will be of little interest to you unless you are a student of dog pathology and/or ophthalmology.

Suffice it to say that, for whatever reason, the dog's vision is poor. If you are myopic yourself, you will have little trouble visualizing what the world then looks like to a dog. If not, you can best visualize it by looking at an object across the room, then without shifting your eyes, try to make out the fine detail of another object near the first one. This won't be exactly right, but it will be near enough.

This may give rise to the question of how a dog can recognize a familiar person at a distance. The simple answer is that he can't, really. What happens is that he has learned to recognize either a general outline, or certain special characteristics—a way of walking, for example. It is much the same process by which you will come to recognize a friend's footsteps. Your hearing isn't any better, it's just that you've unconsciously learned a pattern of noises which you couldn't explain to anyone. You can prove to yourself the dog's lack of distance vision by a simple experiment: put on a differently-shaped hat from any you are accustomed to wearing, and/or a coat whose shape he isn't accustomed to, and then stand still somewhere. Have someone else bring your dog up to you from a distance and, if you are downwind, you'll be surprised at how close your own dog will get before he realizes it's you.

The dog's greater night-vision is at least partially due to a curious structure called "tapetum lucidum", a layer of reflective cells which lies just behind the light-receptor cells of the retina. This is a very strongly functioning structure in cats, and is fully present in many dogs, partially present in some others, and apparently totally or nearly absent in a few. Among other things, this layer causes the eyeshine of animals, by reflecting light back out of the eye. In assisting with night vision, it acts somewhat like the mirror of a reflecting telescope, bouncing back light from the rear to the retina, thus intensifying a dim image. This tapetum lucidum, incidentally, is totally absent in humans, which scotches any speculation on whether people's eyes would shine in the dark if you could just manage to get the light to hit them right. They don't.

The ear is almost identical in structure to the human ear. The major differences are the size of the outer ear structure, considerably greater muscular control, and an angled turn in the outer ear canal which protects the eardrum from damage. The long outer ear structure is of considerable value in one way or another to the dog. If the ear is erect, it acts as an excellent sound antenna, an ear-trumpet of sorts, which can be turned to catch faint sound. If the ear is flopped it is a minor hindrance to good hearing, although the flopped section provides a curtain-like protection against dirt and injury not afforded dogs with erect ears. There is little or no difference except in bulk between flop and erect ears, for a full flop ear can be turned into a completely functional and movable erect ear by the cropping done in certain breeds. Great Danes, Boxers and Dobermans, among others, start life with full, floppy, spaniel-type ears which are cropped in puppyhood to a shorter, somewhat tear-drop shape, which then allows the ear to stand erect and be as movable as an uncropped erect ear.

It is largely in range of hearing that a dog's ears differ. The extended range is almost universally known—it can be pragmatically demonstrated by using one of the widely advertised "silent" dog whistles. Tootle on one of these, and you will hear nothing, or only a faint high peeping. But to the dog it is a shrill blast, audible as much as half a mile away. The whistles are constructed to sound only in the region above 15,000 cycles per second, beyond the normal range of human hearing, but well within the dog's extended range.

Laboratory experiments have shown the top range of a dog's hearing to be about 25,000 cycles—by comparison, the highest note of a piano is 4,186 cycles per second, and very, very few humans can hear sounds above 15,000 cycles. Russian experimenters at one time or another have claimed discovery of canine perception as far up as 100,000 cycles. Nobody else has found sensitivity even approaching these figures.

It is when we get into the subject of the dog's nose and his powers of smell that we approach the incomprehensible. The structure of the nose is similar enough to that of a human, from nostrils right on back. The major difference here is in the much greater length, particularly in the length and area of the turbinates, inner bones covered with erectile tissue which accomplishes the smelling function. All of the difference between human and canine senses of smell cannot be explained merely by a greater turbinate area, but a good part of it is—as witness the difference in smelling ability between the normally long-nosed dogs and such short-nosed breeds as Bulldogs.

What it would be like to smell things as a dog does is almost beyond human comprehension. There are certain humans who have been able to develop highly acute noses—many organic chemists can identify a startling number of compounds and their constituents simply by smelling them, and the famous "noses" of the French perfume industry can perform wonders with a bit of perfume essence. There have been reports of humans with remarkable scent abilities, to the point of being able to tell which coat in a rack belonged to which person at a party, but these are very rare.

The best explanation is by analogy. Imagine a very potent smell; limburger cheese is a good one. If you were to take several objects and have a friend rub limburger thoroughly on one, even several days later you would be able to tell which of the objects had been so treated. A dog can tell, days later, which of several objects you have merely touched with your hand, and in fact with luck he can tell which of several widely separated objects you simply stood near. Every person and every object in the world has its own distinctive smell, easily identifiable, to a dog.

Surprisingly, this extreme sensitivity does not seem to operate by "intensity," if this be the proper word. True, a dog can tell the difference between an old and a new scent of the same person (this is why tracking dogs hardly ever go the wrong way when they come across a track—they apparently can tell the difference in smell between one footprint and the next, certainly a minor difference), but smells which are intense to humans do not seem as bothersome as we might imagine to a dog. Handlers of trained police dogs have found that their dogs can track a suspect even through a factory filled with smell that had the handlers gasping and incapable of smelling anything else.

In all, your dog operates in a world so different from yours that it is difficult to imagine it. He sees differently, hears differently, and smells totally differently. These differences are handy to keep in mind when you must and do treat with a dog, particularly if he happens to be sick or injured.

PUREBRED VS. MONGREL

One of the major misunderstandings about dogs, in the physical sense, is the belief that there is some basic difference between purebreds and mongrels. Straight off, there isn't. There are folktales to the effect that,

among other things, you can tell a purebred from a mongrel by the color
of the inside of his mouth, either that it is all black, or in another version
that there is no black at all. You may hear that mongrels live longer than
purebreds, that they are smarter or dumber, that they are more or less
susceptible to illnesses. None of these is true. Among the various established breeds of dogs there are differences in average longevity, intelli-
gence, temperament, susceptibility or resistance to certain diseases
and conditions. The mongrel tends to be, along with his ancestry, a mixture of these traits. Some purebreds are normally longer-lived than some
mongrels, some tend to die younger than the average mongrel, and so it
goes through any catalog of traits or tendencies.

The only real difference between a purebred and a mongrel is that
certain physical, mental and temperamental characteristics are more or
less guaranteed to be transmitted when two dogs of the same breed are
mated, whereas you get pot luck in the mating of two well-mixed mongrels. For that matter, almost any pure breed you can name was originally a mongrel, by strict definition, for no breed sprang from the ground
in all its purity. The origins of many breeds are lost in history, but others
have a history of only a few hundred years. Doberman Pinschers, for
example, are as pure and elegant a breed as any in the world, but they
did not even exist as a breed one hundred years ago.

Dobermans are probably the most carefully planned dogs in the world.
Some 80 years ago a gentleman named Dobermann, a nightwatchman
in Germany, laid down the specifications of a dog he wanted to breed,
and then proceeded to mix together various existing breeds for the characteristics he wanted. Included in the original Doberman ancestry are
Rottweilers, Manchester Terriers, at least one Greyhound, and touches of
other breeds here and there in the experimental Doberman breedings
before the turn of the century.

True, once the type had been satisfactorily established, Dobermans
were not bred to anything but other Dobermans, and within a few generations the true characteristics held firm and bred true, so that now if
you breed one Doberman to another, you know quite accurately what
the puppies will be like. Equally true, if you were to take several litters
of mongrels and breed them brother to sister, and their offspring brother
to sister and cousin to cousin, you would find that after enough gener-

ations you had established essentially a new pure breed which would result in the puppies looking just like their parents, generation after generation.

All of this is not really necessary, but it will be a help if you understand that there is no essential difference, for a mongrel is nothing but an uncontrolled cross-breeding, while a purebred is a controlled inbreeding after the planned or accidental cross-breeding which established the type, however many hundreds of years in the past.

AGE IN DOGS

Even considering their different life-spans, dogs age and develop at a different rate than humans. There is an enduring general theory that seven years of a human's life equal one year of a dog's—in the overall consideration it is true, in that a ten-year-old dog is about equivalent to a seventy-year-old human. Year by year, however, the theory is badly out of kilter. Dogs grow faster and mature faster, not only actually but relatively, than humans. They also grow more, as a percentage of their birth weight, than humans—but for more on this, see the chart in Chapter II.

A fair working rule with dogs is that the development is twice as fast as that of a human at first (equating seven human years to one dog year), and that the human catches up towards the end. At the age of one year, a dog is about equivalent to a fifteen-year-old human; at the age of two years to a twenty-five-year-old human, at the age of three years, to a thirty-three-year-old, at the age of four years, to a forty-year-old, and then for every dog year, add about five human years. There are of course differences between breeds—the small breeds tend to mature more quickly, both physically and mentally, than the larger breeds, and within the breeds there are obvious differences from individual to individual. But the above can be an aid to you in what to expect in the way of physical and mental development in your dog.

GENERAL CONSIDERATIONS

Overall, the physical differences between dogs and humans are surprisingly minor, and it can be an enormous help to you in your treatment of your dog, in sickness or in health, if you remember this. He is a living, breathing, heartbeating organism very much like yourself. When he is young he is springy and fresh of mind, and when he is older he slows down and gets stiff and crotchety. In between, he eats, breathes, his blood circulates, and the things that affect him are quite like the things that affect you. Treat him as a functioning individual—never think of him as "just a dog," and you will have a happier and healthier dog for as long as you are lucky enough to live together.

CHAPTER II

NUTRITION AND FEEDING

THE FACT that dogs have subsisted, and apparently quite well, for millenia with very little attention given to their nutritional needs can give rise to the question—why bother so much about what to feed a dog? The answer is much the same one which applies to humans. They, too, have managed to live a long time without balanced diets and nutritional studies—but few will question the fact that people live better and longer now that the science of nutrition is understood and applied.

Although you don't need to know much of anything about the technicalities of food elements and nutrition, this chapter does go into these subjects slightly. They are worth your attention largely as a defensive maneuver, for they may help you stave off some of the idiot notions about dog feeding which you can catch in any vagrant wind. If they do only this, they are useful indeed. There are more odd and curious ideas floating around about dog feeding than there are about human feeding, which takes some doing.

Basically, the dog needs the same five major elements as humans to live and thrive: proteins, fats, carbohydrates, vitamins and minerals. Of these, proteins and fats are the two most controllable in a dog's diet, and merit brief discussion.

PROTEINS

The general term "protein" covers many different individual proteins, each of which is distinct and is utilized differently by the body. Each protein is made up of a different combination of several of the basic substances called amino acids. Nutritionist Dr. Clive McCay has suggested the apt analogy of letters which make up words—as with only 26 letters, thousands of different words can be made, so with about 20 amino acids, many different proteins can be made. This is exactly what the body does —it takes the different kinds of proteins from food, breaks each of them down into component amino acids, and then reassembles the right kind and number of aminos, if available, into proteins for body-building. Amino acids not used for protein building are broken down into general body fuel and converted into heat or energy. Some aminos can be manufactured within the body, but in general the system is dependent on outside protein sources.

When a specific type of protein is needed at some point in the dog's body, the system goes over its current stock of amino acids searching for all the necessary ones to build that particular protein, which can be built if and only if all the needed aminos are present at the same time. To return to the analogy of letters and words—a printer must have all the letters in, say, the word "protein" to print that word. He may have warehouses full of type and be unable to print it unless he has at least one each of the required letters all together at the same time. Also, in the general run of printing any text, he will need more of certain letters than others—more "e's" than "z's," for example. The situation is the same with proteins and protein-building in the body.

With this in mind, it is easier to understand why some protein sources are better than others. Animal protein sources (meat, milk and eggs) contain proteins similar to, or identical with, the proteins needed by the body. When animal proteins are broken down within the system, their component amino acids are more likely to be immediately usable. Vegetable proteins generally lack some of the essential aminos, although by combination of enough vegetable proteins, all of the body proteins can be built up eventually—you could make up the word "protein" from the letters in "problem" and "tin," but it would be less efficient.

The unused extra aminos—all the surplus "z's" and "x's"—in vegetable proteins are "wasted" by being converted to body fuel rather than body protein-building, or are excreted. The practical result of all this is that experiments have shown that dogs fed a diet of pure lean meat use the animal proteins therein so efficiently that, while in perfect health, they may defecate only once or twice a week. On the other hand, dogs fed on vegetable proteins only utilize the proteins less efficiently, have far more bulk left over after digestion, and may defecate as often as three times a day.

All of this background leads up to an understanding of the quality of proteins as applied to dog feeding. Many commercial dog foods claim "high protein content," with nothing said about the quality of the protein content. Dog food labels speak almost exclusively of "crude protein" percentage. The percentage may indeed be high, but if the proteins are the "wrong" ones, they will largely be used as fuel and not for body growth and maintenance. This is not a condemnation of either such foods or their labelling procedures—a dog can live and prosper on these "wrong" proteins, but he will have to take in a great deal more of them, his system sorting through more bulk than would be necessary in the case of "right" animal proteins.

FATS

Some time ago there was a prevalent theory that fat was positively bad for dogs, a belief which couldn't be farther from true, but which still lingers with pockets of strength here and there. A proper percentage of fat is as essential in a dog's diet as protein. Fat provides energy in an easily available form. When ingested, fats are broken down into constituent fatty acids (much as proteins are broken down into amino acids) and glycogen. The glycogen is readily converted to fuel glucose, and the fatty acids are stored throughout the body in the form of new fats, these the dog's own body fat.

The dog's own body fats can be synthesized from carbohydrates, but it is considerably easier and more efficient to make them directly from combinations of fatty acids taken from diet fats. Although it is of course undesirable for a dog to become fat himself, sufficient fat in the body is highly desirable as insulation, cushioning for the internal organs, and for reserve stores of food and energy. Just as with proteins, fats of one kind or another are found in very nearly everything—milk, vegetables and grains, but primarily in natural animal fat fed as such.

A good percentage of fat in your dog's diet will, among other things, be helpful in keeping his coat healthy and glossy—in a normal dog, the fat portion should be about 10 per cent, and hard-working, active outdoor dogs can profitably utilize as much as 15 per cent or 20 per cent, both for maintenance and for readily available energy. Therefore, regard with considerable skepticism any dog food claims about "low fat content," which can be made to sound quite convincing and attractive in an advertisement or commercial. Most dog diets actually should have fat added, rather than subtracted.

Insufficient fat in the diet can have an effect on the condition of a dog's skin—in many cases, chronic itching and scratching has been cleared up by addition of fat to the diet. It is one of the greatest misapprehensions many dog owners have, that "dogs just itch," as if itching and scratching were a natural and inseparable part of being a dog. It simply isn't so, for a properly fed and groomed dog will hardly ever scratch. There are other causes of itching and subsequent scratching, of course, but fat in the diet is so widely misunderstood that lack of it will often be the cause.

Just because it is very good for dogs, do not, however, go to the other extreme and add too much fat to the diet. The 20 per cent mentioned above is about the maximum even a hard-working dog should have. If the fat level rises much above that, the dog will begin suffering from protein, vitamin and mineral deficiencies—he gets calories and energy so handily and efficiently from the fat that he does not eat enough of other types of food, and therefore loses the benefits of them. This consideration may, in fact, be behind the false belief that a dog shouldn't have fat—in earlier days, dogs fed exclusively on scraps were likely to get a very high percentage of fat in their diets, and suffered as a result. Someone probably realized that it was an overabundance of fat that was causing the problem, and then, like so many ideas, it got distorted until the belief became prevalent that any fat at all was harmful.

WHAT TO FEED

With these considerations in hand, what should you feed your dog? Considering the natural history of the dog, and his protein and fat requirements, good solid beef is the best possible major dietary constituent. This does not mean that the dog cannot live without meat, that it is the only thing he can eat, or that he cannot profitably eat other foods. It simply means that meat is the best basic food for a dog.

While it is not necessarily true that what you eat when you're sick is the best thing to eat all the time, you will find veterinarians almost universally recommending a high-protein, high-meat diet for ailing dogs. The idea of the meat prescription is to build up the general physical condition of the patient, through a diet of the most efficient food, so that the specific malfunction can more easily be treated. It makes sense, therefore, that a standard and continuing diet heavy in meat will maintain the dog in good condition.

There are of course the ever-present considerations of cost and convenience which militate against meat diets. Beef costs a good deal more than any commercial dog food, and preparing meat for your dog is more trouble than simply opening a can or pouring out a bowl of dry dog food. Your decision on what to feed your dog will rest largely on how much you are willing to spend and how much trouble you are willing to take.

MEAT

In a specific meat diet, the cheapest grades of meat are actually to be preferred to "better" meat, largely because of the higher percentage of fats to be found in such cuts—aside from the factor of expense. Pure muscle meat such as high-grade hamburger is deficient in fat, and extra fats should be added to such a diet, in the form of fat cuttings, lard, margarine or almost any other fat source. Horse meat, an obvious and good choice for a meat source, is excellent for a meat diet, and here there is a special necessity for the addition of fat, as horse meat is quite low in this element.

All high grade muscle meat tends to be low in such factors as Vitamin D and calcium, and a muscle-meat diet should be supplemented with these elements, in cod-liver oil, percomorph oil, organ meats, bone meal, commercial supplements, or any one of a dozen other methods. In the savage state, dogs made up for these muscle-meat deficiencies by eating all of their prey, including organs, skin, hair and bones.

Organ meats of all kinds are excellent nutrition sources, as supplements to a high-meat or any other kind of diet. Liver and kidneys are common additions, but other available by-products such as hearts, lungs and other internal organs are relished by dogs and supply many nutritional necessities. This sort of thing is a little hard for some people to carry out, because of human prejudices against eating such organs, but if you have trouble with the idea, you may be able to arrange with your butcher to grind up an appetizing medley of organ meats and supply them to you in unidentifiable packages which you can then feed to your dog. However little you may think of organs, your dog will love them.

On the line of butchers, it is quite often possible to buy, by the pound, packages of "kennel meat" at very low prices. This will consist of organs, fats, meat scraps of all kinds which happen to be around the butcher shop, and will generally vary in content from one week to the next. If you know your butcher well, and trust him to prepare such mixtures from clean, fresh scraps (without any pork, unless you plan to cook the mixture well), this kennel meat can be a very economical and excellent source of a well-balanced, high-meat diet. Just be sure you know who you're buying it from.

Of individual kinds of meat, pork is the only one which might cause trouble, on two counts. Many veterinarians recommend totally against feeding any pork at all, but many more dogs have been fed pork in considerable quantities, and have gotten nothing but benefit from it. Back of the anti-pork recommendation lie two factors. The first is that pork fat is extremely rich, and cases have been known in which a dog fed substantial quantities of pork fat went into convulsions. This anti-pork recommendation is rapidly being discarded, however, in favor of a simple warning not to over-feed pork.

The other, and major, factor, is the danger of trichinosis. Despite considerable work on the problem, trichina (tiny worms) are still present in some pork. If infested pork is eaten without sufficient cooking to kill the trichina, they will become established in the system. Once established, there is no way known of disestablishing them, short of cooking, which is a somewhat impractical method when it comes to your dog. Therefore, prevention is the only weapon against trichinosis.

As humans are usually extremely careful about cooking pork, scraps from your table will be no danger to your dog, but otherwise tread with care. People tend to be a little less careful with their dogs, and undercooked or raw pork in your dog's diet may well include live and aggressive trichina.

Any other meat can be fed raw to your dog, and he will probably love

it. Raw hamburger, raw small chunks of beef or horsemeat will taste excellent to him. Cooked meat is usually tastier, though, just as it is to you,
and the simplest method is boiling. Simply put ground or chunked meat
in a pot, cover with water, and boil until it is partially or completely
cooked.

A good plan for a meat diet is to feed the cooked meat with about
an equal bulk of kibbled biscuits. When the meat has been cooked,
pour enough of the resulting broth over the kibbles and let it stand just
long enough to soften them without making them mushy. Then mix the
meat and soaked kibbles together, using enough of the broth that has
not soaked into the kibbles to make a small bit of liquid in the bottom
of the bowl—don't over-do this liquid so that the meat and kibbles are
floating in it, just add a little. There is a small problem in timing here;
the meat will have to cool a little, and so will the broth, so it is best to
wait a few minutes after turning the fire off under the meat before you
soak the kibbles. A little experimentation will show you how to do it
just right.

If you want to, you can with very little trouble make a minor sort
of beef stew for your dog, adding a bone to the pot, and a carrot or a
potato, all of which will add to the flavor and make it more appetizing
to your dog, particularly if he is a finicky eater. And anything of that
sort you add to the "stew" will benefit him nutritionally.

DRY DOG FOOD

Many, many dogs have been raised and maintained on diets consist-
ing almost entirely of dry dog foods, and these dry foods can serve
you very well if you prefer them. Moistened with milk or meat broth,
or mixed with scraps, they are appetizing to the dog, and most brands
are very carefully designed for adequate and balanced nutrition, with
the exception of fat content. There are numerous reasons why most of
the dry dog foods are low in fat—among them the non-dietary but
practical problem of high-fat foods staining paper or cardboard packages and making them rapidly very unattractive to the purchaser. A
second and minor factor is the fact that the "fat is bad for dogs" fallacy
is still believed in some areas, so much so that certain dog food adver-
tisements have stressed, as a presumed product benefit, the fact that

the product does not contain "messy fat." That it may not, but it is the worse for the omission. A supplement of fats should be added to any dry dog food diet.

Continued experimentation has shown that the average needs of the average adult dog for the average dry food amount to one pound per day per 36 pounds of dog. The three "averages" in that sentence are there for good reason, for needs vary with the size, age, degree of activity, and even to some extent, the breed of a dog. But the one pound per 36 pounds is a very good basic ratio you can use for general estimation of what you will need.

Many of the dry foods come in meal form, and these are best prepared by mixing with milk, warm water or meat broth. The ideal temperature of the mixture is about 120°, or just enough to be warm without getting hot. Mix the liquid in until the meal has about the consistency of hamburger—any looser and it will be difficult for the dog to eat; never make a mush of it. The pellet and ribbon forms of dry food are also best mixed with liquid to soften them, even if the dog will eat them dry. And add at least one good meat meal per week to any ration of dry dog food, and an occasional bit of fresh liver.

There is one caution about dry dog foods you should observe if you are feeding only one dog, particularly a small one. The vitamin content of dry foods has a tendency to deteriorate sharply with storage. In many stores in many areas, large 25-pound or even 50-pound sacks of dry foods are available, at a saving. However, these are poor buys because of the vitamin-loss factor. In most stores which do a good volume of dog-food business, the stock will be fresh at any given time, but extensive storage in your kitchen cabinet will do the deterioration job as well as storage anywhere else. A good rule to follow is to buy no more than two weeks' supply of dry food at a time—which rules out 25-pound packages for dogs weighing less than about 60 or 70 pounds.

CANNED DOG FOOD

These are also referred to as "pudding" foods, and they are made of cereals such as barley, rice, corn, wheat, oatmeal, mixed with bone meal, supplements, wheat germ and meat. Their major difference from dry foods is that they contain actual meat products, rather than the meat meal used in dry feeds. As one result, they contain a very great deal more water, and have to be fed in larger quantities than the average dry food. Don't be put off by the fact that the labels of these products will specify as much as 75 or 80 per cent water, or "moisture" as some prefer to call it. Meat itself is about 70 per cent water, and if the product uses a good proportion of natural meat, there is nothing in the world the manufacturer can do about that high a percentage of water in the final product.

The average dry food will contain about 10 per cent water as against the average of 70 per cent in canned foods, which leaves 90 per cent solid matter in dry foods as against 30 per cent in canned. From this 30-90 ratio, it is simple to calculate that a dog will need about three times as much gross weight of canned food as dry for the same amount of solid nutrients—the water content counts for nothing in nutrition. This makes the average amount of canned food for daily adult feeding about one pound per 12 pounds of dog.

Canned foods also tend to be low on fat content, although not as low as dry foods, so additional fat should be supplied with a canned-food diet.

LABELS AND INGREDIENTS

Despite such defensive knowledge about nutritional factors as you have gleaned from this chapter, the labels of dog food cans and packages will probably mean very little to you, with their specifications of nutritional constitutents in "guaranteed analyses." There are, however, sources of aid and clarification. One is the table of nutritional requirements for dogs drawn up by the National Research Council, which is reproduced opposite. These standards are widely accepted.

Out of this table, only the protein and fat levels are likely to be of practical value to you in selecting dog food—point-for-point consideration of the vitamin and mineral elements would not only be tedious for the average dog owner, but in fact highly problematical as to value. First, there is the consideration that you as a layman are very unlikely to be able to judge whether a shortage of, say, two-tenths of a milligram of pantothenic acid is a serious deficiency or hardly worth bothering with. There is also the eminently practical fact that many dog food

NUTRIENT REQUIREMENTS FOR DOGS

(*In percentage or amount per pound of food*)

	Meal or other dry dog food	*Canned or wet mixtures of dog foods*
Moisture	8-10 %	70-75 %
Protein— minimum for growth	18	6
Protein— minimum for maintenance	13.5	4.5
Carbohydrate— maximum for growth	70	23
Carbohydrate— maximum for maintenance	75	25
Fat	4.5	1.5
Calcium (minimum)	1	0.4
Phosphorus (minimum)	0.8	0.3
Sodium chloride	1.4	0.5
Potassium	0.8	0.3
	mg. per lb. of feed	*mg. per lb. of feed*
Iron	22	8
Copper	2.5	1
Cobalt	1	0.3
Magnesium	200	70
Manganese	2	0.7
Zinc	2	0.7
Iodine	0.5	0.2
Vitamin A	0.6	0.2
Vitamin D	0.003	0.001
Vitamin E	20	7
Vitamin B12	0.01	0.004
Thiamine	0.3	0.1
Riboflavin	0.8	0.3
Pyridoxine	0.4	0.15
Pantothenic acid	0.9	0.4
Niacin	4.1	1.5
Choline	560	200

labels list pretty much what happens to strike the manufacturer's fancy when it comes to the minor ingredients, although all give the protein and fat percentages.

As to fats, there is an interesting note in the N.R.C. report containing the above table: "Levels of 5 per cent and 11 per cent have been suggested as goals for commercial dog foods. In view of the adverse effects of low-fat diets, the higher recommendation seems more nearly in line with good practical nutrition, although the 5 per cent selected by the committee and listed in Table 1 is certainly sufficient for normal physiological functions."

Using the N.R.C. table, a dog food with as low as 5 per cent fat content can thus state that it is a complete dog food, with the best of possible backing—still, the N.R.C.'s note above supports this chapter's recommendation for higher fat levels.

A rapid glance at the N.R.C. tables may give the impression that canned food, for some magical reason, needs to have less of everything in it, but you will see on a closer look that it simply bears out the fact that about three times as much gross weight of canned food is needed to supply dietary requirements, as indicated earlier.

Most dry dog foods will have at least a partial analysis on their labels, and a few carry the statement that the food meets or betters the N.R.C. standards. Such a statement is a good guide in your choice of a dry food.

You will find that a few canned foods carry on their labels a keystone-shaped small shield which may say either, "Inspected and certified by the U.S. Dept. of Agr. as a normal maintenance dog food," or "Packed Under Continuous Inspection of the U.S. Dept. of Agr." Either of these shields is the best guarantee you can have as to the quality of the food, because the shield means that the food was packed in a plant whose sanitary standards meet the Department of Agriculture's specifications, and whose formula and composition meet those same standards. Not all canners participate in this voluntary program of inspection, and the lack of a shield on the can cannot be taken, by any means, to indicate that the food therein is not perfectly good. The inspection program was set up at the request of a group of the canners themselves, to combat "back-yard" canners who were piling any old scraps into cans and selling them as complete dog food, although some major, highly reputable canners do not participate in the program.

One point well worth noting about both canned and dry dog foods is that they are intended for dogs, not for people. While this may seem somewhat obvious, it is a point that is well borne in mind, for a number of reasons. First, either dry or canned food may look or smell totally unappetizing to you, but a dog's senses and tastes are different, and what appears a mess to you may be, to him, something really delectable. Second, dog food manufacturers, with certainly no evil intent whatever, often make statements about their products which are more calculated to appeal to a dog owner's taste than to a dog's, for the simple reason that it is the owner who lays out the money. Among these are claims about special tastes certain to appeal to dogs which may or may not be true. Particularly curious are the statements about food color—"a rich meaty red"—which can have little enough effect on dogs, who are totally color blind. This latter point is worth nothing when considering dog biscuits, some of which come in many attractive colors, none of which are at all visible to your dog.

BISCUITS AND KIBBLED BISCUITS

There are two major types of dog biscuits, those intended as complete foods, and those intended simply as extras or for a little diet variety. Which type is which will generally be specified on the label. The complete food biscuits are sometimes used as just that, being little more than dry dog food moisturized and then formed into biscuit shape. Some dogs are fed almost entirely on these biscuits, and there is very little to recommend against it, if you are sure that the ingredients are such as to make them a good diet, and provided you add fat.

The regular baked-flour biscuits are the most common variety. These are made of flour, milk by-products, meat meal and supplements, and baked into hard biscuits, not unlike biscuits for humans. If you ever nibble one just for experiment, you will find that it has apparently no taste at all—to you it doesn't, but dogs taste things entirely differently, and most dogs find them delicious.

"Kibbles" or "kibbled biscuits" are simply the same biscuits broken up—the origin of the name is obscure. Usually the kibbled version is used for supplementing another diet, for the smaller pieces are easier to mix with meat or scraps. The shaped biscuits can be fed straight as treats, or moistened.

It is not a good idea to try to maintain your dog on a diet of these biscuits alone, as they are not usually complete foods. Additionally, over-feeding of biscuits very often causes chronic diarrhea in dogs. One problem you may have heard about, though, no longer exists with biscuits. Some years ago, the flour for these biscuits was bleached with nitrogen trichloride, and dogs fed any quantity had convulsions, and some died. This chemical is no longer used in the manufacture of biscuits, and there is no danger in feeding them.

SCRAPS

With the greater availability of high-quality dry and canned dog foods, the practice of feeding a dog almost entirely on table scraps has been drastically reduced over the years. In addition, the trend to smaller families, and particularly to pre-prepared and packaged low-waste foods, has cut down on the volume of scraps available for the family dog. This latter factor points up one of the dangers of a scrap-feeding program for your dog—people raised in large families and in slightly earlier times retain strong memories of the family dog subsisting entirely on mountains of scraps, and attempt to feed the modern dog that way. The usual result is that they find themselves getting "just a little extra" so there'll be enough left over for the dog, and the dog is being fed at human-food prices.

Otherwise, there is very little to be said against scraps as a major constituent of your dog's diet, always provided you eat a more or less sensibly balanced diet yourself. If he has been raised on them, a dog will happily eat all the leftover meat, fat, potatoes, vegetables and anything else that comes his way. Chicken and fish are fine for him, too, if you carefully remove all the bones before giving them to him. Because a scrap diet tends to be high in fats and carbohydrates and low in lean animal protein, you will very rarely have to add fat to this sort of diet, but it is a good idea to give the dog a meal of his own lean meat at least once a week by way of supplement, plus a small daily ration of kibbled biscuit or even full-diet dry dog meal just to help keep things more or less balanced for him. Scraps can of course be added as a supplement in themselves to any regular diet—meat, dry food, canned food or whatever—and will contain many essential nutrients which will do him nothing but good.

FISH AND CHICKEN

Most dogs love either fish or chicken as part of their diet, and there is no reason at all not to feed these items, if a little care is taken, especially with the bones. Botn fish bones and chicken bones, either raw or cooked, have a nasty habit of either sticking in a dog's throat, or splintering and causing tearing of his throat or stomach. Scrap fish or chicken from the table, however, will do him nothing but good, and it isn't a bad idea to give him a little bit of his own, cooked and mixed with his normal ration, if his appetite is flagging—a little variety in the food is appreciated by almost any dog.

Although raw chicken can be fed, you should never feed a dog raw fish. There is an enzyme in raw fish which destroys thiamine, one of the B Vitamins. Eating raw fish often causes a form of paralysis known as Chastek paralysis, which is at best debilitating, and at worst fatal. Thorough cooking of fish inactivates this enzyme, and cooked fish is a perfectly safe and nutritious food.

SUPPLEMENTS

There is considerable current dissension, and probably always will be, about the value of regularly supplementing diets with commercial vitamin-mineral preparations. To start with basics—a dog eating a perfectly balanced diet is very unlikely to need any commercial supplements when in normal health and condition, which excludes the obvious conditions of sickness, and the not-so-obvious conditions of pregnancy, lactation and growing. Nutritionists and veterinarians are to be found on both sides of the regular-supplement fence—one school holding that a normal diet takes care of all nutritional requirements and that supplements are just an unnecessary expense, the other that the expense is in fact small and that supplementation is a guarantee that hidden nutritional deficiencies will be taken care of.

One thing you can be sure of is that a dog fed a good diet, regularly supplemented with a commerical preparation, is very unlikely ever to suffer from any deficiency condition, and will grow and prosper well indeed. It is essential that both specifications be met, for there is a small danger in regular supplementation that the owner will consider the vitamin-mineral standards thus met, and will ignore the necessity for otherwise balancing a diet. In one area there is no question but that supplements are a definite advantage—that of the finicky eater. If your dog is really picky and choosey about his food it is likely that he isn't getting some of the things he needs in his diet, and so they should be given to him in a supplement.

Such simple supplements as cod liver oil or percomorph oil given once a week (a few drops, according to the label and the size of the dog) are excellent sources of some of the vitamins. A half-pound of liver a week for a dog of 20-30 pound size is an excellent natural supplement. Beyond these, there are multi-vitamin and vitamin-mineral supplements intended for human use which are excellent for dogs if used in quantities suitable for a dog's size. On this line, remember that a standard vitamin pill is intended for a human of about 150 pounds, and therefore should be given to a 25-pound dog only once every six days to get the same effect. The liquid multi-vitamins can be controlled as to quantity very easily, and are very good for this purpose.

Finally, there are supplements specifically intended for dogs which are excellent for general supplementary use. Most brands are available almost everywhere. You will find, once you look into the subject, that it actually will cost very little to be sure your dog is getting all the vitamins and minerals he ought to have for the best possible growth, health and life—it is well worth it.

There is, in the use of supplements, a tiny danger of overdosing. Actually, any sane and reasonable person runs so minute a chance of this that it hardly bears mentioning—but the danger does exist. Overdoses of vitamins and minerals will usually be thrown off by the body, but really massive overdoses can cause as serious conditions as deficiencies. The rule to follow is the logical one of giving only as much as is indicated on the label of the product, calculating from your dog's weight. This pattern of dosage, on top of even the most vitamin-packed diet, cannot possibly harm any dog.

FOOD FALLACIES

Aside from the normal and usual differences of opinion you will hear on the subject of diets for dogs—more fat, less fat, more protein, less protein, and so forth—there are a number of specific and quite widespread notions about the positive or negative effects of certain foods on dogs. Some of these beliefs have persisted for hundreds of years, despite repeated and totally convincing disproofs. A few of the major ones are listed here:

Milk causes worms: totally untrue. No matter what stage or form milk comes in, it is totally impossible for it to cause worms. Not only that, but no kind of milk whatever will cause worms—dog, goat, cow, sheep or any other kind of milk. Worms are caused by worm eggs and nothing else, and these worm eggs must be taken into the body by some normal route. True, it is remotely possible that milk might be contaminated with worm eggs or larvae somewhere along the line, but it is a very remote possibility and has nothing whatever to do with the properties of milk as such. This fallacy probably got its start from the fact that puppies drink large quantities of milk, puppies have worms, and therefore milk must be the cause of worms.

Horsemeat causes tapeworms: totally untrue, with the same comments as above. The origin is probably much like the milk-worms theory—dogs eat horsemeat, dogs have tapeworms, ergo horsemeat causes tapeworms.

Raw meat causes worms: again, totally untrue, with the exception noted earlier in this chapter about trichina, trichinosis and pork.

Garlic will prevent or kill worms: this is a somewhat trickier one. Most veterinarians scoff at the idea, but a few quite level-headed people believe that garlic at least discourages some types of worms. One eminent canine nutritionist, in a highly-respected text, says cautiously, "There is some evidence that garlic may destroy certain parasites and bacteria of the intestinal tract." No one, however, will recommend that garlic be used as an anti-worm device, however efficacious it may be against vampires. Feeding a little garlic would probably do no harm other than make your dog socially unacceptable, but the real danger of this belief lies in the possibility of trying to use garlic for worm control and as a result ignoring the proven chemicals and professional treatments which very definitely will control worms.

Raw meat makes dogs vicious: untrue, except for the obvious fact that a dog fed absolutely nothing but meat may very well be badly nourished in general, and as a result a little nervous and edgy about things. The rawest and bloodiest meat, as part of a normal diet, does not bring out any atavistic tendencies or bloodlust in dogs, any more than it does in you if you happen to be a Tartar steak enthusiast.

Sulfur will prevent worms, parasites, and/or keep your dog generally healthy: totally untrue. This curiosity is so widespread and established that you can even buy little blocks of sulfur, some quite cunningly shaped, for placing in the dog's drinking water, with claims that it will benefit the dog. It won't. The sulfur block in the water may be decorative, but that's all. It does happen that sulfur compounds are very good for the treatment of some skin conditions, but such treatments are not carried out by putting sulfur blocks in water.

Raw eggs are good for the coat: totally untrue. It is, in fact, actively bad to give a dog raw eggs. While the egg yolk, cooked or raw, is one of the most efficient sources known of high-quality proteins, the raw egg white interferes with absorption of the vitamin Biotin and hampers or prevents the absorption of certain minerals by the digestive system—so much so that raw egg white is recommended in cases of poisoning, to help prevent absorption of mineral poisons. Cooked egg white, on the other hand, is quite nutritious, but has nothing special to recommend it—and even cooked eggs won't do a thing for your dog's coat, except as they contribute to a balanced diet.

The "raw egg a day for the coat" is such a widespread and widely believed idea that it is worth repeating—raw eggs *do not* benefit a dog's coat and make it shinier or more healthy. They may even be harmful. They may be additionally harmful because raw eggs can cause diarrhea. Cooked eggs are a fine source of protein and some other nutrients, but even cooked, they are not a specific for a good coat—they help only insofar as they contribute their share of nutrients to a good overall diet.

Dogs can't eat or digest starch, especially potatoes: for the most part untrue, with the proviso that the starch be cooked. Dogs can eat, enjoy and utilize a substantial portion of cooked starches in their diets, including potatoes and bread. Raw starch, including potatoes, can cause diarrhea. The belief that starches generally are bad is presumed to originate in the fact that people who fed their dogs chunks of raw potato often saw potato chunks in the resultant stool. Quite right they were, but cooked potatoes in moderate amounts are perfectly fine for dogs, a valuable source of carbohydrates for energy.

There are undoubtedly many more fallacies which have large or small circulation. So many of these are variants on the worms and no-worms theme that it is best simply to keep the general principle in mind that worms come only from worm eggs, and that they are treated only by specific medicines. No food will either cause them or cure them.

Two more general cautions about dog feeding are these:

First, despite all the folklore you may hear to the contrary, dogs are not especially good judges of what is good for them in the way of food. They often have more sense than people about eating when they are sick, but as to nutritional components of the diet, they have as little or less sense than people do. They will happily eat badly balanced diets until they are terribly run down. You should not make the mistake of letting your dog judge what his diet is to be. Figure out what is good for him, and then give it to him to eat.

Second, don't fall into the trap of false cause-and-effect. In both nutrition and medicine, it is a very common error to assume that because one event preceded or coincided with another, it necessarily caused it. It may have, and then it may not have. The food fallacies discussed earlier undoubtedly all had their origins in one form or another of false cause-and-effect. Changes in diets, or the addition of special foods, can often have a very beneficial effect on your dog's health, or at times a detrimental effect, but be sure of the connection before you repeat it or recommend it.

PUPPY FEEDING

For the purposes of the next sections, a puppy will be considered as being at least two months old. You are not likely to get one much younger than that. If you do, or if you are raising younger puppies from a litter, their feeding is covered in the chapter on Whelping and Post-Natal Care.

There is a standard maxim among people who breed and raise dogs for shows—"If you don't get it into them the first year, you'll never get it into them." Professional breeders are interested in making every puppy they raise turn into not just an averagely healthy dog but a dog in absolutely top form and of maximum development. You can't feed a dog into development beyond the maximum potential bestowed on him by his heredity, but if you do that much, you're doing well indeed. There is a good deal of reason in the professional breeders' maxim about the first year, for this is when the major growth takes place. A dog which has been improperly nourished during its puppyhood can sometimes be brought into very good condition by later careful feeding and care, but nothing can replace solid growth and development as a puppy.

The best rule that can be given for puppy feeding is this: give him as much food as he'll take. Another saying, about "a fat puppy is a healthy puppy" is not necessarily true, for even a puppy getting enough crude calories to make him fat may be lacking in certain essential elements, but a puppy in good solid flesh is a fair bet to be better off than a scrawny one.

The amount any individual puppy will require can vary so widely that it is idle to attempt to lay down any hard and fast formula. Nutrition studies suggest that the average adult dog will require a minimum daily intake of 30 calories per pound of his weight to maintain himself in "normal" activity, whatever "normal" means to a nutritionist. Even if this were a good rule of thumb, you would be little better off for it. It would require you to conduct an investigation into the caloric content of such foods as you plan to feed your dog, all of which is not terribly practical.

We get a bit closer to the mark when we find that the average dog may require anywhere from half an ounce to two ounces of food per day (per pound of dog) for maintenance, depending on the type of food and on the size of the dog. A growing puppy would need about twice as much. This still doesn't help all that much with an individual pup, but it does at least begin to set approximate limits.

The real complications set in when you do come to consider your own pup, the only one you're interested in, whatever averages veterinary nutritionists may have come up with. If he is a very active type who lives in the country and runs his head off every day, he's going to need a good deal more food than a quiet pup in a city apartment. If you've decided to get him started in life with canned food, he's going to need about three times as much gross weight of food per day as he would of dry food—remember the fact that canned food has only one-third as much solid material per pound as dry food. What with all the factors involved, it would require pages of cross-indexed tables and charts for you to arrive at any scientifically right amount by reading—thus the basically simple rule that you should feed him as much as he'll take.

Whatever you feed your pup, put down at the first few meals a little more than you think he can possibly eat. Take a reading on what he actually did get down, then for a few meals after that put down just a little more than that amount. You will very quickly learn the amount he wants to eat, and you should then proceed to feed him just about that much. Keep in mind, however, that a puppy is growing minute by minute. The amount he will require one week when he weighs ten pounds will be considerably less than he needs the next when he weighs twelve. Don't stay with any stated amount, but keep experimenting as he and his appetite grow.

FEEDING AT TWO MONTHS

If you have just acquired a puppy of this age, it is best to give him his first few meals according to the instructions of the breeder, or of whomever you got him from. Moving to a new home, leaving his litter-mates, the trip itself—all can be quite upsetting to a very young puppy. It will help him if he is met at his new home by at least one familiar factor, his normal food. Whatever the breeder tells you the pup has been happily eating, go ahead with it until you believe he has settled in and begun to accept his new status in life.

Most puppies will have been weaned at four to six weeks of age, and will be quite accustomed to eating solid food by the time they are two months old. If you plan to feed your dog canned food as his lifelong diet, you can start giving him small amounts with his puppy diet, after you have let him eat his old food for a day or two. Make the changeover gradual—put in a little of the new food with the old, then next meal more of the new and less of the old, and so on through several meals until he is eating his permanent food. A sudden change of diet, aside from any emotional complications, may upset his digestion physically, so don't spring it on him all at once. The same applies to dry food, suitably moistened with evaporated or whole milk.

It is a good idea, at this age, to make at least one of his meals a formula meal of milk and supplements. The formula is an easy one: mix Pablum in whole milk (or diluted evaporated) until you have a consistency of about twice that of heavy coffee cream, and add about one drop of commercial liquid vitamin supplement per four pounds of puppy. Adjust this dosage according to any directions on the label of the supplement you use.

This formula is a good breakfast for the pup, and the remaining three meals of the day (a pup at this age should eat four times a day) can be your own selected food for him. Particularly if your pup is one of the larger breeds, it is a good idea to add a specific canine dietary supplement to at least one of the regular meals. The larger breeds need more calcium and Vitamin D per pound of puppy than the smaller ones, because they are building a much more massive bone structure, and there is danger of rickets in a large pup if his diet is deficient in these elements.

The subject of what to give puppies, particularly at this age, is a hotly contended one. Some authorities will tell you that any and all normally healthy puppies will thrive and grow strong on nothing but plain canned or meal food from the age of two months on. Others firmly believe you should add such things as lime water to a young pup's formula. One group holds that lactose (sugar of milk) should be added to milk, another that the sugar should be reduced if possible and more fat added. In all, it is difficult to steer a steady course between the camps.

You are on safe grounds, however, with the milk, Pablum and supplement meal. In this meal you are dead sure your pup is getting the natural beneficent qualities of milk, rightly called "nature's wonder food," the bulk and nourishment of the Pablum, and a good dose of the essential vitamins. In the other meals, the canned food, dry food, or plain meat will again supply the proteins and fats necessary, and the supplement added will insure that the minerals for growth are getting into him. In none of this will the cost be excessive, and you will be certain that you are laying a solid foundation of growth.

There are two minor points worth consideration at this point— about meat and canned foods. If you are feeding meat, it is better to cut it into bite-size chunks than to feed ground hamburger. The reason is that a puppy wolfs his food into his stomach even more voraciously than a grown dog, and the slightly larger size of chunks assures that the meat will stay in his stomach longer, and will be digested more thoroughly. Minor, but worth considering. And on the line of canned foods, it is well to realize that because of their 70 per cent moisture content, a puppy fed on them will drink less additional water than a pup fed dry food. Minor, but it might be a comfort to you to know, particularly if you are comparing your pup's water intake with a friend's pup who drinks either much more or much less.

There are certain things your puppy quite definitely doesn't need at this point, and looming large among them are the standard vegetable baby foods. Quite a few breeders will include these on their lists of food for puppies, but they are a waste of your good money and feeding time. Not that they can harm a pup, or do him no good at all, but they are simply nowhere as good as food intended specifically for dogs and puppies. Mashed baby foods were designed, naturally enough, for babies, and they tend to be short on meat protein and long on vegetable matter —admirable for slower growing humans, but not up to par for violently growing puppies. The meat baby foods, such as beef or lamb, however, are fine and easily digestible, but they are very expensive to feed as a full diet.

Another non-essential is raw eggs. Just in case you skipped the nutrition section of this chapter, here again is the reason—raw egg yolk is a fine source of protein, but raw egg white impedes the absorption and digestion of certain nutritional elements, and as such is actually harmful.

FREQUENCY OF FEEDING

As you will have seen from the above recommendations, puppies at two months should eat four times a day. This schedule works out fairly conveniently, with one meal in the morning, one at noon, one in the middle of the afternoon, and the last one late in the evening. There is no need to be rigid about a time schedule, but the meals should be spaced about five hours apart and will naturally fall into the breakfast-lunch-supper-late supper pattern. The reason for this frequent feeding is that although the young pup needs a large amount of food, his stomach is small and simply cannot hold enough to carry him throughout the day as an older dog's can. The parallel with humans holds well here, for babies and young children are much the same—voracious appetites combined with relatively small capacity.

Older pups will eat less often. At 5-6 months he may be down to three meals a day, to two at 8-9 months, and to only one daily feeding at one year. Cut out any meal he regularly shows little or no interest in, and increase the quantity of the remaining meals. Don't go by averages, but adjust the number of meals to your pup's individual needs.

FEEDING AT THREE TO FOUR MONTHS

If you get your pup at this age, again follow, for the first few days, the feeding instructions of the breeder. After that, or continuing the diet of the two-month-old, go on with the same diet described in the preceding section—four meals a day, one of milk formula and three of solid food.

Give the pup as much room-temperature (or slightly cooler, but not iced) water as he wants to drink, but supply it only at mealtimes. This is more for purposes of house training than health, as a puppy of this age probably hasn't yet acquired much control over his bladder. If he is given water only with meals, he will tend to have to urinate shortly thereafter rather than at any old time. The amount of time it takes for bladder pressure to build up will depend on the individual, with a fair average being half an hour—you will soon learn by observing your own pup's schedule.

At this stage, perhaps even earlier, you may run into the problem of the finicky, fussy eater. When a puppy is first in your home, he will probably gobble his food as though eating might go out of style tomorrow. It is a natural thing, for he has been accustomed to competition with his litter mates, and in that situation, to paraphrase the military maxim, he who gets there fustest and eats fastest gets the mostest. After a few days or weeks in your home, he will catch on to the fact that there is no longer any competition and that he can take his own sweet time getting the food down.

It is a very good idea, therefore, to make a firm practice of not leaving any meal on the floor for more than fifteen minutes. If he has begun to treat his food in a disdainful manner, returning to nibble now and then, he will get a considerable surprise the first time you take up the meal and there's nothing there to nibble on. It's a hard thing to do at times, because his pitiful expression and unhappy vocalizations make it a great temptation to give it back to him, or leave it there just a little longer, but if you give in the first time, the battle is lost and you may have a picky eater for life. Stick to it, and after a few times, he will get the idea that if he's going to eat, he'll have to get busy when the food is available. He does have to get the food into him, but missing one meal, or even two or three, won't hurt him. It will just make him hungry enough to attack the next meal with fervor.

It merits repeating: if your pup misses as many as three meals, it won't hurt him. Let him get good and hungry. If, however, he goes without food for a full day, and then next morning shows no interest in eating, there is a good chance something is wrong with him. Call your vet and explain the situation, or take the pup in for an examination—a normal, active puppy simply will not go for a full day without food and not turn up ravenous the next morning, no matter how spoiled he is.

Disinterest in food when you first put a meal down can sometimes be overcome by giving him a taste. If it is the formula meal, dip your finger in it and hold it in front of his nose to get him to take a lick of it. Quite often a puppy will then decide to dig in. Or if it's the solid meal, take up a teaspoonful-sized chunk in your fingers and feed it to him by hand. Puppies go for this sort of attention, and after a chunk or two will decide the stuff's pretty good and they might as well set to and eat it. Don't, however, fall into the trap of hand-feeding. It is right and valuable with a sick dog, but any healthy puppy should never be fed by hand. It can become a habit that will have you in its grip the rest of his life, particularly if you are at all soft-hearted, and who isn't?

Puppies are very sensitive organisms in many ways, and particularly in the way of picking up tensions present in you. If you are having the beginning of a feeding problem, and you get all sick and nervous about it, and over-solicitous, and worried, he will pick that up out of the air better than the best parabolic antenna will catch radio waves. It *is* a matter of some concern, but the best approach is a casual one.

It is hard to believe, but there are cases, almost entirely in the world of professional show dogs, where a four-year-old or older dog is still being force-fed. This is a step even beyond hand feeding—a small wad of food is formed, and then literally shoved down the dog's throat. In each case, a promising puppy got finicky about eating, and his owner, anxious to get food into him, began making up pellets of food and poking away. That sort of thing is all grand fun for the dog, for he gets loads of attention at each meal, and once the habit is established it is hard to break. As the dog gets older, it gets harder and harder, for his appetite is not so ravenous as a pup's, and he can go for days without food if it suits his purposes, causing considerable anxiety on the part of his owner. There are no known cases of a dog simply dying of starvation if force-feeding is discontinued, but some have wasted away for a week or more in the face of determined owner efforts to put an end to the situation. Usually the owner's determination gives way before the dog's, and the force feeding goes on. Don't get entrapped by this sort of thing. No healthy dog should have to be force-fed, or even simply hand-fed. If it has gotten started, take the pup to a vet for a thorough examination. If he is certified healthy, then set yourself to outlast your pup. Put his food down at the appointed intervals and wait until he gets hungry enough to eat it. He will.

FEEDING DISHES

Although a healthy, hungry puppy can eat from anything up to and including an old derby hat, it is worth giving some thought to a proper feeding dish for him, just to make things easier for both of you. The major consideration is the shape of his nose. There are three general shapes—flat, blunt and pointed. Flat-nosed dogs like Bulldogs can eat out of almost anything they can get their faces into—a shallow pie pan or dish is good. Blunt-nosed dogs like Cocker Spaniels can eat very handily out of the deep special dog dishes shaped something like a volcano. Their blunt noses don't get in the way when they're digging for food, and the volcano shape of the dish is very handy for keeping their ears out of the food. The sharp-nosed breeds, such as collies, need a flatter, shallower dish. Their nostrils stick out somewhat in front of their mouths, and in a deep dish they are likely to get a noseful of food before they can get to it to eat it. This is unpleasant for a dog, and he may refuse food or be finicky about it if fed from such a dish.

FEEDING AT FIVE TO SIX MONTHS

This is a period in which most pups really make noticeable growth and need their nutrition. Up to now, pups only seem to grow a little every time you look the other way. Near six months, they seem to grow right before your eyes, shooting up and getting gangly and leggy, losing the puppy fatness they may have had.

As noted before, the number of feedings per day will depend on the individual pup, but by this time he should certainly be down to three, and possibly to two. On either two meals or three, the morning feeding should still have as its basis milk plus the vitamin concentrate, but at this age most pups will appreciate something less mushy than Pablum as the bulk part of the morning formula. Ordinary breakfast cornflakes in the milk are good, and crumbled shredded wheat makes another tasteful and nutritious "filler." Don't, however, give him any of the bran cereals.

FEEDING AT SEVEN MONTHS TO ONE YEAR

From this point on in a puppy's growth, you can feed him pretty much as though he were an adult. By now he will almost certainly be down to two feedings a day—a main heavy meal in the evening, and a breakfast of milk and cereal. At seven months, his total food consumption will be approaching that of an adult. Though not full grown, he will be eating about the same amount as an adult would—as he gets bigger and heavier, the total intake will stay about the same (always depending on his activity), but with increasing maturity the ratio of food weight to body weight will become compensatorily smaller.

RATES OF GROWTH

It is impossible to predict the proper rate of growth for any individual dog, but this factor is often of such concern to the owner that a chart of average weights at one-month intervals is included here. If your breed is not represented among those listed, you can still use the chart quite well by finding out what the average dog of your breed weighs at maturity, then using the line for the breed nearest yours in final weight, or making your own approximate line between breeds if yours falls right between two of the charted ones. If your breed weighs, say, an average of 68 pounds at maturity, then simply draw another line on the chart, halfway at all points between the lines for German Shepherds and Setters. The resulting line will be a fair approximation of the growth schedule for your puppy.

It is important, however, to keep in mind that each of the very neat and symmetrical lines on the chart is a smoothed-out averaging of the records of a number of dogs. Some of the individuals varied widely from the norm in one direction, some individuals varying widely in the other. According to the original data charts of Laurence Alden Horswell, who compiled the chart, the weights of individual puppies tended to stay quite close to the average curve until six months of age, and then began to vary quite widely in some cases.

Remember also that there are bigger and smaller strains within breeds, and your puppy is much more likely to end up weighing about the same as his parents than any breed average. During the first six months, however, his rate of growth should stay fairly close to the charted curve for his breed, or average adult weight of his breed. If his weight falls markedly below expectations during those first six months, take a good long look at the way you've been feeding him, or better yet, take him to your vet for an examination.

The major inter-breed phenomenon you will immediately notice on examining the chart is that the smaller breeds mature much more quickly than the large ones. Pomeranians may reach their full adult weight at eight months, when Great Danes are at only two-thirds of their adult weight.

APPETITE PROBLEMS

If at any time during the first year your pup seems to show a flagging appetite, don't worry about it in the beginning. There is one period when he is teething, somewhere between three and four months, when his

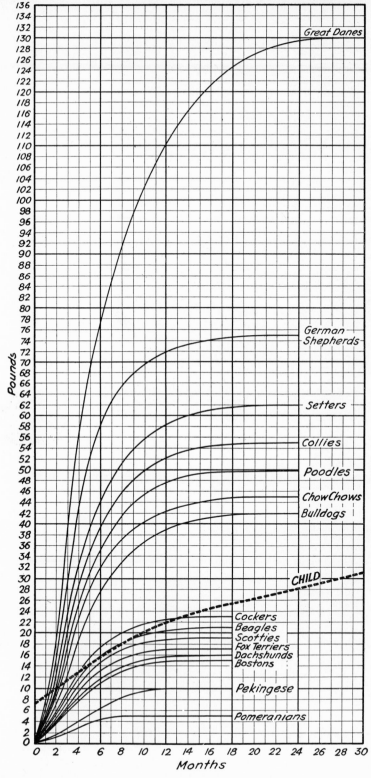

By courtesy of Lawrence Alden Horswell

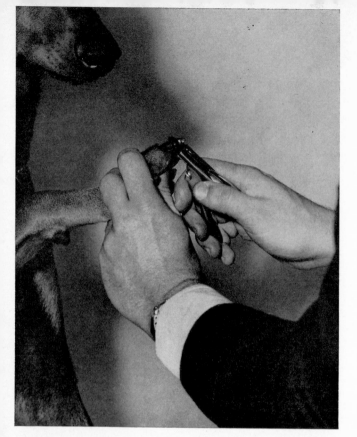

Left: Nail clipping (see pages 56 and 95)

Below: Grooming implements: clockwise—nail clippers, combined brush and slicker, manual coat clippers, curry comb. (See pages 58 and 89).

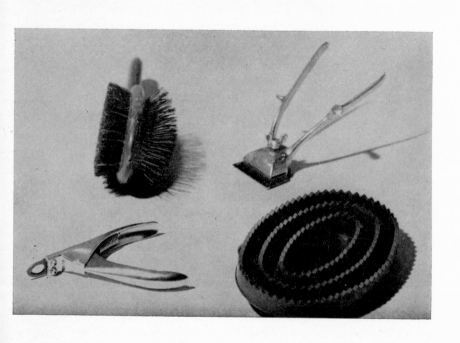

appetite will drop sharply. It is normal, and all puppies go through it. There will be other times—when he may have a mild cold, or a slightly upset stomach, or just be feeling out of sorts in general. If the lack of appetite goes on for a few days, and you see no signs of ill health, such as dull eyes, general listlessness, diarrhea, you can try giving him a few Brewer's Yeast tablets—not to be confused with bulk yeast. These tablets are generally available in drugstores, in bottles of 6-grain (369 milligram) tablets, with nothing on the label about appetite stimulation. They are good for the purpose, though. Once a day for two or three days, give your pup the tablets, one to each ten pounds of body weight. Many pups will eat them out of your hand, or you may be able to salt them throughout his food if he is eating enough to carry out the deception. Don't continue with them much beyond three days if they show no effect. After that much time, it is worth a trip to your vet—a week of seriously depressed appetite quite probably indicates something wrong that should be looked after. The vet may supply you with specific tablets for the purpose, or even give your pup an injection for appetite stimulation, if there seems to be nothing wrong that requires specific treatment.

Many people begin worrying about their dogs' appetites when there is really no need to. Remember that if you live in the city or in any other situation in which your dog's amount of exercise is severely limited, he can't be expected to eat as much as a normally active country dog. If he seems healthy and is not getting thin on what seems to you to be too little to eat, you're probably wrong about how much he should be eating.

SNACKS AND TIDBITS

Dogs are very much like humans in regard to between-meal snacks. They really shouldn't have them. If you are not a snack eater yourself, it will be easier to keep the temptation out of your dog's way, but if you habitually nibble bits of cake, candy or doughnuts, you are very likely to fall into the habit of giving him "just a little bit." It is bad for two reasons. First, it interferes drastically with his balanced diet, even as it does with a human diet—a snack lowers the normal appetite for a balanced meal. Second, if you get into the habit of giving him a little of whatever you're munching on, it will develop into a habit of his that can become annoying and lead to a serious breach of relations between you. Once he gets the idea that it is his natural right to share snacks with you, you will never be able to enjoy another snack in peace. There he will be, with those big brown eyes turned on you like soulful searchlights. He will poke his nose at you and at the food. Some pups badly spoiled in this way get downright demanding about it and you will be tempted to shout at him to scram, and relations can become severely strained. It can also be embarrassing when you have guests, and your pup starts climbing over them, poking and licking at any food they set down on the coffee table for a moment.

It is far better never to start the whole process. This sort of advice is probably the most widely ignored in the world, for there seems to be little harm in giving him just that little bit just that one time. He will be interested in the smell of any snacks you may have, and will inevitably try to investigate at first. But if you give it firmly to be understood that there is nothing doing, that snacks are strictly for humans, and hard lines to you, dog, then he will shortly abandon the idea and mind his own business. Dogs learn fast about such things, and he will leave you alone in the future. But if you start even a little bit, it is like a breach in the dike. It can get out of control before you realize it.

There is nothing wrong with giving him an occasional snack or tidbit of his own in the form of some kind of dog biscuit, but establish a hard and fast rule from the beginning that he gets this sort of thing only in his feeding area and doesn't carry it about into the house to munch on there. For one reason—biscuits chewed in the living room will inevitably leave crumbs and attract ants and other undesirables. For another, it is an eminently good practice to teach your dog to eat nothing but food given him in his feeding area.

FOOD REFUSAL AND TABLE MANNERS

The idea of teaching him not to eat anything outside of his feeding area has several purposes. First, if he learns this lesson thoroughly, he is far less likely ever to pick up any poisoned food from the yard or street. There are, unfortunately, people who hate dogs enough to leave poisoned food around for them, and a dog who will pick up anything edible in sight is fair game for a dog poisoner. Also, there is accidentally poisonous food, in garbage and elsewhere.

Secondly, if he does not take food at random, he is less likely to be lured away by a dognapper with a handful of hamburger, or to get friendly with a potential burglar who comes bearing tasty gifts. It is all for his own protection and yours.

You can start on this training by simply never letting the situation arise from the first. If there is nothing for him to eat around the house except in his dish and at mealtimes, he will not get the idea that anything is fair game. Next you can progress to leaving a bit of hamburger or a tasty biscuit on the floor where you can keep an eye on it. If he attempts to eat it, tell him "No!" very firmly, and don't let him have it. Keep this up until he ignores any food lying about on the floor of the house. Then go through the same routine outside when you have him on leash and can prevent him from grabbing the food and running. From this you can progress to having a friend offer him food both inside and outside the house—simply insist that he not take it, and after a while he will get the idea and turn down food anywhere but in his bowl.

Along with this he should acquire basic table manners. This will help in teaching him food refusal, but it is also an end in itself. Basically, simply never give him anything from the table while you're eating. Here again it may be hard to resist. All the wonderful aromas of roasts and steaks and hamburger and chicken and fish will inevitably draw him to the table like a magnet, and the searchlights will go on again. He will give the impression that he hasn't been fed for a week, and how could you be so cruel? It isn't cruel at all—simply sensible. Once he comes to understand that all that acting isn't getting him anywhere, he will learn to ignore you once you've sat down to your own meal, and life will be easier all around.

Guests can cause a problem here, but if you explain that you're teaching him not to beg at table, they'll generally go along with you and keep things away from him. There will be a few who insist they've had dogs for generations and know all about it, and that just one little bit of steak fat certainly can't do him any harm. Be staunch, and don't permit it, or you'll be in for a siege of retraining.

ADULT FEEDING

The opening sections of this chapter, covering nutrition and types of possible diets, have covered the constituents of your dog's food. What remains to be said is that adult dogs are best fed only once a day, and this time is usually in the evening. It is an entirely natural pattern for a dog, tracing back to the savage state when the hunter filled his stomach as best he could whenever he could make a kill, and then went away somewhere to digest and wait until he got hungry again. The reason for the time being evening is that the dog will be able to rest and digest his food during the night—the exception here being dogs who are kept largely as watch dogs for night duty around the house. For exactly the same reason, they should be fed their meal early in the day so that they can sleep and rest during the day, and then be alert during the dark hours.

While a puppy should have water available to him only at mealtimes, the adult dog can have a bowl of water available at all times, because he will have been housebroken and will have enough control over his bladder to wait for his regular walks.

IN GENERAL

Care and attention to feeding and nutrition can seem like much ado about nothing. If you look at, or think about, all of the stray and pet mongrels you've known who seemed to be in good enough health without anybody ever bothering much about what they ate, you may wonder if it's worth all the trouble this chapter would seem to incur. The best answer is to point to the show dogs you may have seen around or at dog shows—it is very likely you will have marvelled at their outstanding good condition, health and vitality. A great deal of it comes from careful, good nutrition, and if you'd like your dog to be healthy and robust, good nutrition is the clue. Certainly there are healthy strays, and healthy un-cared-for mutts, but remember that those you see are to be placed against those you don't see—all the ones who died young, or whom you don't remember because of the universal human tendency to remember only the examples which bear out a thesis. You have just your one dog, and can't take chances with the laws of averages which dictate that on random diets some dogs will be healthy but others won't. Feed him right up to the hilt, and you'll never regret a moment or a cent of it.

CHAPTER III

PUPPY CARE

The considerations of the health of a puppy are in some ways like those of feeding. Certainly a good many millions of puppies have grown and prospered far out of sight of any veterinarian and protective needle. Your pup just might, too. But also, untold millions of puppies have sickened and died of the ravages of various canine diseases—those pups you seldom hear about, that might have lived had basic care been taken. The human race managed to survive centuries of negligible medical care too, but the mortality rate was fearsome, particularly among children. Nowadays few people would dream of taking the chance of not having their children inoculated against various childhood diseases.

Whatever the statistics about the chance of survival and health without preventive measures, it will mean little to you if your pup is one of the few who contribute to the black side of the statistical tables. There might be only one chance in a thousand that your pup would get a certain disease if unprotected. But it would be small comfort to think about the 999 other healthy pups if yours lay dying.

VETERINARIANS

It must be noted at the outset that your vet is the most important factor in your pup's well being and health, so it is imperative that you give some thought to your choice of a veterinarian and your relations with him.

In many communities, there is one vet within reasonable travelling range, and so the choice is pretty well made for you. When there is a choice it is best to make as extensive an investigation as you can before you need a vet. An astonishing number of people never bother to think

47

about picking a doctor for themselves until they're sick and don't have time to choose. The same situation, of course, obtains when it comes to a vet for the dog they own. If possible, take a hard look around for the best veterinarian in your area, long before you ever imagine you will need him.

The situation is not unlike that of finding a good doctor. Veterinary societies will not recommend any individual veterinarian, except for reasons of geography, because of ethics and professional courtesy. So you will be thrown onto your own resources. If you get a puppy from a breeder, ask him who he thinks is a reliable vet in the area. Ask your friends who have owned dogs for years. Don't be surprised if you get contradictory opinions, for most people who have considerable to do with dogs tend to have strong convictions about particular vets. One may praise a vet to the skies, another condemn the same man as a butcher who shouldn't be allowed to treat a goldfish with a head cold. You're not likely to find such contradictory views, but take all recommendations and dis-recommendations with a grain of salt.

Aside from a man's reputation, take note of the office and clinic he maintains. It isn't an infallible guide, but you can get a clue if the vet you are considering works out of a rat-hole and handles your dog while the ashes from his cigar dribble down the front of his white jacket. New dog owners often have an impression that veterinarians are not really professional men—that they are some sort of horse doctor who happens to treat dogs on the side and therefore doesn't need much of a clinic and office. This couldn't be farther from the truth—a veterinarian is just as much a professional man as a doctor, and has exactly the same reasons for maintaining a clean, pleasant, attractive office.

On the other hand, however, don't be over-impressed by an office full of shiny gadgets. Just as an example, two of the top veterinarians in Manhattan are diametrically opposite insofar as the outer aspects of their practices go. One operates in a fairly dingy side street, alone except for a kennel assistant who handles clipping, bathing and kenneling, and in a small office behind a drab waiting room opening from the sidewalk. The other is head of a spotless clinic, complete with receptionists, assistants, kennelmen, X-ray room, operating room and enough equipment to run a small human hospital. Both are individually superb veterinarians.

The best general advice is this: once you have more or less picked a man, by reputation or however, watch him with a close and beady eye on your first visit with your dog. Watch for a firm but gentle touch with your dog—a competent vet is never afraid of a dog, never handles one roughly or callously. Do not, however, interpret it as fear if the vet insists on putting a gauze muzzle on your dog before conducting his examination. This is standard practice with many vets who have been badly bitten by some dog whose owner took oath that he would never, never put tooth to anyone. Once the vet gets to know your dog he'll abandon the muzzle, but many insist on it during a first examination.

Look for a willingness to explain things to you, at least in a general fashion. A vet who refuses to discuss your dog's conditions with you as an intelligent adult can be presumed to have a reason for his unwillingness, which reason is probably either uncomplimentary to you or to the vet. *Canine Medicine*, a highly respected textbook for veterinary students, gives the following advice to its readers:

> "The safest, most dignified way for the clinician to indicate his qualifications to his client is to perform a creditable examination and to base on this a preliminary report in simple conservative language. The attitude that details of the case are 'none of the client's business' is a curiously perverted one which fails completely to recognize the fact that the client, as the owner of the patient (and as the payer of the fee), has a right to know what is wrong and what will be done.
>
> "Possibly a few practitioners hesitate to enlighten their clients because of a fear of revealing 'tricks of the trade.' Modern veterinary medicine is not based on 'tricks' and it is absurd to think that information imparted in a few minutes could make a quack of anybody."

The feeling for a good veterinarian is really something you acquire by experience. Just remember to keep your eyes and ears well open when you visit your prospective vet, and don't be fooled by a line of scientific bafflegab. You're a human and he's a human, whatever degrees he may have, and you should be able to make a reasonable working judgment of him as a man, and from that get some idea of what he is as a vet.

Once you've got a vet, stick with him as much as possible. Some people have an unfortunate tendency to "doctor shop" and in the process nobody ends up knowing their full history. If you get a vet and stay with him, trusting him, he will get to know you and particularly the medical history of your dog, and will be better able to help you when you need his help.

It is not all a one-way street—if you expect good veterinary care, you will have to cooperate fully with your chosen veterinarian. First, train yourself to be aware of symptoms and unusual conditions in your dog, and to observe them accurately and remember them or write them down. General disease symptoms are discussed at some length in the chapter on Adult Care, which you may want to look at now, even if your puppy is very young at this point. Accurate reporting of your dog's symptoms and details of any past illnesses are highly important to a vet. Here again is a quote from *Canine Medicine*:

> "The importance of history as an aid to diagnosis can hardly be exaggerated. Information as to the nature and time of onset, early signs, circumstances under which symptoms were first noted—anything which may have directly or indirectly related to the ailment for which the dog was presented for treatment is important to the clinician and should be brought to light by him."

To which the additional comment is obvious—if you present a clear and ordered picture of what has happened, so that the vet doesn't have to "bring it to light," everything will be that much easier for him. Some few owners actually take the attitude that it is the veterinarian's job to find out what's wrong, saying in effect, "If I knew what was wrong with the dog I wouldn't be here, so find out for yourself." It is highly unlikely that any reader of this book will end up in this camp, but it is mentioned simply to show what veterinarians do come up against.

There is another tendency, unfortunately much more prevalent, to being uninformative about unsuccessful home attempts at treatment, or falsifying the early signs of disease because the owner is ashamed of having let it go so long without treatment. Don't think veterinarians don't know about such things—again, *Canine Medicine* says, "And, unfortunately, there are clients who purposely misrepresent the history of the case in order to conceal their own neglect or ill-advised efforts at treatment." If you have let something go too long without treatment, or have fumbled with medicines and treatments you didn't understand, it was wrong of you, and your vet may give you a dirty look or two and a lecture. But if it is any owner's decision that his dog should suffer rather than he because of his mistakes, then he shouldn't be allowed to own a dog in the first place.

It is an excellent idea to take your dog to the vet's office for periodic general examinations, just as you ought to visit your doctor's office every once in a while for a look-over even if nothing seems to be the matter. It is, in fact, even more sensible with a dog, for your dog can't effectively communicate to you the fact that he has had a minor pain in his side for months, or that he is beginning to grow a crop of some intestinal parasite which doesn't show up until he is seriously ill. Consult your vet about regular examinations, and don't think you're being foolish if you bring an abundantly healthy dog to a vet time after time. You're not wasting the vet's time—he is in business as much to keep your dog healthy as he is to treat sick dogs. If periodic exams show your dog is in fact staying healthy, so much the better.

WEATHER PROBLEMS

The best time of year for a puppy to be born is in January or February, if he is going to live in the colder sections of the country. That way, you get him in March or April (at about two months of age) and he has the entire summer and fall to be outside while he's growing up. By the time cold weather sets in, in October or November, he will be nine months or ten months old and considerably better able to withstand the rigors of cold and snow.

Unfortunately, things are not always arranged so conveniently. Many pups arrive as Christmas presents at the age of three months and have to endure the icy blasts of winter in their first few months of going outside. It can be a problem, too. Even pups with long, thick coats will suffer if they live in a heated house, then are plunged into the outside freezing cold. It's all very well to say, "doesn't matter, he has his own fur coat," but imagine how you would feel if you wore your heaviest over-coat inside, got as well adjusted to the heat as possible, then were thrown outside on a freezing day. The adjustment is a little easier for a dog, or a puppy, but the principle applies.

Much as he may love to romp and play in the snow, be a little careful about the length of time you expose your puppy. Bring him in fairly quickly after he has relieved himself, and most important, dry him off well. Particularly if he has short hair, it wouldn't hurt to have a sweater for him. The idea of a sweater for a dog seems hilarious to a great many people, but it isn't. If you do get him one, be sure it covers his chest— the most important area to keep reasonably warm. Some of the dog sweaters you will find in pet shops are all very fancy and as attractive as such an item can be, but they leave the chest bare for some curious reason. Make the sweater a practical one. The same goes for a coat if you prefer it. Coats are not as efficient as sweaters for a puppy, and the majority available in stores cover only the back, so shop carefully.

Hot summer weather brings its problems, too. Dogs and puppies suffer quite severely from the heat sometimes, and have heat strokes. There are several things you can do to help prevent heat problems.

First, do not, repeat *do not,* shave off his coat! There is a long-standing idea that this is something to be done automatically in the summer. Actually, it is harmful. It probably stems from people realizing that they themselves are more comfortable with less clothing in the summer, and seems very logical, but it is a misapprehension. Dogs sweat hardly at all, dissipating their heat largely in the moisture of the breath, so taking the coat away does not help cool a dog by aiding perspiration evaporation. The coat actually helps protect a dog against heat, even as the long robes of an Arab are a protection against fierce desert sun and heat. Keep the coat on. What you can do is brush it vigorously every day to remove dead hairs and undercoat which may be sticking to the skin. That will help. A very dense coat can be thinned out with thinning scissors, a special kind which cut only a few scattered hairs at each stroke. Or ask a professional to do a thinning job for you. But *do not* shave your pup to the skin. Aside from the above considerations, shaving can, for reasons not fully understood, cause subsequent baldness in some dogs.

Your puppy will probably cut down his eating all by himself in the summer, so don't worry if his appetite seems to fall off. Feed him a little less in any case, and keep him supplied with fresh, cool water, changing the contents of his dish a half-dozen times a day to make sure cool water is always available. And of course, keep him out of the hot sun as much as possible—except for the coat, treat him pretty much as you treat yourself when the heat sets in.

Rain is another problem altogether. Dogs don't think much more of going out in the rain than humans do. Some are quite adamant about it, but they do have to go out nonetheless. It won't hurt your puppy to get rained on. If it happens, just make sure you dry him thoroughly with a rough towel when he comes in, paying particular attention to his chest. It's difficult to get a dog thoroughly dry as the towel tends to dry just the coat and leave the skin wet. But rub him thoroughly and he'll love it—it's like a prolonged petting. In fact, with very little effort you can train him to wait on the porch for his drying, or to run straight to the kitchen or bathroom, wherever you keep a towel for him. He'll get to expect it so much that he'll stand in his appointed drying spot and complain if you forget.

There is very little point, in either rain or snow, in dressing your pup up with a raincoat and/or the little bootees you find in some pet shops. Just be sure he gets dry and warm as soon as you bring him home, and don't keep him out too long. There is one thing to watch out for if you live in an area where the city, or a private individual, puts rock salt on icy sidewalks. Puppies and dogs who walk on the salted ice sometimes get chunks of the rock salt stuck between their pads, and when they come home, lick it off and swallow it. A very little rock salt can make your dog very sick, or even kill him, so watch out for it. After coming in from a walk on icy salted sidewalks, go over his pads with a towel to dry them and clean out any salt that might be stuck there—paying particular attention to drying between the pads.

BATHING

You will hear and read a lot of contradictory things about bathing your pup, for opinion is sharply split—one faction claiming you should never bathe a puppy, another that it cannot do him any harm. In a curious way, both sides are right, improbable though that may seem. The "never bathers" are right because many pups have died from complications resulting from colds after a bath; on the other hand, the "bathers" are right provided you take a modicum of care with the bathing. As you see, the point turns on the care you take.

As a good general rule: don't bathe him until he's a year old. Even in good weather, there's an ever-present danger that he will catch a cold afterward, and a cold is a deadly enemy of a puppy. Most pups simply don't get all that dirty, and don't need baths—there is definitely no need for a regular Saturday night plunge. Or any plunge for that matter. If he does seem to be getting very dirty or smelly, you can sponge him off with a damp rag, or a rag wetted with witch hazel to get the surface dirt off his coat. It's generally not the skin that gets dirty and needs cleaning, it's his coat—but when you soak him in a bath, the skin gets good and wet, too, and that's what leads to colds.

If something comes up that makes it absolutely necessary to bathe him, you can do it if you go about it sensibly, and he is at least four or five months old. If it's cold or even cool outside, take him for a walk just before the bath so he can empty himself and be able to stay inside the house for several hours after. Then go ahead and bathe him with warm water. Afterwards, dry him off thoroughly with good rough towelling, making sure you get the skin, not just the coat dry. Be sure to get his chest dry, for that's the vital spot. Then keep him in a warm room, off the floor if possible, and definitely out of drafts. In good warm weather you can even do the bathing outside, towel him dry and let him romp in the sunshine to finish the process. See the chapter on Adult Care for proper techniques of bathing a dog.

If your puppy does catch a mild cold as a result of a bath (or for any other reason) and you don't think it is serious enough to take him to your vet, try giving him a small shot of brandy, which will help. A twenty-pound pup can be given a teaspoonful of brandy mixed with two or three teaspoonsful of water or milk. You may be able to persuade him to drink it from a bowl, but if not, give it to him as though it were a liquid medicine, a technique explained in the chapter on First Aid and Home Nursing. Adjust the teaspoonful dosage up or down for the size of your pup.

CROPPING, DOCKING AND DEWCLAWS

Dewclaws are the "thumbs" your pup may have on the inside of each front leg, part way up the leg. Some few pups are born with none, most have them only on the front legs, and a few have them on all four. Like the human appendix, they are no earthly good and can be harmful, so they are cut off many pups shortly after birth. They can be harmful in a number of ways. First, positioned as they are, they can scratch or damage a dog's eye when the paw and leg are rubbed over his face. It doesn't happen often, but it has happened. The nail of the dewclaw is often neglected at toenail clipping time, and it can grow around and become painful to the dog, because there is no chance to wear it away in normal walking and running. The dewclaw can catch on brambles and under-brush, or other things, and be torn or disjointed, again causing consider-able pain. So they are better off and done with.

The trouble, so far as you're concerned, is that the de-clawing is best done at the age of two or three days. By the time you get your pup it will probably have been done already. Still, if not, even at two, three or four months, the operation is feasible, and can be easily handled by a competent veterinarian. If your pup's dewclaws are giving him trouble, or you think they might, talk it over with your vet.

At the same time the dewclaws are removed on pups, many breeds have their tails docked, which is the technical word for "cut off at one point or another." It rarely happens with mongrels, of course, but quite a few of the pure breed standards call for docking. Done at two days of age it doesn't seem to hurt the pups at all, provided it is done right. If you happen to have a breed of the short-tailed variety, don't think he has been tortured in having his tail docked, or that anything out of the way has happened to him.

A little later in life, some breeds have their ears cropped, again a tech-nical term, this meaning "trimmed to a certain shape." Among these breeds are Boxers, Great Danes and Dobermans. The best age for ear cropping is about six to eight weeks; if you get a pup of an ear-cropped breed, it should have been done before you got him. In some cases breed-ers leave it up to the new owner. If you are going to have it done, see your vet as soon as possible, for every passing week makes it more difficult and dangerous.

None of these operations should be attempted by anyone but an experienced veterinarian. When ear cropping, for example, is done by a vet, the operation takes place under complete anaesthesia. Aseptic pro-cedures are employed, bleeding is controlled, the ear is properly sewn, and there is very little danger and no pain at all to the puppy. Later, when the puppy comes out of the anaesthetic, the ears may itch and bother him a little, just as an appendectomy scar bothers you. If ear cropping strikes you as cruel, it can only be pointed out that thousands of "ear jobs" are done every year by the most ethical vets; the American Kennel Club, which will not countenance cruelty to dogs, supervises and approves the showing of cropped breeds; and the ASPCA, that formidable protector of animals, has never stopped or attempted to stop the practice.

Ear cropping is still illegal in a few states, but in most it is permitted, provided it is done under anaesthesia and by a licensed veterinarian. New York and New Jersey are among the states which have legalized cropping only recently. Curiously enough, in England, where sensitivities about dogs run high, ear-cropped dogs are not eligible for shows, yet dogs with docked tails are.

CARE OF THE NAILS

As soon as you get your puppy, take a look at his nails to see if they need clipping. They very likely will, and even if you don't see the need, you'll probably feel it, for a young puppy's nails, untended, get needle sharp. For proper care, you should have one of the guillotine-type of nail clippers made specially for dogs—a curved sliding blade neatly nips off the tip of the nail.

The earlier you start regular nail care, the better. You get your pup used to the procedure while he is still young and impressionable, you save him possible pain, and you help prevent the nails from getting unmanageable, for if left alone too long the quick tends to grow farther out and it then becomes painful for the dog if the nails are cut to the proper length.

You can tell when his nails need clipping, first, if they are puppy-sharp. As he gets a little older, look at him as he stands still. If the nails touch the floor, they need clipping. And if the nails click as he walks on bare floors or concrete, they very definitely need clipping.

It is best, for the first few times, to have someone else help you with the job, for the puppy will object to it—not that he knows what it's all about, but he won't like the restraint involved in holding a leg still long enough to nip the ends off of four nails. If someone else holds both the pup and one of his legs, you can concentrate all your attention on taking off just the right amount of nail. But if you are doing the job alone, hold him in your lap or beside you on the floor, take hold of a front leg just above the foot, and let him get used to the idea of being held. Also, it is a good idea to let him sniff and nuzzle the clippers, to learn that there's nothing harmful or dangerous about them.

The first approach is an extremely important one—be firm but very gentle about it, and never scold him or shout at him if he wriggles and objects. You must simply let him know that it is something which has to be done, and that it will be that much easier if he cooperates. Puppies who are harshly introduced to nail clipping often panic at the thought for the rest of their lives, and fight and howl every time the clippers come out. At the other extreme, a puppy rightly introduced and gently handled will get to the point of actually enjoying clipping because of the extra attention it means.

Once you have the puppy's foot still, and him calmed, take off just the tip of his nail—it would be a good idea at this point to read the section on nail care in the later chapter on Adult Care. Puppy nails will probably not need filing, but otherwise the advice on the care of an adult's nails applies to a puppy's. Inexperienced owners tend to under-do the clipping rather than overdo at first, which is all to the good, as you can't hurt the pup that way. As you gain more experience you will find just the right amount to cut off.

It can hurt, and badly, if you attempt to take too deep a cut with the clipper, so be careful until you learn to gauge things. If you do cut too deep, the nail may start bleeding. It's nothing to worry about unless it should become profuse, which is unlikely. You can stop the bleeding by pressing a cloth or tissue to the nail for a moment. A small wad of cotton soaked with ordinary hydrogen peroxide is very effective, or even a styptic pencil, but remember that the pencil will sting, just as it stings you. Most times, the bleeding is minor enough to stop by itself, but in any case, keep your pup off his feet a few minutes, and keep him from licking the nail for a while.

Don't let this possibility of minor pain and bleeding scare you away from regular nail care, however. It isn't like cutting a human finger—the construction of the dog's nail is such that there is a blood supply in the nail itself. Minor cuts heal perfectly and without danger. With even a slight bit of practice, you will never have any problem, and nail-cutting and filing which does not go deep enough to reach the quick is no more painful to the dog than cutting and filing your own nails is to you. He doesn't even feel it if you do it right.

GENERAL GROOMING

Along with regular nail care, regular care of your puppy's coat will help him. Whatever the length of his hair, it is a very good idea to brush him on a regular schedule—once a week at least. Start him as soon as you get him, and he will come to accept regular brushing and in fact will actively enjoy it.

Starting with your very young puppy, it helps to make a game out of the brushing. Let him sniff and poke at the brush as much as he wants to. Then, holding him gently, brush away with easy strokes, just hard enough to do some good to the coat, and to work out any dandruff and dead hairs he may have accumulated on his skin. As you go along and he becomes familiar with the idea, you can very easily train him to stand, either on the floor or on a table. "Stand" training is simple—just put him in a standing position and gently keep him in that position, repeatedly telling him to "Stand, stand," and praising him even when he doesn't do it right. Again, never be harsh. Don't expect it to work miracles right away—it takes time. But as long as you're gentle and praiseful about it, he'll learn, and will soon be standing like a veteran while you go over him with the brush.

Grooming affects not only his appearance, but his health. Fleas, ticks and other unpleasant skin parasites are far less likely to set up house-keeping in a cared-for coat which is clean. And even more important, if you are in the habit of working on him regularly, you are far more likely to find any parasites which might be on him—for they do get onto the best groomed dogs. Additionally, you are more likely to notice any skin conditions such as eczema, ringworm or mange, and be able to catch and treat them before they become serious problems. And further yet, it is good even if it only sets up a habit pattern on your part. A well-groomed dog is generally well cared for in other respects, as the owner has gotten into the habit of making regular checks on his dog's health.

GENERAL HEALTH

Aside from specific symptoms of specific diseases, there are a number of general ways you can check on your puppy's health. Here again, except for the obvious human-canine differences, you need only look at your puppy approximately as you would at a baby or child—much the same picture of health or illness will be apparent.

The positive signs are these: good appetite, alertness, healthy coat, bright eyes, pink gums and tongue, normal puppy activity. All of these you can check at a glance and by simple observation. The reverse of any of them should lead you to suspect something wrong—listlessness, dull eyes, pale gums, lagging appetite, dull and dry coat. No single symptom or combination necessarily means a specific ailment, but they are the things you should keep an eye on.

More specifically, you may want to keep something of a check on your puppy's temperature, particularly if he shows any of the negative signs listed above. But first you must abandon the universal notion that a cold nose and/or cool ears mean that all is well with the pup, or that warm ears and/or nose mean he is running a temperature and may be sick. Neither of these is true. At best, you can say that a very cold nose and ears just might indicate lack of dangerously high temperature—if it reassures you to feel his nose, then go ahead. But it won't tell you anything really, for a dog can run an illness temperature and still have a cold nose. One thing is for sure—although doctors can get an idea of the absence or presence of temperature in a human by feeling the forehead, it is a safe bet you have never seen a veterinarian feel a dog's nose to check his temperature in the course of an examination. Take it from the people who know—it simply means little or nothing. And as far as warm noses go, you will soon find that your puppy's nose will be warm whenever he wakes up. It has nothing to do with his health; it's just the way things happen when a dog sleeps, particularly if he has curled his nose into his paws. So discard any ideas of checking temperature this way.

The way to do it, of course, is to have a thermometer and be able to take a rectal temperature whenever you want to make a check. Any ordinary clinical thermometer will do—have a special one for the pup and keep it well separated from any others you might have around the house. To use it, smear a little butter or lard or mineral oil on the bulb end as lubrication for easier insertion. Then, making very sure the pup is held still, insert the thermometer about half way into his rectum, keeping it there for a minute. Ease it in gently, for the sensation is a strange one for the pup, and he may object. Hold the protruding end of the thermometer only loosely—just enough to keep it in and steady. When you take the thermometer out, have a piece of tissue or cotton ready to wipe off the end before you read it.

The dog's normal temperature is 101.7°. Puppies tend to run a normally higher temperature than adult dogs, just as children have higher temperatures than adult humans. For puppies, a good average temperature is 102.5°. Remember, however, that this is an average. It will vary somewhat from pup to pup, and from season to season, and rises and falls slightly according to the hour of the day. A reading as high as 103° in a puppy may mean little or nothing. But once it gets any higher than that, it is time to suspect definite illness of some sort, and to get in touch with your veterinarian. If you should find a temperature as high as 106°, the situation is probably very serious, and you should waste no time at all in getting an examination of your puppy. You may save his life by prompt action. If you are unable to get to a vet quickly, see the Adult Care chapter for temporary control of fever.

Taking rectal temperatures seems like a messy and generally unsavory business to a good number of people, but it really isn't so bad. If you have raised children, you'll probably be used to it, and will be able to take your pup's temperature quite skillfully. If you haven't, try it anyway. It's a small thing to do when the life and health of your puppy might be at stake—temperature is one of nature's surest indicators of ill health, and something serious may show in it long before it becomes manifest in other symptoms.

Another excellent check is the condition of your puppy's bowels and stool. In the normal puppy, the bowels may be moved often, and this is to be expected. The thing to watch out for is erratic timing. It is quite within reason for a pup not to defecate for as long as a day and a half, but this will probably not be too serious—constipation is only rarely an indication of trouble in a dog or pup. But if the constipation continues, or recurs with any frequency, again take a good general look at him and consider taking it up with your vet.

The surest indicator of trouble is diarrhea. By the time a puppy is two months old (and you will rarely have one younger), his stool should be consistently well formed. Again, it is not out of the ordinary for a pup to have an occasional loose movement, but if it happens more than once or twice in succession, suspect trouble inside. A normal stool is fully formed and light to dark brown in color—the normal color will depend on his diet. If it is mushy, and expecially if it is largely liquid, and if the color becomes dark and tarry, or very light in color, something is going wrong with the digestive processes and internal accommodations of your pup. This is a good time to give him a thorough check-up yourself, and to take his temperature. It may well turn out to be nothing but a mild stomach upset, perhaps brought on by a change of diet or an emotional upset, but it never hurts to check.

When you see the first signs of diarrhea, you may want to try giving him Kaopectate (available in any drugstore) to help control it. A good dosage is one tablespoonful to a twenty-pound pup, varied according to the size of your puppy, and given every four to five hours until the stool becomes formed. If the diarrhea is only the result of a temporary upset, the Kaopectate will help control it. But if the dosage does little or no good, or if the diarrhea begins again after it has been controlled, suspect illness and at least check by phone with your vet, describing the condition, to see whether you ought to take the pup in for a check. Don't give Kaopectate for more than two days straight without your vet's okay— always check with him if the diarrhea has not been controlled by that time, and check with him earlier if it seems to be getting worse despite the treatment.

Vomiting is an obvious indication of problems, but this symptom has unnecessarily worried more puppy owners than almost any other. Don't take this to mean that vomiting isn't serious—it is. But it may mean very little except that the pup ate something that he had to get rid of. If your pup throws up food occasionally, or retches up a little frothy yellow liquid, it very likely means that something hasn't agreed with him or that he is disturbed by something—that he is nervous and possibly frightened. The main thing to watch for in vomiting is the after-effects. If the puppy recovers in a few moments and appears normal and playful, then there is probably nothing wrong. If you find vomit on the floor, and can find no other signs of illness in the pup, again it indicates that it was probably the result of nothing but a minor upset. But if the vomiting is repeated, or if it ever contains blood, or if the puppy is depressed, shaking, terrified, drooling or otherwise in an abnormal condition immediately after the vomiting, get in touch with your veterinarian as quickly as possible. One of the possibilities is poison, on which there is a discussion in the chapter on First Aid. Vomiting of froth, if continuous or chronic, and continued or chronic vomiting of just-swallowed food or water may indicate leptospirosis or other kidney diseases. Leptospirosis is discussed later in this chapter.

WORMING

This most common problem of puppies is the subject of a great deal of misunderstanding, probably because it is such a common problem. It has been estimated that 10 per cent of all puppies born in this country die of the effects of internal parasites, so worms are certainly not to be taken lightly. Yet a puppy who has the proper observation and treatment is extremely unlikely to be seriously affected.

Several of the major misconceptions about worms should be cleared away first. They are:

1) Worms can be caused by specific foods. Totally false in the sense usually meant, which is that items such as milk or horsemeat can cause worms. What is true is that worm eggs or larvae can be eaten along with contaminated food of any sort, if the eggs or larvae have been deposited in or on the food. But no food or drink of any sort *causes* worms by itself.

2) It is a sure sign of worms if the pup drags his rear along the ground. This one is partially true. Particularly with tapeworms, moving segments of the worms in the rectum and around the anus cause irritation, and to relieve it, a dog may try, largely ineffectively, to "scratch" the area by rubbing it on the ground. This dragging, however, is much more likely to be a sign of congested anal sacs, the pain of which the dog attempts to relieve this way.

3) Every puppy should be wormed just as a routine. Very definitely not true. Although worm infestation is so prevalent that most puppies eventually must be wormed, many born of a worm-free mother never have worms of any sort at any time and live quite happily without ever being wormed. Worming should only be done after a definite diagnosis of worms in a stool specimen.

4) It's easy to handle the problem with a few commercial worm pills. Very dangerously false. Although there are worm pills and medicines on the market, they should absolutely not be administered by you. Worms are a serious problem, and there are specific medicines for specific worm infestations. To be effective, some of these medicines are mildly poisonous and extremely dangerous to the pup if administered by an inexperienced person. Only your veterinarian should handle worming.

5) Garlic or onions will cure worms. Not true, but a little tricky. See the discussion of this in Chapter II.

6) Puppies (and grown dogs) just have worms, and a few don't really hurt them. Dangerously false. This one is the reverse of #3, which dictates that routine worming should be done on all puppies and dogs. Both are manifestations of a way of thinking of dogs—as if they were some sort of machine, like a car, which ought to be routinely greased at given intervals. Although dogs are highly susceptible to worms, worm infestation is by no means an integral part of being a dog. As stated earlier, some dogs go through life without ever having a worm, and they are that much better off for it. If your dog has a worm infestation, however minor, it should be treated, for the worms are harming his health and vitality. If left untreated, even a minor infestation can become serious, and if the ravages of the worms are widespread enough in the dog's or pup's body, he will not recover his full health even after the worms have been completely eliminated by successful treatment. His stomach and intestines may be so badly damaged that he will have trouble with them for the rest of his life.

There are four major worms which affect puppies—roundworms, tapeworms, whipworms and hookworms, in approximately ascending order of seriousness. Infestation comes from eating food infested with worm eggs or larvae, from contact with eggs or larvae in feces or on the ground or from contact with another dog infested with worms. In both the latter cases, transmission usually occurs when the puppy picks up larvae on his coat or feet, and ingests them by licking himself, or by licking off larvae from the other dog's coat.

Roundworms: by far the most common, and fortunately the most easily treated. One of the usual signs of roundworms is a hearty appetite which does not produce any gain in weight, combined with a distended, rounded abdomen which is is often confused with fatness. Even a cursory examination, though, will reveal that although the belly is rounded, the puppy is not fat in other areas, and may even be thin to the point of emaciation. The appetite may fall off due to a general rundown condition, the coat will be dull and shaggy, and pale gums and other mucous membranes will often be seen in severe roundworm cases. There are roundworm medicines commercially available, the Piperazine compounds, which can be given with safety, but which should be avoided until and unless you have gained some experience with dogs. Roundworm symptoms can mask those of other conditions, and you should have a veterinary diagnosis and okay on any worming before you go ahead with it.

Hookworms: Less common than roundworms, but quite deadly to a pup if untreated for long—hookworms probably cause more puppy deaths than any other worm. The symptoms are depressed appetite and often extreme nervousness and tension, combined with anemia (seen through pale gums), listlessness and the characteristic symptom of very loose, bloody diarrhea which is extremely difficult to control.

Tapeworms: The symptoms of tapeworm are much more obscure than those of roundworm or hookworm. The appetite is usually good with little gain in weight, but there is seldom any associated anemia or constant diarrhea, and the abdomen is not distended. Slight signs are alternating diarrhea and constipation, and a vague abdominal discomfort which few owners will notice. Diagnosis of tapeworm is almost always made through noticing tapeworm segments in the stool, in the puppy's bedding, or in the hairs around the rectum. These segments look very much like grains of rice, pinkish white when first passed, turning to brownish as they dry. If you suspect any worm infestation and are unable to detect strong symptoms of any kind, keep a close watch on the puppy's stool for these segments, and on the puppy for the characteristic "sledding," dragging his rear along the ground. Tapeworm infestation is difficult to cure, and should be handled only by a vet.

Whipworm: Until quite recently, whipworm was the most difficult of all worms to cure completely. Whipworms concentrate in the caecum, a structure roughly similar to the human appendix, and there they are highly resistant to most orally administered medicines. But recent veterinary research and development has produced a chemical, often injected rather than given orally, which works throughout the body on the whipworms and in most cases drives them out with great success.

The symptoms of whipworm are somewhat obscure, the most notable being chronic and profuse watery diarrhea characterized by an unusually foul smell. General unthriftiness and emaciation, combined with nervousness, are indicators of possible whipworm. There is one curious indicator which does not appear in all cases of whipworm and in fact can be caused by other conditions, but which will point a large, blinking neon sign at the possibility of whipworm if you see it with your dog. This is a "three-part" stool, in which the beginning of the stool in a single defecation is solid and well-formed, then becomes soft and mushy, and finally becomes watery with blood present.

Watch for all worm symptoms. Even without them, you should have a routine worm examination done by your veterinarian. For this he will need a stool specimen. This too strikes some people as a grim way to go about things, but it will help your vet and save time if you are able to bring him the specimen. It isn't hard or particularly unpleasant—simply locate your pup's most recent stool, scoop up a small bit with a wooden spoon, tongue depressor, postcard or file card and put it in a clean small jar, with metal screw cap if possible. If you have more than one puppy, be very sure the specimen you take is from the pup you're going to have examined, and even if you have only one dog be sure the stool isn't from some passing neighborhood dog. Wrap the jar with a piece of aluminum foil and drop the package in an out-of-the-way cool place until it's time to take it and the pup to your vet's office. It is only by examination of a stool specimen that your vet can definitely establish the presence of worms, determine the type, and administer the proper medicines.

Some types of worm medicine require that the puppy be starved for as long as 24 hours before their administration—and totally starved, for if there is any food in the stomach or intestine when the medicine is given, the puppy may die. Therefore, if your vet gives you such instructions, follow them to the letter! Soft-heartedness on your part could very easily lead to the death of your pup. Although water can usually be given with safety, do not give milk or any other drink but water. And watch that he doesn't eat any bits of food that might be on the floor, or swipe any food during the night.

Depending on your willingness, and the vet, you may either leave your pup for worming, to be picked up a few hours or a day later, or you may take him home as soon as the medicine is administered. The vet may even give you the necessary pills, with instructions to administer them as soon as you get home, or next day if pre-worming starvation is necessary. If you do give the pills at home, use the method described in Chapter V, and watch carefully that the pup does not manage to retain a pill in his mouth and spit it out a minute later.

When the pup gets home, or after you give him the pills, be prepared or you may defeat the purpose of the treatment, which is to get completely rid of the worms. If you live in the city, the best way to handle the situation is to put the pup in a box completely lined with many layers of old newspapers—in the country, keep him outside and preferably in an area distant from your yard. The worms will pass out of him in his stool, and this stool may be sudden and loose. It will definitely be full of worms and worm eggs, mostly dead, but including a few survivors, particularly if you use the Piperazine compounds, which knock the worms out but do not kill them. As soon as the puppy defecates, if in the house, take up all the soiled papers and destroy the bundle, preferably by burning. Outside, just get him away from that area right away or he may be reinfested by contact with the stool.

In roundworm treatment, puppies sometimes vomit up worms, and this vomitus should be destroyed with just as much dispatch as a worm-laden stool—keep an eye on this possibility, particularly if you are worming him in the city, as the vomitus is not as noticeable as a stool, and you might just miss it.

The puppy will void several times after the administration of worm medicines, and you should be very careful about the stools for at least a day. To complete the worming—to get gid of any larvae which were not hit by the original medication and matured afterwards—you may have to repeat the worming in a week or two weeks. In the meantime, before your puppy is let out, his run area should be thoroughly treated to destroy such worms and eggs as may be in or on the ground. Simple boiling water soaking the ground thoroughly will help kill worms, but the best treatments are solutions of salt or sodium borate (Borax or Borascu). Prepare the salt solution by mixing one-and-a-half pounds of salt per gallon of boiling water, and apply a pint of this solution per square foot of ground, sufficient to saturate the ground to a depth of about two inches. Sodium borate can be prepared with about one pound per gallon of water, applied one gallon per ten square feet. As you can see, none of these treatments is simple—the salt solution treatment of a run only 5 by 12 feet would require more than 10 pounds of salt and preparation of more than 7 gallons of solution. And, of course, any such treatment is sudden death for grass or flowers, so it can only be applied to bare runs to which the pup is restricted. If he has the freedom of the yard, there is little you can do but hope he doesn't pick up the worm infestation again. One thing you can do, though, in the case of a house dog, is to scrub his quarters thoroughly with disinfectant or the salt solution, throw out all his old bedding and thoroughly disinfect any toys and eating utensils he has.

As a general precaution, with or without worms and treatments, the yard area should be kept scrupulously clean of his stools—the surest method of reinfestation is the puppy rolling in old feces, or even stepping accidentally in them, and later licking his paws.

COCCIDIOSIS

This is one of a number of protozoan and bacterial invasions of the intestines—difficult to recognize specifically, and resistant to treatment. The symptoms are much like those of worms—diarrhea, becoming looser and more watery and containing blood and mucus, combined with unthriftiness, emaciation and dehydration. Severe forms can sometimes be recognized by a slight cough and discharges from the eyes and nose. It has been estimated that most dogs in this country have at least a few coccidia in their intestines—in some cases these and other protozoa or bacteria suddenly start to get out of hand, for reasons which are poorly understood. Coccidiosis is one of the most common causes of chronic diarrhea in puppies, and although it may be fatal in itself, it is most usually dangerous because the weakened condition it causes leaves the puppy wide open for other problems, particularly distemper. Diagnosis can only be made by microscopic examination of a stool specimen, and treatment can be handled only by a vet through administration of antibiotics. The possibility of coccidiosis is another reason you should never ignore severe or continuing diarrhea in a puppy.

TEETHING

Puppies are generally born without any teeth. The milk teeth begin erupting from the gums at three to four weeks, nicely coinciding with early weaning to avoid damage to the nipples of the nursing bitch. This set of small, sharp teeth stays until the age of about three or four months, when the teeth begin to fall and are slowly replaced by the larger, blunter permanent teeth.

There is no set schedule which can be applied to every puppy, but the fourteenth week of life, when many of the milk teeth have fallen out, is usually the height of teething. Do not be worried if at about this time you find tiny teeth on the floor. Puppies usually swallow most of the milk teeth as they loosen and fall out, but some do occasionally fall to the floor and are left there. At the same time there may be a little blood on his gums, or you may find blood on a toy or on your hand if your pup plays at chewing on you. This too is natural and nothing to worry about, unless of course the bleeding continues and is profuse, a condition which is very rare.

The normal mechanism is this: the puppy teeth lose their connection with the jaw, and are pushed out by the emerging permanent teeth. Within a day or two after any individual puppy tooth goes, you may be able to see its permanent replacement slowly forcing its way out of the gum. Occasionally, the puppy teeth hang on. The permanent teeth don't stop for this, but force their way out around the retained milk tooth, and can grow in crooked or misaligned. During the teething period, check your pup's mouth regularly to see that the milk teeth are coming out and that no permanent teeth are being misdirected. It is an even better idea to have your vet check the progress of teething, but you can tell pretty well by yourself if all is going well in your pup's mouth.

Puppy teeth which are causing trouble to the permanent teeth can be pulled very easily by the vet, so if you suspect any trouble along this line, take the pup to the vet for a thorough check.

Teething is a difficult time for a puppy, just as it is for a child. The gums are sore, and the entire system is upset. This is a period in which the appetite can be expected to fall off, and your pup may run a slight fever and have mild diarrhea. If this sort of symptom shows itself around the thirteenth, fourteenth and fifteenth weeks, it is probably not at all serious —just the normal run of teething, always provided any diarrhea is mild. Before teething is begun, your pup should be protected against distemper. He will be weakened at teething time, and distemper can strike here more ferociously than at any other time in his life. If he is unprotected and gets even a mild case of distemper, the chances are very good that his teeth will be marked with ugly black-brown rings and pits for the rest of his life—a common phenomenon known as "distemper teeth."

Although in about nine cases out of ten, such "distemper teeth" are actually the result of distemper, they can also result from any debilitating disease or deficiency condition which interferes with proper nutrition during the eruption of the permanent teeth.

At teething time and just before, it is an excellent idea to let the pup have a good hard natural bone, one of the artificially hardened bones you will find in pet shops, a hard, thick scrap of natural leather or a commercial leather toy—anything he can work and chew on to ease the pain of his gums and to help in the loosening of the milk teeth. Aside from helping him, you will be helping yourself, for it is during teething that many pups become destructive around the house, chewing on furniture, shoes and other forbidden items, just to help themselves along in teething. If you supply him with good chewing material, the problem will be lessened.

After the fourteenth-week crisis is over, teething goes on at a slower rate until he is about eight months old—the permanent teeth are in and growing to nearly mature size. After the fourth or fifth month there should be no more trouble with teething upsets or symptoms.

TOYS AND BONES

Any of the items mentioned above as teething toys will serve quite well for normal play use by a puppy. So, for that matter, will almost any sort of ball. Give him an old tennis ball, an old handball, or the hollow red rubber balls of slightly less than tennis ball size you will find on dime-store counters. These are a dull, almost powdery red when new, and the rubber is fairly thick—don't confuse them with the many varieties of thin-rubber hollow balls you'll find, nor with the many sizes of balls with painted designs. The paint on these latter comes off very easily, and although it is specified as non-toxic, these balls shouldn't be given to a puppy.

The major thing you must watch out for when you are giving him a toy is the possibility of his tearing off pieces and swallowing them. With some things, swallowing will do him little or no harm—leather, for example. A good hard leather toy will be almost entirely consumed by a puppy over a period of time, and will do him no harm.

Rubber is the main danger. Some commercial dog toys are made of relatively soft rubber, which can be torn very easily even by a puppy. There are also soft, spongy dime-store rubber balls that shouldn't be given to a pup—these are solid rubber, but very soft, of about the consistency of the rebound balls attached by a string to a paddle. Small pieces of rubber are indigestible, and can very easily become lodged in his intestine, blocking things off thoroughly. If this were to happen, your pup could die before you could do anything about it, so be careful about giving him rubber toys. Test any potential toy with your fingernails, to see if it is easy to get bits off it. Some hard rubber toys and balls are fine, but test them first yourself.

You should very definitely never give him anything wooden to play with, nor anything involving long threads or lengths which might be swallowed. The wood is obvious, as splinters can cut his mouth or throat easily. The long lengths of thread or whatever may not damage him (although there have been cases in which thread or string snagged in the intestine and caused a considerable length of the intestine to be pulled up like an accordion, requiring surgery which was not always successful), but they can cause discomfort to him and a messy situation for you. If a long thread or bunch of threads is swallowed, it usually goes through the stomach and intestines largely intact, and then issues forth from the rectum in a length. It is not uncommon to see a puppy trying to complete his defecation with a length of thread halfway out his rectum—he will possibly become frantic at the strange sensation and run around trying to brush it off. It is bad enough when this happens outside the house, what with the necessity of you helping him get it all the way out—if he manages to run inside the house in this condition, it is easy to see how messy it could become.

Bones are a puppy's prime delight. Give him any of the large beef bones —the long heavy leg bones or the heavy knuckle ends—either whole or in sections as cut by the butcher. Give them either raw or boiled just a little to bring out the flavor of such meat as is left on them. Either way, he will go into transports of delight, particularly at chewing and licking out the marrow of a lightly cooked long bone. He will grind and chew away at them, and you will probably see considerable wear and tear on the bones which looks as though it must be harming his teeth, but it isn't.

All chicken and fish bones, either raw or cooked, should be strictly avoided. These small and splintery bones can catch in his throat, with highly unpleasant results. Also avoid the smaller and more splintery beef bones, such as the ribs, steak and chop bones.

The major problem with bones is that they can be very messy, particularly if cooked. Simply train him to keep them either out of the house, or strictly in his own play area.

Another item you should very definitely not give him to play with is an old shoe. This won't hurt him physically, but it can have very bad after-effects and will lead to some damage to him through punishment for chewing on your good shoes. A puppy's mind is a simple one, and he cannot make the distinction between old shoes and new ones—if he is allowed to chew on one shoe, then he is allowed to chew on all shoes, so far as he is concerned. The same applies to anything else—don't open up a category of playthings for him unless he is to be allowed to chew on anything in that category.

CARSICKNESS

While most puppies learn to love riding in cars, there is often a difficult transition period during which they throw up very shortly after the car starts moving. It is not surprising at all if you look at it from the pup's point of view—he is thrust willy-nilly into a strange-smelling object which then proceeds to roll and jolt him, accompanied by exhaust smells, loud noises, and the unnerving sight of the previously stable world rushing and turning past him. Part of the problem is simple motion-sickness, but a good portion is psychological.

If you encounter this problem, it must be attacked by gradual stages. First, make sure your pup is not fed for at least three hours before you take him riding. This takes some of the load off his stomach, and if he does have to vomit, it will be neither so dramatic nor so messy. Then begin very gently and sympathetically. Get him into the car, let him be near you on the front seat (reserve any restrictions to the back seat for later when the sickness problem is over) and start very slowly for a short drive, perhaps no more than around the block.

Keep a close eye on him for the first signs of sickness—it is far easier, of course, if somebody else does the driving and you devote yourself to comforting him and watching for symptoms. These first symptoms are a slightly fixed expression in the eyes, and particularly drooling and excessive swallowing, with licking the chops. Once these appear, the actual vomiting is not far off. As soon as you see them, stop the car and let him out for a run, to relieve himself, and just to get settled again. It may be tedious at first—you may have to stop several times during even the shortest first trial trip, but he will eventually get over it.

Work the lengths of the trip up slowly, and as the trips begin to get longer, if you see the first signs and symptoms, try to distract his attention with a favorite toy or simply by talking to and playing with him—this will often put off the crisis while you build up the length of the rides. All this sounds like too much bother, really, just for a car-sick dog, but a little concentrated work now will save you a great deal of trouble later.

The vital factor here is his relaxation and confidence. Do not, under any circumstances, get mad at him, shout at him or anything of the sort. If he does throw up before you can stop and get him out of the car, clean it up, be kind and reassuring, and then go on again. During the first rides, cover your lap and the seat of the car with an old sheet or blanket, or newspapers—this will make it easier on your temper, and easier to clean up afterwards.

If he simply cannot seem to get used to riding, you can try tranquilizers as a last resort—but get special dog tranquilizers from your vet, don't try dosing the pup with human tranquilizers, aspirins or even the most modern seasick remedies. Give your pup the pill, allow about 45 minutes for it to take hold, get him in the car and start off again. Don't worry about this method—that you'll be getting him into some kind of habit, and that you'll have to keep a stock of tranquilizers on hand for him every time you want to take him along in the car. Tranquilizers have an interesting effect: they lessen the tension one or two times, and the dog somehow comes to associate riding without the old tensions, and after a few tranquilizer rides he may be able to take it like a veteran, without any drugs at all. Still, use this technique only as a last resort—it is far better if you are able to cure him by patience and gentle introduction to the subject.

DISTEMPER

Distemper is a fearful killer of puppies, and there is no exception to the rule that every puppy should be inoculated against it. There is an antibody in a bitch's first milk which will protect her pups against distemper until shortly after they are weaned, if she has an immunity herself, either natural or administered. For a time after weaning, the pups are partially protected by the fact that a very young pup is generally fairly well isolated from the world and from contact with other dogs, but even this isolation is far from foolproof protection. Distemper is a virus disease, and the virus can get around in astonishing ways.

Veterinary thinking about distemper protection has changed considerably within the last few years. At one time, it was thought that vaccine inoculation of a dog provided permanent immunity, and a puppy's vaccine shots are still widely referred to as "permanent" shots. Unfortunately, no vaccine known at present does give permanent protection, as has been discovered by the development of blood-sample testing for immunity. Depending on the individual dog, the vaccine, and other factors, a supposedly "permanent" shot may give protection for as little as six months, and few dogs will be distemper-immune for more than three years as a result of having had vaccine.

One exception to this is the "street exposure" theory, which holds that a dog, once successfully immunized, maintains a life-long immunity through constant exposure to live distemper virus in his contacts with other dogs. While this may work very well with dogs living in large cities, or otherwise in constant contact with other dogs, it unfortunately does not work too well with suburban or country dogs who, although certainly in contact with others, may not come into contact with a distemper-carrying dog for some time. This sounds as though it would be the most desirable of circumstances, but actually it isn't. If such a relatively isolated dog were one whose combination of factors resulted in only a short-term immunity, his lack of repeated "street exposure" might allow the antibody level in his blood to fall to such a low level that, when he finally did meet a distemper carrier, the new virus, rather than reinforcing immunity, would infect him with an active case of distemper, causing at best serious illness, and at worst, death. It has unfortunately happened, in some cases where an adult dog, as old as eight or nine and thought to have been permanently immunized during puppyhood, has caught distemper and died of it.

Unless you are raising a litter of your own, or get a very young puppy, you will probably not be faced with the problem immediately—many pups are sold already inoculated with "permanent" vaccine. (The term "vaccine" will be used herafter to refer to what are ordinarily, and incorrectly, called "permanent" shots, to distinguish them from puppy protective serum.) If your pup has not had vaccine, you should consult with your vet right away about them, and get the facts from the breeder on whether the pup has been given anti-distemper puppy serum, and if so when the last serum shot was given.

Vaccine is generally not given until a puppy is nearly three months old. Before that a puppy can be protected temporarily by the serum. Serum shots provide protection for from ten to fourteen days each, and will carry your pup over until vaccine can be given. The one hitch about serum is that vaccine cannot be given until the veterinarian is sure that the effect of the serum has completely worn off, and so he will ordinarily wait until a full fourteen days after the last serum shot, perhaps fifteen to be sure, before he will give vaccine. If the puppy serum provided protection for only ten days (and nobody can tell), then there is a period of up to five days when your pup is wide open to distemper. During those five days you should be extra careful about exposing him to the outside world, and to other dogs who can carry the distemper virus without showing any effects of it.

There are several systems of vaccine shots, calling for varying combinations of vaccine at varying intervals. Different veterinarians will swear by different methods, and the best thing you can do is leave the method of inoculation entirely in the vet's hands. He will also be best able to advise you on the necessity of later "booster" shots of vaccine, to be sure that full immunity is provided your dog throughout his life.

Distemper is a dreadful disease, and if your puppy should get it, the chances for his survival are small. A number of pups have lived through mild cases, but even then many of them have been left with crippling after-effects, generally in the form of "chorea," a spasmodic and intermittent jerking of some muscles, for which there is no relief short of death. There are treatments for the disease, but their value at present is problematical. Largely, the veterinarian treating distemper will attempt to prevent secondary attacks by other organisms—one of the most serious menaces to a pup weakened by distemper. Antibiotics and other drugs may be injected to combat secondary infections, but there is currently no specific drug to combat the distemper virus itself. Even supportive and secondary-preventive treatments are often fruitless. Meningitis and encephalitis often afflict the sick puppy, and once the nervous system is so gravely involved, the chances for survival, particularly survival without crippling after-effects, fall almost to zero.

If your pup should get distemper, it is best to follow the advice of the vet as to whether to try treatment, or to put the pup to merciful sleep. It is as serious as that. Many people (including the author) have buckled down to nurse a distemper-stricken pup night and day, to give him every advantage, determined to save an innocent pup who never had a chance, against long odds, only to go through weeks of torment both for the owner and the puppy, ending in final defeat. Some few pups have pulled through severe cases and shown no after-effects at all, but such instances are rare.

The symptoms of distemper may include: loss of appetite, diarrhea, nausea, sensitivity of the eyes to light, frequently gumming over of the nose and eyes with a sticky discharge, a dry cough, and sneezing. Notice that diarrhea, that almost universal symptom, is present at the beginning of nearly every case, and is often the first sign to the owner that something is wrong. Photophobia (sensitivity to light) is a very common early symptom, but one which is hardly ever noticed except by dog owners of long experience. Keep this symptom in mind when watching your puppy, particularly as he reacts to strong light, sunlight, or the sudden turning on of the lights in a darkened room.

Distemper can be spread with terrible ease. The breath of a sick dog is enough to transmit it to a well one. And remember that a dog with the virus present may never show the signs, as a non-affected carrier. Even if a dog is due to come down with a mild or serious case, he can be normal and healthy in appearance for as much as five days before he shows the first signs himself, but still be capable of transmitting the virus during this incubation period. The virus can be transmitted through the urine, feces, saliva or nasal discharges of a sick dog or carrier. It can travel through the air for an undetermined distance.

One general belief about distemper, though, is not true—that you should not bring a new puppy into a house where a dog has died of distemper until six months have elapsed. It has been fairly well established that the virus does not live outside the host dog for more than about a week at normal house temperatures, and that four weeks is a safe interval to wait before bringing a new pup into the house. For extra safety, you could make it six weeks, but no more than that is necessary. You should, however, be sure that the new puppy is well protected against distemper, and that in cold weather particularly he not be allowed outside during the critical period of transition from serum to vaccine protection. Although the distemper virus dies quickly in warmth, it actually thrives on cold, and winter is the most dangerous distemper season.

It is a good idea, also, to be careful about the new pup's exposure to neighborhood dogs (and visiting dogs of friends, and even visiting friends who own dogs, for distemper can be carried in some cases by the owners of a sick dog or a carrier) until he is well and thoroughly protected by his vaccine shots. The dog who had distemper before and died of it very probably got it somewhere in the neighborhood, which means that the area will be dangerous to an unprotected pup.

HEPATITIS

Hepatitis is another killer of puppies, although you will not hear as much about it as distemper. This is largely because in the past it has been generally diagnosed as distemper, and deaths due to hepatitis were listed as distemper deaths. The initial symptoms are much the same—failing appetite, listlessness, high temperature (104-106°). As the distinction between distemper and hepatitis has become more widely recognized, some of the specific hepatitis symptoms have been identified—the mucous membranes, especially of the mouth, often become bluish, indicating toxemia or general poisoning of the system; the abdomen is often tender and the afflicted puppy has a tendency to hump himself up to relieve pain in the abdominal area; the stool is often dark and tarry at the onset, there is vomiting and diarrhea.

The disease is particularly frightening to a puppy owner because it can strike almost without warning. One day a puppy may seem to be in the best of health, the next morning near death. The chances of recovery in young puppies are not good, but as age increases, the chances improve. Hepatitis may respond somewhat to treatment with serum, but it is far better to have protection in advance. This protection comes from a recently developed vaccine which seems very effective in bestowing immunity. It may be given separately by your vet when the puppy is about three months old, or it can be given in a combined distemper-hepatitis shot which is becoming more common.

A virus disease like distemper, hepatitis is transmitted very readily from one dog to another. Again, seemingly healthy dogs can spread it. Dogs who have had hepatitis and recovered seem able to transmit the virus, either through direct contact or through their urine or feces, for as long as five months after their recovery. It can also be spread by humans, although humans are not affected by canine hepatitis. This is one of the reasons breeders and kennel owners are sometimes very cautious about letting puppy shoppers come into too close contact with their litters—it is eminently possible for a human to carry the disease from an affected kennel to a healthy one on a shopping tour.

LEPTOSPIROSIS

Leptospirosis has in recent years been the subject of considerable veterinary work, to the point where there is now a vaccine preventive, greater surety of diagnosis, and some hope of effecting permanent cures through the use of antibiotics. Only a few years ago, there was no preventive at all, and the best available treatment consisted of penicillin injections alone, a procedure now frowned on by many vets because, although penicillin wipes out the leptospirosis organisms in the bloodstream, it may leave them active in other areas of the body and make an active carrier of a cured dog.

The disease is one which directly affects the kidneys. It may be picked up through contact with the infected urine of another dog (the most common source of infection), or in some cases through contact with the infected urine or droppings of rats. The usual transmission takes place when a dog sniffs the urine of an infected dog, and his nose touches the urine. He may also contract leptospirosis through eating food contaminated by rats, or even by simply living in a rat-infested structure—in these cases, the dog may lie down in an area contaminated by rat urine or droppings, get a little on his coat, and then in licking his coat pick up the leptospirosis organisms.

The symptoms of leptospirosis include: a change in the color of the urine, to deep yellow and in some cases orange, often accompanied by a noticeably intensified urine smell; continued and chronic vomiting of frothy white or yellow bile or of recently ingested food or water; muscular stiffness, particularly in the hind legs, accompanied by a reluctance to rise from a sitting or down position; and pain in the area of the kidneys and abdomen. Severe and advanced cases often show jaundice (yellowing of mucous membranes, skin and eyes) and marked dehydration, although any dog whose case has gone untreated until such symptoms show themselves has little chance of recovery and cure. By such time, he will almost certainly be a victim of uremic poisoning (the kidneys, functioning poorly, allow poisonous wastes to enter the bloodstream) and will at best suffer chronic uremia for the rest of his life, which will itself be shortened.

The vaccine now available provides good protection against leptospirosis, and many vets now recommend that it be included in the normal course of puppy care, along with shots against distemper, hepatitis and rabies. The duration of the protection is uncertain, and is definitely not permanent, at least in the present stage of its development. A shot may give protection for from six months to a year, but it is difficult to tell exactly how long the protection will last. The ideal system, of course, would be such a shot every six months, but very few people will carry out such a program. Next best is at least a yearly shot, which can be given in conjunction with an annual rabies shot and thus entails little extra trouble. This program might just provide total protection, and at the very least will provide protection for half of each year. These protective shots should always be given regularly to dogs who come into close and continued contact with many other dogs, as happens in the case of pure-bred show dogs.

Unfortunately, leptospirosis can be transmitted to humans, either by an infected dog or by infected rats. If you live in an area in which there is any sort of rat problem, it is extremely desirable to have your dog protected, for his own sake and for prevention of transmission of the disease to you via him. As the disease can also be contracted through cuts or abrasions of the skin, simply petting an infected dog who may have a little of his own or a rat's tainted urine on his coat could just possibly result in a human case. It is more than a little unlikely, but humans have gotten the disease from dogs.

Also, in rat-infested areas, if you are feeding your dog dry food kept in cardboard cartons or paper sacks, discard any sacks or other containers which have been broken into by rats—infected rat urine or droppings may be present in the food, and if your dog eats it, he may come down with leptospirosis.

RABIES

This is more generally considered as a problem of adult dogs, but as it can be prevented by beginning a series of periodic vaccinations at about six months of age, it is worth discussing in this section. Rabies is also a virus disease, but it can be transmitted only by injection of the saliva (or other excretion) of an infected dog into the tissues of another animal. Its real danger is that it is not restricted to dogs but can be transmitted to, and by, most other animals, including cattle, horses, sheep, goats, cats, pigs, bats and humans.

Through vaccination programs, rabies is far less a danger now than it was in the recent past, but it still exists as a serious menace. Department of Agriculture statistics show a total of over 86,000 cases in the ten-year period ending with 1954. Out of these, approximately 65,000 cases were in dogs—over 6,500 cases per year on the average. Against an estimated total of nearly thirty million dogs in this country, this is a small enough percentage, but percentages are of little comfort to the owner of a stricken dog.

Fortunately, public-health education has almost entirely done away with most false beliefs and superstitions about rabies, including the notions that dewclaws on a dog indicate he is immune, that dogs "go mad" only during "dog days," or that there are any mystical cures for rabies, such as "mad stones." All of these notions are minor and linger only slightly in the present day, but if you run into any idea about rabies that it is transmitted by anything but bites, or that there is any preventive other than vaccination, or any cure at all, you can be sure it is totally false.

The most serious problem is the possibility of rabies in any dog or puppy which bites a human. In every reported bite case, rabies is considered as a matter of routine, because of the violent and terrible consequences of the disease. If not caught and treated in time, the disease is invariably fatal, and fatal in a particularly terrible way, for the victim dies in racking, spasmodic convulsions. The dog, in every case of a bitten human, must be examined for the possibility of rabies, unless, and it is a big unless, the owner can prove that the dog has been vaccinated against rabies within the past year. In many cases and many localities, even a vaccinated dog may be held for quarantine and examination, but vaccination is sometimes considered definite proof that the dog cannot be harboring the virus, and that the bitten human is safe. Otherwise, the standard quarantine is one week, for a dog can transmit rabies in his saliva, if he is infected, nearly a week before he himself begins to show discernible signs of the disease.

By far your best course is to have your pup vaccinated against rabies as soon as your veterinarian feels he is old enough, which may be anywhere between the ages of six months and a year. The protection will be good for from one year to three, depending on the type of vaccine. The vet will give you an identifying tag, which should be on your dog's collar at all times, and a certificate showing the date of the vaccination, which you should keep very carefully in a safe place and ready for presentation if your dog should bite anyone. Vaccination protects not only your dog but also you and the people around you.

As to the disease itself, there are two forms—dumb rabies and furious rabies. Both forms generally show the same initial symptoms—a marked change in behavior, increased irritability, avoidance of noise and light, sudden refusal of favorite foods, inability to drink, and a peculiar change in voice which results from partial paralysis of the vocal cords and muscles of the throat. In the furious form, the excitability increases rapidly, and the dog will become sullen and unresponsive to his owner's commands or entreaties. As his throat becomes more spastic and inflamed, he will become completely unable to eat or drink. This latter symptom gives rise to the misnomer "hydrophobia," meaning "fear of water." The rabid dog does not fear water, but actually is desperate for a drink. His throat is, however, so spastic that he is unable to swallow. At the same time, excess salivation is present, and the jaws often show dribble and large amounts of foam in the traditional picture of the "mad dog." As the furious rabies case progresses, the dog begins to roam, attempting to bite anything in his way— anything attacked will be bitten and the virulent saliva injected into the wound. It is vitally important never to attempt to handle a dog suspected of rabies! If you ever suspect it in a strange dog, get out of the way. If you suspect it in your own dog, do not attempt to handle him beyond confining him as conveniently as possible, then report the circumstances to your veterinarian and let him arrange for all handling and treatment.

If you have been bitten by a strange dog, as might happen in the case of breaking up a fight between the stranger and your own dog, get the owner's name and address if at all possible. Most important, though, scrub the wound thoroughly with strong soap and warm clean water. Tincture of green soap is one of the best possible types to use, and you should have it on hand in any case for treatment of your dog—it is available in almost any drug store. Get the soap into all parts of the wound and keep washing for as long as twenty minutes. This is no sure guarantee that rabies infection won't occur, but it may do the job. If bitten by your own dog, and there is the remotest possibility that he may carry the rabies virus, follow the same procedure. Then get medical treatment.

The progression of dumb rabies is different in its later stages. The dog becomes completely listless and often partially paralyzed. The jaw and throat are very often paralyzed, and the dumb rabid dog will either lie quite still with his jaws "frozen" open, or wander very weakly and un- aggressively, again with the jaws open. Death follows within three or four days. In both forms, once the disease has become established, there is no possible treatment or cure.

Symptoms of rabies are in many cases very much like those of other conditions—a foreign object lodged in the throat will result in similar symptoms, eclampsia in nursing bitches is often mistaken for rabies, and distemper complications, including convulsions with associated foaming and champing at the mouth, are often thought to be sure signs of a rabid dog. Any convulsion will bring the thought of rabies to mind, but here you can rely on one guide. If your dog ever has a convulsion and recovers from it and appears normal, he is not rabid. You should never handle a dog suffering a convulsion, but once the convulsion has passed, if it does, the danger is past. A rabid dog progresses to severer convulsions and death, and never appears normal after the first onset.

ACCIDENTS

The major possibilities of accident are taken up in the chapter on First Aid, but there are certain areas which are the special province of puppies —electric shock, swallowing dangerous objects, and falls and sprains.

It is not common for a puppy to suffer electric shock, but it does happen, and it is an extremely unpleasant thing when it does. The most common cause is a curious young puppy roaming around the house and finding an attractive electric light cord which he proceeds to chew on. If he chews through the insulation, there is a short circuit across his mouth, and he can suffer terrible burns. The best prevention for this is coating all the available wires in the house with something extremely unpleasant to the smell and taste. Any of the commercial "keeps dogs away" preparations will be effective, or you can use musterole or citronella. If the accident should happen to your puppy, pull the plug immediately, before touching him. Then treat for shock (see First Aid) and apply artificial respiration, if necessary. Although the short circuit generally results in burns it is seldom fatal.

Swallowing small objects around the house is another unfortunate habit of puppies. Dice, cinders, jacks—a long assortment of items have passed into puppies' stomachs, and for the most part have been naturally passed out or removed successfully by a veterinarian. If your pup shows signs of sharp pains in the stomach, this is one of the first things to suspect, and he should be rushed to a vet who has X-ray facilities. Many times, even quite dangerous objects can be taken right back out the throat by a sort of long forceps. In extreme cases, the foreign object may have to be removed through an operation.

It is rare that the owner sees the offending object go down, but if you should happen to see your pup swallow something that isn't good for him, you can try to get it out by forcing him to vomit. A word of caution, though. Make sure you know what it was that went down before you try getting it back up that way. Inducing vomiting is never something to do routinely, and if he brings back up something with sharp edges, vomiting may be the worst possible thing for it—the sharp edges may have got down okay, but just might catch and cut something on the way up. So take care. It is always better to see a vet about such things, but in emergencies you can use the standard mustard-and-water emetic to get him to empty his stomach. Mix a tablespoonful of dry powdered mustard with a standard glass of lukewarm water, then force as much of it down your pup's throat as you can. It won't take much for him to throw up, and with luck the offending object will come up with everything else.

Falls and sprains are another puppy specialty. Particularly in the early months of his life, a pup has little or no sense of height, and would just as soon jump off the roof of a ten-story building as off the sofa. You should never allow a puppy freedom in any situation where he could be severly injured by a fall. Even in short falls a puppy can be injured. As he gets bigger and explores the world around him, and uses his new muscles, he will try to jump off a sofa he has barely been able to climb up on, or off a table or a porch. When he lands he may severely twist a leg or shoulder, and you will know about it quickly enough from his shrieks. Generally, the noise is more due to the shock of the fall than to actual pain, but it pays to investigate carefully.

If he has taken a fall, hold him very carefully and feel each of his legs gently to check for breaks. Compare one front leg to another, which is the best way of seeing if anything is out of line in either one. Compare the back legs. Move each of the legs very carefully through its normal arc. You will soon be able to feel, or tell by his reaction, whether anything is seriously wrong. If any of the leg bones seem to be broken, you should of course get to your vet immediately. If any of the motions of the leg cause him severe pain, there is the possibility that he has wrenched the joint, perhaps even dislocated it. This too should be treated professionally. But if he simply whimpers when you touch the injured part, and seems able to navigate, even though limpingly, it is probably nothing more than a pulled muscle or a bruise. Most cases are nothing to worry about. He will limp around very valiantly for the rest of the day, but a good night's sleep will see the end of it. It is possible for you to miss diagnosing a broken or badly wrenched bone, but only for the first day. If, on the day after the accident, your pup is still complaining about the leg and seems unable or unwilling to put his weight on it, very definitely take him to your vet for a check.

MENTAL HEALTH

This will strike many people as perhaps a curious and completely out-of-place section for a book on the care of dogs, but care can and does go beyond the merely physical. It is safe to say that more puppies are ruined as future companions through poor psychological treatment than are damaged by physical neglect. There are millions of spoiled, browbeaten, confused, ill-trained dogs in this country, and they are a trial to their owners and to everyone else. And they aren't necessary.

This section is not intended to be about training, but you will find that your pup will be happier, and you will be happier with him, if you follow some of the basic rules of good dog training, even if he never so much as learns to sit up.

The first thing to remember in handling a puppy is that he is an extremely impressionable and easily molded young creature. Once he has left his litter and his mother, almost all of his learning about the world and the way he should conduct himself, and what he can expect from the world—all these come from you. He has no other sources but instinct and experimentation to provide him with attitudes and codes of behavior. Therefore the responsibility on you is considerable—the adult dog will reflect very distinctly the way the puppy was handled.

Remember that he is an individual, not just a toy for somebody. He has a mind of his own, his own desires and "thoughts," and will respond best if he is treated as an individual. True, a puppy is extremely childlike, and even a mature dog does not have a mind capable of a great deal of independent thought. But if you allow him a certain essential dignity, everybody will benefit. This means that he should be left alone, to his own devices, part of the time, to live his own dog's life. Don't constantly coddle him, and, on the other hand, don't constantly restrict him and expect him to live very moment at your beck and call. Just let him be a dog.

More specifically, if you will remember the following points, you'll find that your pup can grow up to be a good and responsive companion, unafraid of the world, and a joy to be with.

1) Never instill your own fears and nervous habits into him. Most dogs who are afraid of thunder, for example, are taught to be afraid by nervous owners. When it thunders, even if you are mortally afraid, grit your teeth and smile and pretend nothing is happening. It may even do you some good. Most dogs who get frantic about the telephone and doorbell learn this by watching their owners, who jump out of their chairs and jitter when something rings. Be calm about things, and your dog will be calm, too.

2) Never punish a dog for something he did in the past, unless it was the very recent past and you can make it abundantly clear to the dog why he is being reprimanded. If you think about it a moment, you'll see the logic of it. First, it is obviously ridiculous to punish a dog for doing something yesterday. He simply can't remember and make the connection, and all he'll know is that you're being harsh for no apparent reason—if it happens often, he'll get edgy about you and come to expect the worst at all times. Similarly, you can't expect a dog to remember in the evening something he did in the morning. And it follows right down to a few minutes ago. A dog, especially a puppy, simply doesn't have that sort of memory. Once a thing is done, it's over for him, and recriminations five minutes later are a mystery. So don't make the mistake of punishing him after the fact.

Don't read this as saying you must be permissive about his misdemeanors. If you catch him at something, there is no reason in the world you shouldn't let him know about it. And if, for example, you find that he was tearing up your best shoes a minute ago, you can hold them in front of his nose and give him the business about shoes in general. The presence of a damaged object will not establish that he did wrong, but he will get the idea that, from your scolding in connection with it, he shouldn't touch that object in the future. But never, never try to get him to remember something abstract he did in the past, like barking too much. He just can't make the connection. All it will teach him is that you're capricious and likely to come at him hollering and swinging at any old time.

3) Be consistent. There is nothing that will confuse a puppy quicker than being allowed to do something one day, forbidden the next, and then allowed it again the day after. The dog's mind is such that only with great difficulty can he learn that some things are allowed at some times and not at others. They can learn versions of this, but if at all possible, keep a consistency about what is allowed to him. Don't allow him up on the couch sometimes and not others—he won't understand it. Don't let him chew quite happily on something, and then next time shout at him to stop that nonsense. Don't let him take scraps at the table when you are alone, then whack him when he begs from company. If you are going to forbid him something, forbid it firmly but gently from the first, make it stick, and he'll learn what to do and what not to do and won't go through life always uncertain about everything.

4) Very important and very specific—never, never punish him for anything when you've called him to you or when he has come to you of his own accord. This is the worst possible mistake you can make. Imagine yourself in his situation. A friend calls to you, and you go over to him. When you arrive, he chews you out thoroughly, or whacks you a good one right in the teeth. A day passes and it happens again. On about the third day, when your friend asks you to come over, you're going to be fairly reluctant to come, no matter how pleasantly he calls. Your dog feels the same way about things. If there's a likelihood he's going to be punished when he arrives, he's going to take care either that he doesn't arrive, or that the arrival is delayed as long as possible. And who can blame him? If he has done something wrong, you must always go to him to administer whatever chastisement is appropriate. If you can't get there, let it go until next time.

This applies particularly to dogs who tend to run away, or at least are reluctant to come when you call them. If he is running loose, and you call and call and call, and he only comes after the twentieth call, don't shout at him. Welcome him warmly, or the next time he'll be gone longer. You can see what's happening if you look at it again from his point of view. He's had a good run, and now he finally comes to you. Wham, you clobber him. He doesn't connect it with the run, or not having come the first nineteen times you called him, but only with the most recent thing he did, which was coming. That's the way a dog's mind works. In this case, the same thing applies to your catching him. It's hard to catch a runaway dog who doesn't want to be caught, but it can be done. If you do sneak up on him and grab his collar, don't be unpleasant, for the same reasons given above. He'll associate it with being caught up with, and the next time he'll take care that you don't get near. Be nice, and make him want to come to you, or just never allow him to get away. That's the only way.

5) Much of the previous advice boils down to this: be dependable. A puppy or a grown dog is looking for a leader, someone he can trust and follow happily. As you own him, you're supposed to be that leader. If you let him know that he can trust you completely, he'll go through the fires of hell for you. If he can't trust you, you and he are going to have troubles of one sort or another for all your lives.

There are of course many more rules of handling and training, but if you faithfully follow these, and try to think of the way a dog acts in terms of the way you would react to a situation, you'll find that you have a much greater chance of having a dog who is genuinely fond of you, trusts you, and who will do what you tell him. When you take your own reactions as his model, remember, however, that he is illiterate and doesn't understand much English. He can't find out by comparative reading that, faulty though you may be, you're a pretty good type when compared to other people. And you can't explain to him next day that you made a mistake or were just feeling grouchy and didn't really mean it when you whacked him. Work on it—and it'll keep him in good mental health, and good to have around.

CHAPTER IV

ADULT CARE

For MOST dogs, the major part of the care you will ever have to give is external—keeping his coat in moderately decent condition, his nails clipped, his ears and teeth clean. While millions of dogs have lived and died who have never been brushed, bathed or barbered—and managed to get through life in fairly good order—both you and your dog will be happier, and he healthier, if you pay even a minimum of attention to his grooming and general health. If you have ever seen a purebred show dog on the streets, or in a dog show, and marveled at the beauty of his coat and his appearance of good health, you've seen the difference between a cared-for dog and one nobody much bothers with. True, show dogs have a great deal more attention given to them than you are likely to be willing or able to give to your own house pet, but even a small part of that attention will do a large amount of good.

As to general health, it is not the function of this book to make you a home diagnostician of serious diseases, although a dog can suffer from as wide and severe a variety as a human being. Just as with your own and your family's health, about the best you can do is watch for obvious deviations from normal—and this will be a large step forward in the care of your dog. A great many human illnesses go undetected until they become severe or are accidentally discovered, and it happens even more often with dogs, for the average owner is relatively inattentive to minor signs and symptoms. What this chapter *will* cover is recognition of symptoms as symptoms, although you may not know precisely what they are symptoms of, recognition and treatment of external parasites, points of general care, and the grooming that will not only help him but help you keep an eye on his health.

GROOMING THE COAT

For comfort and general health, one of the best things you can do for your dog is to groom his coat regularly. Long-haired dogs will very quickly show the results of inattention, through snarled, dirty and matted hair, but even dogs with short, flat coats will benefit greatly from regular grooming. Not only will it largely eliminate the need for baths, but it will cut down on the amount of shed hair floating around the house, and will make regular examination for skin conditions and parasites almost automatic.

Short-haired dogs are the easiest to groom, but they are often the most neglected, simply because their short hair does not mat and snarl and show obvious signs of lack of attention. Brushing alone will do a world of good, but currying will increase the benefit at hardly any extra cost in labor. Most good pet stores carry a rubber curry-comb, very similar to the standard item used on horses. It is usually of hard rubber, oval, and consists, on the business side, of three concentric oval rings of hard-rubber teeth which look much like big saw teeth.

Currying should be done about once a week—take the curry comb and use it much as you would a brush, starting back of the ears and working down the neck, along the back and sides and down the legs. Dig in fairly firmly with the curry—it is almost impossible to hurt the dog's skin with it, and for it to do the job you should really give him vigorous strokes. The curry comb will bring out large amounts of dead hair and especially undercoat. If your dog is an adult and you use a curry on him for the first time, you will be amazed at the amounts of shed hair and undercoat which come out the first time you use a curry. Highly recommended, a curry will cost you under two dollars in most stores.

Next comes brushing, and once a day is not too often. Almost any hairbrush will do the job, but you can get a special dog brush if you feel inclined. Brush vigorously with it, just as you curried, always working with the "grain" of the coat, and you will find that soon your dog's coat will glisten and shine.

With a dog of whatever size, do the currying and brushing outdoors if it is convenient and the weather permits, simply to avoid the problem of what to do with all the loose hair you'll stir up. Otherwise, have the dog on spread-out newspapers to catch the worst of it. If your dog is a small one, it is a good idea to train him from puppyhood to stand quietly on a table for his grooming; large ones should be trained to stand still on the floor.

Dogs with medium hair should be brushed exactly as short-hairs. With these dogs, the curry comb may be useful, but longer hair will often respond better to a wide-toothed comb, or even to what is sometimes called a "slicker" brush, a brush whose bristles are thin metal fingers set in a flexible rubber backing. Such a brush should be used with care, for you must get it close to the skin to get all the dead hairs out, and, being metal, it can scratch and damage the skin unless you observe a little caution.

Long-haired dogs are another problem entirely. These should without question be brushed and combed daily, for their hair will otherwise mat and get messy in short order, particularly if they are active outdoor dogs. Combing these dogs is no longer a simple matter of running the comb through the hair—there is simply too much of it. The best technique is to take a small section of hair, slip the comb through it at skin level, and pull the comb out towards you. If you do the grooming regularly, even this more complicated combing will not really be tedious at all, for it will take only minutes to comb out the minor snags and snarls. Brushing can then be done in much the same way, working on small areas at a time, and finally giving the dog a thorough surface brushing to complete the job. If you have a long-haired dog who has gone ungroomed for some time, and you've worked at him with comb and brush, don't be discouraged by the magnitude of the job and decide it isn't really worth all that trouble. It can be very hard the first time, but it will get easier and easier with each succeeding grooming as you get the coat under control and get the techniques perfected.

Clipping and trimming are yet another minor complication in the life of the owner of a long-haired dog. Some breeds should be trimmed— Poodles and Cockers among them. There are special show clips for these breeds, and methods of clipping and trimming them which are beyond the scope of this chapter. In any case, to learn to do it yourself takes person-to-person instructions from someone skilled in the art of trimming. But the rule which applies to such dogs is that even a bungled job of clipping is better and easier to care for than none at all, so with a clipper, either manual or electric, there is no reason you shouldn't try to do the job yourself. There is only one thing to keep in mind —clipping and trimming don't mean shaving. If you try to do the job yourself, just trim, leaving enough hair to cover the dog, don't shave him right down to the skin.

All of this is, in a way, "preventive" grooming. If you have neglected a long-haired dog and his coat is matted and snarled, or if even a well-groomed dog should come in with cockleburrs well and snugly distributed through his coat, there is nothing for it but some patient work with comb, slicker brush and scissors.

Mats and snarls are best attacked from the top. Take hold of the hair under the mat—this is to keep from pulling on the dog's skin when you apply pressure to the mat. Begin, with the comb, to work on the end of the mat farthest from the skin. By teasing at it with the comb and alternately with the slicker brush, you should be able to break it up little by little. Then, as it clears up, you can begin to run the comb from the skin out in easy strokes, finishing the job for that particular mat. It is a good idea with a really severely matted dog to spread the work out over two or three days, several short sessions a day. This way it will be easier on you and your temper, and easier on the dog, who will not have to stay still for quite so long at a stretch, and whose skin will not be subject to quite so much punishment all at once—however carefully you try to hold onto the hair below the mat, some of the tugging on the hair will be transmitted to his skin, and he won't appreciate it overly.

In some cases of extremely bad mats or snarls, you may simply have to cut the hair below the mat and wait for it to grow out. It's messy, and your dog will look peculiar for a while, but if you simply can't get the snarls out, or can't put in enough time on them, then you'll have to cut. The hair will grow back, and if you start a regular program of grooming, you won't be faced with the problem again.

Cockleburrs and other similar items are treated much like mats and snarls. Hold the hair under the burr to keep the pressure and tugging from hurting the dog, and then try to tease and comb it out. It is often helpful with burrs to cut through the body of the burr itself several times (parallel with the strands of hair) to help break it up. Patient work with comb and slicker brush will solve most burr problems, but again, in extremes, you may have to cut to get them out successfully.

When you do, do as much combing and teasing the hair away as you can beforehand so that the hunk of hair you have to cut out with the burr will be as small as possible.

Particularly when working on burrs, don't neglect to check under the dog's legs—in the "armpits"—for those are favorite spots for burrs to hang on, and in such spots they are particularly irritating to a dog. These are best removed by careful cutting. If burrs have caught in the hair around male or female genitals, again cutting is the best treatment, but of course cutting with caution. In such cases, always hold the clump of hair with your fingers between the skin and the scissors, so that you run no danger of cutting the skin.

Chewing gum, tar, paint and other unpleasant items which may get involved with his coat can be softened and removed with turpentine, but first check the skin just below the spot for cuts or abrasions, and afterwards scrub the area with soap and water to get the turpentine off the hair and the skin. Never use turpentine around the eyes, or around the genitals or rectum.

BATHING

The first general rule about bathing a dog is—don't, unless there is good reason to. Even country dogs who are outside much of the time will hardly ever need a bath, provided they are kept more or less well groomed on a regular schedule. Not only does your dog not need regular baths, but they may even do him harm. Some dog soaps and flea-soaps can be irritating to the skin, and it is not uncommon for an owner to bathe his dog with such soaps, see that he is scratching and trying to ease a skin itch, and then unwittingly complicate and worsen the problem by bathing him again and again with the same substances in trying to help the dog.

Even for relatively ungroomed dogs, which yours shouldn't be, there is no reason for a regular schedule of bathing—if he gets ordinarily dirty, you can keep him generally clean by wiping his coat with witch hazel, or using one of the commercial dry dog shampoos, most of which are quite effective. But even the best-groomed dogs do occasionally get themselves thoroughly dirty, and if so, then bathing is in order, and can be done quite painlessly.

Proper training for the bath is essential from the first, and this assumes that your dog is under at least nominal control—that he will go where you tell him and stay where he is put with a minimum of fuss and bother. Put him in the bathtub, or in a washtub, and prepare him for the bath by putting a small wad of cotton in each ear to keep most of the water out, and one or two drops of mineral oil in each eye for the same purpose. Then with a sponge or spray attachment, wet him down thoroughly, right to the skin, with lukewarm water. It is best to start with an empty tub—plunging a struggling dog into a tubful of water is what causes most of the folklore about dogs hating baths. The majority of dogs get edgy about being plunked forcibly into water, and don't really like standing or sitting about up to the navel in it. So start out with the tub or washtub dry—leave the drain open and, in a washtub, try not to let the level of the water get too high.

Once you have him thoroughly soaked, work up a lather with any good regular soap you have around the house, and scrub him thoroughly in a normal manner, being always careful not to get soap in his eyes, and keeping water out of eyes and ears as much as possible, even if they are properly protected with cotton and mineral oil. Then rinse away the soap—two complete rinses are good—very thoroughly. Remember that it is a lot harder to rinse all the soap out of even a short coat than off your relatively bare skin, so do a good job of rinsing. Then towel him off well with a rough towel. Here again you can get the surface of his coat more or less dry with a superficial towelling, but it takes work to get the coat satisfactorily dry down to the skin. (The situation is closely analogous to washing and drying your own hair, and should be treated very much the same.) After that, if you have a hair-dryer around, use that on him to help complete the drying job, and then if it is at all cool outside, keep him indoors for at least an hour, and after that only let him go out for periods up to fifteen minutes for the rest of the day. If the weather is warm and sunny, let him romp outside and dry off in the sun, but reserve this (and outside washing) only for warm days.

If you are careful and gentle about bathing from the first, you will find that your dog doesn't really mind the procedure all that much.

DIPS AND SPRAYS

Although dips and sprays are generally used for the elimination of external parasites, their application fits neatly into the subject of general skin care and bathing. A "dip" for fleas, lice, ticks, mange mites or any other parasite is used very much like an ordinary bath. Many people are confused by the term "dip," associating it not illogically with sheepdip and having a mental picture of literally dipping a dog into a vat of some curative liquid. Aside from the difficulty of preparing a big enough vatful for even a small dog, the same cautions apply as in bathing—dogs just don't like to be plunged into vats of anything, and it wouldn't work out too well.

Therefore, a dip is handled by putting the dog into tub or washtub and soaking up spongefulls of the dip solution, pouring it over the dog until he is well soaked. Here again the eyes and ears should be protected by mineral oil and cotton respectively, and extra care should be taken that none of the dip gets into his eyes, where it might do considerably more harm than soap and water. If the odor of the dip is obnoxious enough that you'd prefer not doing it indoors (and the stink of some of them, particularly those with a sulfur base, must be smelled to be believed), you can do the dipping outdoors on the ground or in a large washtub. The major disadvantage of doing it on the ground is that you don't have the advantage of the run-off solution collecting in the bottom of a tub, where it can be sponged up again and poured over him again in case your original pot of solution runs short.

When his coat is thoroughly soaked with the dip, towel him more or less dry, enough so that the coat itself is dry on the surface, but unless the instructions tell you otherwise, leave the skin and the inner part of the coat wet, so that the dip can continue its action. Don't rinse the solution out, for the same reasons, unless specifically instructed to do so. Use the same overall method if what you are using is described as a "bath" rather than a "dip."

Sprays are something you should use with considerable care—flea and tick combatives are becoming quite common in aerosol cans, and seem very handy to use. They are indeed handy, though ordinarily quite expensive considering the amount of active material you get for the money you pay, but this is characteristic of any aerosol product and can't be held against dog sprays specifically.

If you do use a spray, again the two major injunctions apply—spray thoroughly enough to get the material right down to the dog's skin, and be very, very careful about getting the spray into his eyes. Even if the can tells you it won't hurt him, don't get it in his eyes, ears or nose. Cotton in the ears and mineral oil in the eyes will help, but you should still spray with caution, and carefully cover his eyes when you are spraying the area of head and neck. It is better, in fact, not to spray his head at all, unless absolutely necessary, which isn't likely. You can always cover this area by squirting some of the spray onto a cloth and wiping his head and neck with the soaked cloth, just as you would use a dip. If you are doing the spray in a confined space, or outside where the wind is likely to carry the vaporized material towards you, be a bit careful about breathing the stuff. Once you are done, gently towel the surface of his coat to get it more or less dry, and leave the skin and the base of his coat damp.

CARE OF THE NAILS

Your dog's condition of life dictates how much care you will have to give to his nails. Dogs who are on city streets and pavements a good deal of the time usually keep their nails well worn and filed down in the course of running and walking on concrete, and country dogs who are outside on grass and dirt most of the time, while their nails tend to be longer, also usually keep them in shape by simple abrasion. It is the house-dog pet, who spends much of his time indoors walking either on wooden floors or soft rugs, who will need the most attention.

The rule for cutting and filing nails is that they should be done as often as they need to be, which doesn't sound very helpful. Nonetheless, there is no regular schedule which can be given for nail care, simply because of the differing conditions of different dogs' lives. If your dog walks on bare floors, you will be able to hear when his nails need cutting —they will click continuously and noticeably on the floor. A well-trimmed nail should not make any noise when the dog walks normally on a bare floor, a working rule you can use quite well to determine whether you have nails under control.

Nail cutting is easier with two people, of course, but even by yourself you can do it. For the front legs the best procedure is to hold the foot firmly in your left hand, or if he is skittish about it, tuck his foreleg under your arm (if he's big enough) with him at your back, and hold his "wrist" firmly. As illustrated, put the oval of the clipper over the nail so that the nail comes through from the side away from the blade, and the blade slides *up* at the bottom of the nail. This all seems very awkward and unnecessarily complicated when you first do it, but it is the right way and results in cleaner cutting and considerably less chance of splitting and mangling the nail.

When you clip, clip only a little at a time, even if the nail has been badly neglected—this is to be sure that you do not get too far up on the nail and cut into the quick, a very painful business for the dog. Dogs with light and white nails often have a quick dark enough to be seen through the nail, and with these you can easily avoid it, but in dark-nailed dogs the quick is invisible except to an expert, so your best bet is simply caution. Nip off only the tip, and then a day or two later nip off a little more, and then a little more, and when you finally have the nails at the proper length, it will take infrequent clipping and very little general care to keep them in perfect shape.

After each clipping, it is a good idea to file the nail at least a few strokes, to round and smooth it off so that it doesn't catch on rugs or fabrics, and doesn't split through catching on anything. You can use almost any medium of fine wood-file for this, a coarse nail-file, medium sandpaper on a block or a medium grade of the relatively new steel sandpaper. With the latter two particularly, be careful that you don't sand and cut the pad or surrounding skin while you're working at the nail, but aside from this caution, there is very little harm you can do with filing. You will find, as you approach the quick, that the nail changes from hard and brittle to soft and relatively pulpy—this is the signal that you have filed quite far enough. Some owners like to do filing only, for fear of hurting the dog with clippers, and although it is more work, this method is as satisfactory as combined clipping and filing. Do not, however, if you plan to file only, succumb to the temptation to use a sanding bit in your quarter-inch drill, or even one of the small sanding bits on the tiny drills you can find at some pet stores. This sort of sanding, if it is to be used at all, is strictly reserved for experts. The very high speed of the electrical sanding bits is such that if you are not careful you can cause considerable pain and damage through the heat of the friction between the fast-whirling bit and the nail.

It is one of the surest bets in the world that when you are first at it, and even occasionally when you have become an expert at clipping, you will clip a little too far up on the nail, hurting your dog and causing the nail to bleed. If this happens, and it will, don't worry about it too much. Console your dog, and either go on with great care, or leave off for that day. If the bleeding is slight, the only thing you need do is try to keep your dog off his feet for about fifteen minutes until the blood has had a chance to coagulate, and keep him off rough concrete sidewalks for the rest of the day if possible. If the bleeding is more copious and appears not to be stopping of its own accord, hold a piece of cotton over the nail for a few minutes to help the coagulation. You can also try a styptic pencil—but remember that it may sting. An excellent method involves hydrogen peroxide, in the standard strength available at any drugstore. Soak a small piece of cotton with peroxide, and hold it over the nail for about a minute. There is a chemical called Monsel's Solution which old kennel hands use for such bleeding, and it is potent stuff—if you are able to get a supply, all you have to do is dip a cotton swab in it and daub the bleeding nail lightly. Never, incidentally, use Monsel's to stop the bleeding from a skin wound, as you may hear recommended—it will cause discoloration of the skin. However, this solution is extremely difficult to get hold of in many areas, for it must be made up by a pharmacist, and most pharmacists neither stock it nor are willing to make it.

THE EARS

As with human ears, the primary dictum about dogs' ears is the familiar maternal caution not to put anything in smaller than your elbow. This is because in unskilled or even semi-skilled hands, which means yours, enormous damage can be done to the ear canal and the ear drum by poking things in, around and at them to clean or treat them. Humans often blithely ignore this advice with themselves, and use hairpins and matchsticks to clean wax out of their own ear canals, and with unpleasant frequency puncture the drum or seriously irritate and infect the canal, which results in, at best, impaired hearing. Whatever you do to your own ears, don't do it to your dog's.

This warning having been established, it is perfectly all right, and in fact desirable, to check and clean your dog's ears every now and then, if needed. Dogs with erect ears suffer ear trouble much less often than those with hanging, floppy ears, because the flap retains moisture and dirt and prevents air from getting to the inside of the ear. If your dog gives you some reason to believe there is something bothering him about his ears—usually by pawing continually at one or both ears, scratching them, rubbing them against things, or even showing more rapture than usual when you scratch or rub them—it's likely they need, at least, a cleaning. It may be only dirt and accumulated wax, in which case you can take care of it quite easily. Take a small wad of clean cotton, and with this on the end of your little finger, swab the ear out gently. To avoid irritation and to help with the cleaning, wet the cotton with a little mineral oil or rubbing alcohol, and you will find that you can do a good cleaning job. Before you do this, though, check carefully for burrs, grass and weed awns, or any other sharp and sticky items that may be lodged in the ear—if you go swabbing happily away and grind any of these into the inside of your dog's ear, it may cut or infect the sensitive skin therein.

As you will have seen, the inside of a dog's ear consists of a number of flaps and ridges of cartilage and skin, some of them forming little "valleys" in which dirt and wax are often accumulated. If you can't clean these out with even a very small bit of cotton on your finger, use Q-Tips or any other small cotton swab on a stick. Because of the temptation to use these to go deeper into the ear and into the ear canal, many veterinarians would prefer that dog owners didn't even know such things as Q-Tips existed. However, as people do know about such things, and are very likely to make the connection, it is best simply to say that these stick-swabs can be handy for external ear-cleaning, but only if you realize, fully and completely, that you can do really nasty damage if you poke them into the ear canal. Do not, under any circumstances and for any reason whatsoever, go deeper into the ear than about half an inch away from where you see the visible part of the ear canal end at the bottom of the dog's ear. With this caution firmly in mind, there is no reason you shouldn't use Q-Tips for cleaning out the "valleys."

Some breeds of dogs have little or no hair on the inside of the ear, while others, such as Poodles and the Terrier breeds, have thick hair which can cause considerable trouble. If this hair is too thick, it can hold moisture inside the ear quite efficiently, which leads to such unpleasantries as infections, and the hair and the resulting moisture will often hold gobs of dirt inside the ear, and clog up with wax which would ordinarily work itself out of the canal and out of the ear. This ear-hair is best kept under control by what seems at first an inhumane method, but really isn't—yanking it out. To do this, simply reach into the ear with thumb and forefinger, and take a small amount of the hair and yank it out with a sharp, quick motion, much the same as you would, or should, use to take adhesive tape off yourself. Done quickly and adeptly, it doesn't hurt the dog at all. Repeat this a few times with small batches of hair (not much at a time) and take out only enough to somewhat clear the ear canal—don't try to strip it bare. The proper technique is a bit difficult to learn, but once learned is simplicity itself—it is an excellent idea to get direct instruction from your vet or from a breeder of your breed of dog.

As to accumulations of wax in the ear canal, you may read or hear that it can be removed easily by putting in some sort of softening oil and then massaging the ear gently from the outside to loosen the wax. True, it can be done this way, but it is something you shouldn't try except under the expert guidance and with the recommendation of your veterinarian, for several reasons. First, you don't know whether your dog's ear trouble really is nothing but impacted wax, or something worse which will develop complications while you ignore it and treat for wax. Second, it is easy to injure the ear canal by rubbing it from the outside—rubbing hardened wax against the sensitive canal, or even rubbing the canal walls against each other too much when the wax has become softened.

Regular inspection of your dog's ears should include a careful look for ticks, for the ear is one of the tick's favorite hiding places. If you do find ticks, remove them by the method described later in this chapter. One reason you should pay somewhat careful attention to your dog's ears, and to him, if he shakes and scratches at them overmuch, is the possibility of ear mites. Mites are something only your vet can diagnose, but their symptoms are much the same as those of any ear trouble—shaking and scratching, and in severe cases irritability and overall nervousness. Treatment of ear mites should be left strictly up to the vet.

THE EYES

The normal care of your dog's eyes involves only wiping away such small discharge as may appear every day at or near the inside corner of each eye. This is very much akin to the "sand" that you wipe away from your own eyes in the morning, and a small amount means nothing at all in a dog. Simply brush it away with a tissue or a piece of cotton. Unless you are specifically advised to do so by your vet, don't bathe your dog's eyes regularly with boric acid solution or anything else—the more you leave the eyes alone, the better off they will be.

Signs of disorder in the eye are a sudden increase in the discharge from the eye, or a beginning of discharge in a dog which normally has none. This symptom is quite often one of the earliest and most noticeable signs of Vitamin A deficiency, so give a thought to the balance of your dog's diet if his eyes start mattering. Constant scratching or pawing at the eye may indicate foreign matter in the eye itself, or injury or abnormal growth of the eyelids. As explained in Chapter I, dogs have a partially functioning nictitating membrane or "third eyelid," a translucent membrane which can slide partially or completely over the eye from the inside lower corner of the eye. In the normal eye it is hardly ever noticeable, except that when your dog has just wakened you may see it sliding back, or if he sleeps with one or both eyes partially open, the nictitating membrane will often be visible between the lids—it can look quite eerie. This is nothing abnormal, but if you begin to notice any extension or enlargement of this membrane under other circumstances, it is best to have your vet do a thorough eye examination, as the membrane may be infected or inflamed.

THE TEETH

Fortunately, dogs hardly ever have the normal human trouble with cavities—their major problems are broken and worn teeth, and the formation of dental calculus. The most common causes of broken teeth are chewing on hard objects such as metal or stones, and fighting. Once your dog's adult teeth have come in, you should familiarize yourself with the way they look normally, and check them every once in a while for broken tips or crowns, something which the dog himself might not feel or notice until the breakage went further and exposed the pulp of the tooth to decay and subsequent pain. In particular, check your dog's teeth if he has been in a fight, even if he tore the other dog into seventeen small and distinct pieces and seems not to have a scratch on him. In their preliminary clashes and in the heat of the fight, the teeth of two fighting dogs will often crash together, and even the winner may suffer a broken tooth. If you do notice anything broken, the only thing you can do is take him to the vet for possible treatment—early treatment may save the tooth, or if the case is severe enough to require extraction, the dog may be saved serious infections, pain and complications.

Dental calculus is a problem of almost every dog, its severity depending largely on the dog's diet and his ability to keep his teeth clean by gnawing on bones or other hard objects. Wild dogs very seldom have calculus trouble—calculus is the hard deposit of material at the base of the teeth, at the gum line. It occurs in humans, too, and you have probably had to have your dentist chip away your calculus at one time or another. Dogs kept on a soft diet of human-type foods are the most subject to calculus problems. One of the solutions to the problem is to have a synthetic bone or hard-rubber toy available most of the time for your dog to chew on, and he will help hold down the problem himself as the hard bone or toy chips and rubs the calculus away in the normal course of events. Hard dog biscuits also are helpful in keeping calculus formation at a minimum. But even with such practice, you may have to have your vet do an annual or semi-annual chipping job. The major part of the calculus will form on the outside surface of the tooth, so the job can be done quite efficiently without even having to get the dog's teeth apart. A really thorough chipping job, including the inside, might require that the dog be put under anaesthesia. This is inadvisable in some cases, and so you may have to settle for an "outside only" chipping.

Calculus and the brownish stains which often discolor a dog's teeth can be prevented, at least in good part, by regular brushing of the dog's teeth. This sort of thing strikes some people as being mildly hilarious, but it is nonetheless something that ought to be done. One of the troubles with the situation is that people are often advised simply to brush the dog's teeth, and immediately and naturally have a mental picture of toothbrush and paste, which is not at all the way to go about it. The proper method is to take a small bit of clean cotton, or a small piece of rough toweling, wet it and dip it into ordinary table salt (as an abrasive) and scrub the outside of the teeth with a firm up-and-down motion. Don't overdo the vigor of the brushing, as you can irritate or harm the gums; careful firmness is the procedure. Even the insides of the teeth really should be worked on, but this is quite a bit to expect, and in any case the major problems of calculus and staining are on the outside of the teeth. Brushing needn't be done daily, as the major problem here is not food particles which may decay and cause cavities, but simple cleaning and loosening of beginning calculus formations—weekly is a good interval.

There is one tooth condition about which you can unfortunately do nothing at all, and this is distemper staining. Distemper most often strikes dogs when they are puppies, and when the permanent teeth are coming in and first growing—it leaves its characteristic mark of dark rings and pits on the teeth. If your dog has had a severe case and recovered, his teeth may be quite badly disfigured, and even a mild case which you may have thought was just a general puppy upset will often leave discoloration. Other diseases can also cause staining of the teeth—discolored teeth do not necessarily mean that you dog has had distemper.

FLATUS, MOUTH AND BODY ODORS

The subject of the various odors which may emanate from a dog falls halfway between grooming and health. The common and widely known "doggy" odor, for example, is largely the result of lack of grooming. True, it is not completely for this reason that dogs smell like dogs, but if you have ever been to a dog show, or have known people who have a well-cared-for show dog, think back over the amount of doggy odor you *didn't* notice. It may come as a surprise to you to remember that there was very little if any odor. There is the additional factor of length of hair—short-coated breeds, if left relatively ungroomed, usually smell less than the long-haired, but this again only points to the coat and skin as major factors in dog odor. Try giving your dog one good bath if he is really smelling up the house, and then keep him well groomed, with daily brushings and combings, and the chances are excellent that the major part of his odor will disappear. Various diseases and infestation can also cause specific odors, the most notable being sarcoptic mange which often causes a musty or mousy odor, but these are very much minor elements.

Really obnoxious bad breath in a dog is usually due to diet, but can also indicate infections of the teeth or mouth, or disturbances of the stomach. Dogs fed a diet high in meat will often have a smell of slightly decayed meat on their breaths, which comes from the digestion of meat in their stomachs. It is usually very mild and you won't notice it unless the dog really breathes into your face, and it indicates nothing about health. If it increases and is offensive, it can almost always be lessened or remedied by a change of diet, at least a lowering of the meat content.

Sour and acrid breath will usually indicate, just as in humans, digestive upsets—this is something to be concerned about if it is constant, in which case you should see your vet about the possibilities of some chronic stomach disorder. Continually unpleasant breath can be the result of decaying teeth and infections of the gums which you may not have noticed, and, if such odors are unaffected by a change of diet, again indicate a trip to the vet.

Uremic breath—an odor of urine in the breath—will often be a tip-off to a uremic condition in the dog. This may be the result of any number of kidney conditions, and uremic breath should be a signal for an immediate trip to the veterinarian.

Finally, there is flatus, otherwise referred to as "passing wind." It is not too common a problem in dogs, but one which can be considerably offensive when it does occur. It is often attributable to diet. If your dog is so affected, try various changes of diet to see if you can eliminate it. As with bad breath, the most common offender is meat, and a reduction in the meat portion of the diet may solve or at least reduce the problem. High levels of fat in the diet, desirable as they are for nutrition, are often guilty—fat tends to slow digestion, and when undigested fat passes into the lower intestines, some putrefaction occurs, resulting in offensive odors.

The problem also occurs in excitable and nervous dogs, whose psychic upsets reflect in visceral tensions and churning, just as with humans. Flatus will be one of the least of your problems if your dog is that nervous and upset—the whole syndrome will best yield to calm treatment and attempts at removal of the causes for the excitability and nervousness. It isn't as easy as all that, for some dogs are just high strung and nervous by natural temperament, but you may be able to ease the situation some, and in any case it may help to know that this is a possible cause.

BLOAT

Excessive gas in the stomach may cause a very serious condition known as acute gastric dilation, or bloat. It most often occurs in very large dogs, with Great Danes being the principal victims. The onset of bloat is so sudden that, if it happens to your dog, you may not realize he has the condition until his stomach is enormously dilated by the gas and needs extremely rapid emergency treatment. Bloat usually happens in warm weather, and follows the eating of large quantities of dry food, drinking of large quantities of water, aided by violent exercise just after the meal. If you are observant, you may notice your dog becoming very excited and energetic immediately after such a dry meal combined with the large amounts of water—very soon the bloat victim becomes apathetic and his stomach begins to swell. He goes into shock, standing with his legs spread apart, and his breathing becomes shallow and weak. There is no home treatment for bloat, but if you see the beginning symptoms, and particularly if the abdomen begins to swell, get a vet immediately. The condition is so serious and dangerous that the vet may have to take such strong emergency measures as pushing a wide-guage hypodemic needle directly into the stomach through the abdominal wall to relieve the pressure of the gas. Bloat is very often fatal, but rapid aid can help. If the dog does recover, surgical correction of the cause of the condition may be necessary.

TEMPERATURE

As indicated in the previous chapter, your dog's temperature is one of the surest indicators of his state of health, but temperature ranges are little understood by the average dog owner. The average temperature of the adult dog is 101.7°, comparable to the 98.6° average human temperature. In considering this figure, several factors must be kept in mind, the first, that it is an *average*. Not every dog's normal temperature is 101.7°. It is a figure arrived at by averaging the normal temperatures of thousands of dogs, some of them slightly above, some of them slightly below that figure. Therefore, a perfectly normal dog under normal conditions may have a healthy temperature which varies by as much as half a degree either way from the average.

In addition, normal temperature varies with the size of the dog, the time of the day and the season of the year. Large sedentary dogs tend to have lower normal temperatures than small, active breeds. The temperature is slightly higher during the day than at night, and higher in the summer than during the winter. Taking all these factors into consideration, a variation of a full degree from 101.7° may be considered within the normal range, provided the circumstances point to such a variation in your dog.

You will rarely encounter a subnormal temperature, except in the case of a pregnant bitch just before whelping—it is the rises that you have to look out for. Anything above 103° is an almost certain indicator that trouble is beginning somewhere inside him. As recommended in the previous chapter, it is a good idea to have a rectal thermometer around the house, and to use it when symptoms of illness appear. You won't know specifically what is wrong with him from his temperature, but it will warn you that you had better take steps, and knowledge of even one previous reading (preferably a series of readings) may be of enormous help to your veterinarian in diagnosing your dog's illness. Many diseases and conditions have characteristic patterns of changes in temperature. For your own guidance, a temperature of 104° is borderline—it may result from a minor illness or upset which might never have to be brought to a vet's attention, but beginning with 105° you very definitely should call the vet, for there is serious trouble either present or on the way. Even below that, in the borderline range, it is a good idea to have a vet's attention.

Aside from being an indicator of illness, fever itself can be damaging to the system. If your dog starts running a high temperature, above 104°, during the night or at any other time when you can't get veterinary help shortly, you must take steps to help bring the fever under control yourself. For this, ordinary aspirin is the best possible medicine. A good fever-control dose is one grain of aspirin every three hours per seven pounds of dog. Calculating grains of aspirin is easy, for every standard aspirin tablet consists of five grains. Thus, a 35-pound dog should be given one standard aspirin tablet every three hours. If you have a smaller dog, it is easier to divide one tablet by crushing it and then taking approximately the portion of the tablet indicated by the size of your dog. Or you can use the children's aspirin tablets, which are one and one-quarter grains each. If you are in doubt as to the number of grains per tablet, the label of every bottle or package specifies this amount.

You can administer the aspirin whole, or, if for any reason you have difficulty, crush the aspirin (in the right amount) in the bowl of a teaspoon, add a little water, and give it to him by the lip-pouch method described in the First Aid chapter.

Warning: do not use aspirin indiscriminately, or as a substitute for veterinary attention! Use it only for temporary control of high fever until you can get to your vet, for the fever, harmful though it may be of itself, is also an indicator of other things which need treatment.

STOOL AND URINE

The dog's stool and urine are also excellent indicators of his state of health—the stool in many situations, and the urine specifically in the indication of fever. A dog's normal stool is firm without being hard, fully formed and of a light, medium or dark brown color. Both the normal color and consistency of the stool may vary because of diet, the most common characteristics being a reddish color as a result of eating certain commercial dog foods, and a dark to nearly black color as a result of a high percentage of horsemeat in the diet. A sudden change in the major constituents of the diet may cause a change in the normal color, and may even temporarily cause diarrhea or constipation to a mild degree.

Any persistent or severe diarrhea, however, should be regarded as a strong indicator of problems—so many internal disorders can and do cause diarrhea that it is impossible to list them. If, however, your dog suddenly suffers from diarrhea, it is wise to keep an eye on things for a day or two, and then get professional attention. Mild cases are usually nothing to worry about, but if the stool at any time becomes liquid or watery, and the dog is barely able or totally unable to control himself and hold his evacuations for the outside, then it is almost certain that something is wrong.

The color of the stool can also vary with drugs your dog may have been given—iron preparations causing a darkened to black stool, for example.

But any changes should be regarded with suspicion. An orange to yellow stool may be an indication of infectious diseases, pale gray stools may indicate lack of digestive enzymes, bleeding in the stomach or upper intestine will cause the stool to become black and tarry, and bleeding from the lower intestine or rectum will show itself in bright red blood in the stool. On this latter point, if you see blood associated with the stool in tiny quantities, it may be only the result of a minor irritation of the rectum or colon, but the continued appearance of blood, however small the amount, is cause for veterinary examination—the most common causes being severe whipworm infestation or colitis.

The urine is considerably more difficult to observe, but can at times be an indicator of otherwise unsuspected fever. The normal color is light yellow to amber, and its normal odor is slight. If you observe that your dog begins to pass urine of a deeper color, intense yellow to near orange, and that the odor is strong enough to attract your attention, it is possible that he is running a fever, and a check with the thermometer is in order. Darkening of the urine may also indicate leptospirosis—see Chapter III. Of course, in the relatively rare cases where there is blood in the urine, any other dramatic discoloration or any abnormally foul odor, veterinary attention is indicated at once.

CONSTIPATION AND DIARRHEA

Of the two possible departures from normal stool and elimination, constipation is the least serious. It usually results from a change of diet, or some minor intestinal upset, and is in general nothing to be concerned about. A perfectly normal and healthy dog may go for two or three days without defecating, and finally suffer nothing more than a little discomfort in passing the accumulated feces. It is generally best to leave constipation alone, but you can help things out a bit on the second day with a small dose of Milk of Magnesia or even ordinary mineral oil, both non-irritating laxatives. A good dose of either is one teaspoonful per twenty pounds of dog, not more than twice a day. Do not, however, except on the advice of a veterinarian—which is unlikely—dose your dog with any other form of human laxative or cathartic. One reason is that it may poison him, possibly fatally. Some human cathartics contain strychnine sulfate, for example, and even a tiny amount of this drug can be fatal to a dog. Other human laxatives depend for their action on chemicals which irritate the intestinal walls, and if your dog has some infection or irritation of the intestine already, such laxatives will only complicate matters. In any case of constipation, consult your vet if the condition persists for more than three days, and Milk of Magnesia or mineral oil do not help—or if the dog at any time shows abdominal pain or pain in the rectal area beyond normal minor discomfort in straining to defecate.

Diarrhea is a far more dangerous condition than constipation. It is, first, almost always a symptom of some internal disorder, and, second, a danger in itself. The direct danger of diarrhea is due to the fact that, whatever its cause, it results in a loss of fluids from the body. This loss, if continued, becomes acute dehydration, which in turn can cause or contribute to shock. Therefore, it is important to take close notice of any diarrhea condition in your dog, and to attempt to bring it under control. Controlling diarrhea will do little or nothing for the condition which caused it originally, but is important in itself.

Mild diarrhea—very soft to liquid stools—may indicate nothing more than a temporary stomach upset, or even simply nerves and tension in the dog. The best control is Kaopectate, a standard diarrhea-control product for humans. The chemicals in Kaopectate actually absorb water themselves (the proper chemical term is *ad*sorb, which is slightly different from *ab*sorb, but this is chiefly of interest to chemists and the like). In mild diarrhea, give Kaopectate every four hours, the dosage according to the size of the dog (approximately 2 teaspoonsful per twenty pounds of body weight) and continue this dosage until the dog passes firm stools, or until it is obvious that the diarrhea is so much out of control that it will require veterinary attention. Do not continue beyond two days of unsuccessful attempt to control diarrhea with Kaopectate, and do not continue if the stool becomes watery or liquid.

Mild diarrhea which can be brought under control with Kaopectate is not something which should concern you too much. If it occurs infrequently, think nothing more of it. But if the diarrhea gets out of control, turns watery or liquid, or even if relatively mild diarrhea is chronic, then arrange for a veterinary examination. If there should be a sudden onset of profuse, watery diarrhea and you cannot get to a vet immediately, but all means give Kaopectate until you are able to get to the vet, even if it seems to do no good at all—however, you should not give Kaopectate simply as a substitute for veterinary attention in such cases.

In the home control of mild diarrhea, the dog should be allowed his normal consumption of room-temperature water, however contrary to common sense this may seem. He needs fluids to replace the fluids lost in the diarrhea. Cut out milk, which is mildly diarrhetic, and add cheeses and cooked rice to the diet. Also, if possible, let him out or walk him more frequently than usual, for his bowel control will be weakened by the diarrhea. More frequent outings will not only save you some cleaning jobs, but they will help counteract the bad influence of diarrhea on his housebreaking training.

COPROPHAGY

This is a nice word for a very unpleasant habit of some dogs—picking up and carrying, and even eating their own stools or those of other dogs. It is extremely disgusting to many owners, but, although it can of course not be condoned, it must be realized that a dog's attitude to feces, and urine, is entirely different from a human's and does not involve any revulsion or dislike. It is important to bear this in mind, because coprophagy does not mean that the dog is depraved or disgusting or anything of the sort—dogs just feel differently about such things. Remember that to them, urine and stools are simply "things," and that their individual smells serve dogs as notifications that strange dogs are in the neighborhood, and tell them other things.

Coprophagy, however, must be curbed, and this means an attempt at discovering the reasons behind it. There are many theories as to causes, and you will have to do a bit of thinking about your own dog before you discover what it is in his particular case. One theory is that coprophagy indicates mineral deficiencies in the dog's diet—that he eats stools to recover the unused minerals in them. Nobody has proved this, but enough veterinarians believe it that you should give a thought first to such possible deficiencies.

Other theories hold that dogs often begin this habit out of boredom— it is, in any case, more common among dogs who are confined to runs and have little opportunity to play with other dogs or people. Another theory holds that it results at least partially from hereditary instincts to retrieve—he simply finds a stool lying about, picks it up to retrieve it, and the habit develops.

If dietary supplementation doesn't cure the habit, the only course is simply to remove the temptation. If your dog is confined to a run, clean the run daily if not more often, to be sure that no stools are lying about for him to take. If he has the freedom of a yard, keep the yard well cleaned at all times, and train your dog to use either one corner of it for his defecations, or to use a field or other area. The best solution of all is to take him for daily walks to a distant field or street for his defecation, and keep it up until the habit-pattern is broken. Of course, the daily walks will do both of you good anyway, and there's no reason to stop them even when he is cured.

One further theory that is sometimes mentioned in connection with coprophagy is that it may be associated with worm infestations, particularly hookworms. This ties in with the mineral-deficiency theory, because severe worm infestations often create deficiency situations in the dog, and he may take to eating stools to make up as much as possible for those deficiencies. It is well worth checking this possibility if your dog does begin to practice coprophagy.

ANAL GLANDS

At each side of the dog's anus, there is a small pocket which is variously referred to as the anal gland, or anal sac. Secretions from true glands empty into these sacs, and may eventually accumulate in such quantity as to cause pressure on the walls of the sacs, with subsequent irritation and pain to the dog. The major symptom of this over-accumulation is seen when the dog rubs his rear constantly on the ground, sliding or "sledding" along in an attempt to relieve the irritation and pain. This not uncommon activity is one of the most mis-interpreted symptoms occuring in the dog, attributed almost universally by folklore to worms. The symptom can be caused by worms, but more often it will be an indication of anal gland trouble, and should be watched for. A secondary symptom is continual licking or biting at the anus. If allowed to go on for too long, anal sacs become infected and lead to serious trouble. They can also result in chronic infections of the mouth and other parts of the body—the dog licks infective material from the glands and may then deposit it on other parts of his body by licking there.

Although treatment of the anal sac problem is usually quite simple, it is better left to the veterinarian, who can empty the sacs by simple pressure in the right place. The material in these sacs is unbelievably foul-smelling, which is one of the major reasons you should not attempt treatment yourself. In addition, the contents of the sacs will never be cleaned out as completely as when the job is done by a vet. Often the ducts are obstructed and the sac ruptured, causing a local abscess which can only be treated by a vet. But if you feel up to trying it, be sure to have large wads of cotton on hand, and preferably wear rubber gloves. Then, with the dog well under control, cover your thumb and forefinger with cotton and press gently, just below and to the left of the anus, and then below and to the right, to empty the glands. The material will issue from the anus itself, and you should be careful to have cotton in place to collect it. If you don't apply pressure at the proper spot the first time, you will shortly find by a little experimentation just where to press. But remember to be gentle and considerate while doing it, as the area is already painful to the dog—and don't go on for more than a few minutes if you're having no success, but take the dog to your vet.

DISEASE SYMPTOMS

This book cannot hope to make you an expert diagnostician of dog diseases—if it or any book could, veterinary colleges would shortly be out of business. There are, however, any number of indications that *something* is wrong with your dog, a variety of symptoms which can tell you to be on the alert for others, and to be ready to call your vet for help and treatment. In the following formidable list of symptoms, there is an occasional mention of specific diseases and conditions which might be the causes of the symptoms, but do not interpret these mentions as indicating that they are the only causes of the associated symptoms, or that the symptom necessarily indicates that your dog is suffering from that disease. Many symptoms, including those listed, may mean only minor and temporary upsets, but the mentions are made to show you that apparently minor and often ignored symptoms may be indicative of really serious conditions. In reading over this list, keep in mind that one symptom may mean little, but that a combination of several is almost always an indication that a visit to your veterinarian is definitely in order.

Stool: radically changed in color without a change in diet, loose to the point of liquidity, or chronically loose, bloody.

Urine: changing to dark in color, strong odor, bloody.

Vomiting: occasional vomiting of yellow, frothy bile may indicate nothing more than nervous upset, vomiting of recognizable food may indicate only rejection of that food—in either such case, vomiting can be considered as a temporary symptom provided the dog gives no other indication of discomfort and recovers his normal attitude and appearance quickly. If such vomiting is continuous or chronic, however, there is good reason to suspect leptospirosis. See Chapter III for a more detailed discussion of vomiting and leptospirosis. Continual or severe vomiting, especially if blood is in the vomitus, along with associated pain, disorientation, apathy, trembling, weakness, or shallow breathing, should be considered a serious symptom.

Coughing: may indicate nothing more than a mild cold or sore throat, or that something is stuck in the dog's throat, but the dry, hacking, "bone-in-the-throat" cough is another widely misinterpreted symptom. It quite often indicates the beginnings of one of the distemper-type diseases, or may be the result of worms having migrated to the lungs, causing local irritation.

Coat: dull, dry, rough, excessive dandruff or shedding.

Skin: any obvious lesions or reddening, possibly with associated loss of hair, hot to the touch, any change in color, very dry or flaky.

Eyes: dull, clouded, bloodshot, accumulations of gummy matter, photophobic (extreme sensitivity to light)—the latter two often indicative of distemper or similar diseases.

Nose: runny, clogged with gummy mucus. Warmth or coldness of the nose is not an indicator of normal or abnormal temperature.

Gums: pale, bluish, bright red.

Breathing: weak, rapid, shallow, heavy and panting when not associated with an obvious cause like heat or exercise.

Personality: any change in the dog's basic personality should be watched carefully. Any dog will be happy and excited one day, and quiet the next, indicating nothing but change of mood or circumstances. But you will be familiar with your dog's overall personality and character, and any basic change should be watched with a wary eye—one of the first symptoms of rabies is such a character change, and not always to the worse; shy and aloof dogs infected with rabies may become suddenly friendly and affectionate in the early stages. Don't get over-suspicious about this, though—rabies is quite rare in this country.

Trembling, excitability: when not associated with immediate and obvious causes such as fear or other stimulus.

Apathy: general "I don't care" attitude, if it persists, may indicate a great many internal disorders.

Scratching, biting: aside from the obvious possibilities of fleas or other skin parasites, constant scratching or biting at himself, particularly if it is aimed continually at a particular spot, may indicate internal pains in that area.

Again, any single one of these symptoms may indicate nothing but a mild local condition, but if you see one, be on the alert for others, and be prepared to report them accurately to the vet. It is not a bad idea to keep a written note of symptoms, including the time of onset or at least when you first noticed it, how symptoms have progressed, and duration if they have ceased. Doctors almost universally frown on people who come in with lists of their own symptoms, for the good reason that if a human has to make a list to remember his own aches and pains they couldn't have been all that severe. But in veterinary care, you are reporting for the dog symptoms which he cannot express himself, no matter how vivid they are in his memory, and keeping a written note is a good idea.

Not included in the above listing are such obvious symptoms as specific local pains, convulsions and others which are so self-evident as indicators of trouble that it would be idle to include or attempt to list them.

It is worth noting, along the line of symptoms, that dogs can be hypochondriacs, just as humans often are. One veterinary text points out:

> "Although the attitudes and symptoms exhibited by dogs, in the vast majority of cases, are honest manifestations of subjective symptoms, most practitioners will agree that canine hypochondriacs and

malingerers exist. Real injury or illness at home may bring such a showering of affection and choice food that the dog will repeatedly feign illness to obtain these benefits. Some pets are quick to perceive this possibility of reward."

Therefore, do not conclude that your vet got his degree from a mail-order house if he tells you your own little dog is just faking it in order to get attention—it does happen with dogs, who are more human than even tried and true dog lovers believe in their most sentimental moments.

EXTERNAL PARASITES

Over two hundred years ago, Jonathan Swift wrote, in another context, a verse which has excellent application to this section:

> So, naturalists observe, a flea
> Hath smaller fleas that on him prey;
> And these have smaller still to bite 'em;
> And so proceed ad infinitum.

How far it proceeds ad infinitum, nobody knows, but Swift's verse points out one of the great dangers of the major external parasites, aside from the direct irritation of the dog—that they are often carriers, scientifically termed "vectors," of various diseases. Fleas, ticks and lice may carry such items as tapeworms, heartworms and Rocky Mountain spotted fever, to name only a few. Their direct effects are the obvious ones of irritation of the skin, and as a result of this, scratching which may remove hair, irritate and thicken the skin, and cause a chronic condition of irritation, especially in warm weather. In addition, all three of the major parasites, if left untreated, may spread through a house and attack the human occupants, with consequent unpleasantries. Even the most cursory inspection will advise you of the presence of fleas or ticks, and an occasional close examination will guard against lice.

FLEAS

There are distinct varieties of fleas, including dog fleas, rat fleas, cat fleas, human fleas and sticktight or hen fleas, none of which, despite their special names, have more than a slight preference for their designated hosts—they will quite happily fasten to and feed from dogs, cats, rats, or humans if they have the chance. Fleas are recognized by the traditional excessive scratching, by close examination of the dog's skin where fleas can often be seen, and in unfortunate circumstances, by a sudden access of bites on yourself, usually beginning on and sometimes limited to the ankles.

Fortunately, if caught in time, fleas are easily disposed of, with baths or powders or sprays or dips. Many varieties of preparations are available commercially, and if used according to directions will result in effective flea control—see the earlier sections of this chapter for the proper methods of using sprays, baths and dips. But if you suspect fleas are causing all the irritation your dog shows, and you've de-flead him once, then again, and he still itches and scratches, don't keep on bathing him repeatedly. The flea preparation you're using may be irritating to his skin, or you may have misdiagnosed the trouble in the first place. If it doesn't stop, have a vet look him over for possibilities of other skin problems.

It is when fleas have been neglected long enough to establish themselves in the household that there can be trouble. The female flea, having fed herself on your dog, will then leave him and deposit her eggs almost anywhere in the house, and these will soon hatch into more fleas to contend with. The eggs themselves can survive a winter if well hidden, and infant and adult fleas can live for several months in cracks and crevices if conditions are right. If you are suffering from a general infestation, in which the dog is being re-infested by resident fleas after you clean him up, or if you are being bitten yourself, you will have to exert yourself to break the cycle. Take the dog outside and give him a good flea treatment, and then keep him outside while you go over the house. Vacuum everything in sight—rugs, floors, walls, chairs, sofas, bedding, drapes— and vacuum up a little flea powder as you go along just for good measure, and to knock out the fleas you have caught in your machine. Then give the house a thorough treatment with a good residual insecticide— one which leaves a residue which kills insects when they come in contact with it later. Be careful, though, to use an insecticide which will not be poisonous to your dog if he should happen to lick some of it up, or roll in it and then lick his coat—also use caution about where you put the stuff, with this in mind. Finally, bring your deflead dog back into the house and encourage him to roam and lie about all over the place. The idea is that any surviving fleas will leap on him with glad cries and be in a position for you to make what you hope will be the final extermination. After a day or two back in the house, take him back outside and do another flea removal job on him, and this ought to solve it. It is rather unkind to use him as your final flea-removal agent, but it doesn't hurt him, and in any case it's his fault to begin with.

No one has yet proved it, but there are suspicions that some dogs are natural flea hosts, while others have partial or even full immunity to fleas —something to do with body chemistry, just as some humans are bitten to death by such animals as chiggers, while others never are bitten. Investigating along these lines, veterinary researchers have developed a vaccine-type inoculation which will confer temporary flea immunity. Other work is being done on developing a food additive which will accomplish the same purpose. By the time you read this, one or both just might have been perfected, which would be a blessing indeed.

LICE

You are very unlikely ever to have to worry about lice, but as lice are usually passed by contact, there is a remote possibility that your dog might acquire an infestation by cozying up to a lousy (and this is the proper and original meaning of the word) stray. The symptoms are very similar to those of flea infestation, with the general minor difference that a serious lice infestation may have more of an effect on the dog's coat and general condition—he may appear "unthrifty," a dog term which is best explained as "poor looking, ragged."

Close and careful examination may reveal the lice themselves, heads buried in the skin if they are of the sucking variety, and possibly moving about on the skin if of the biting variety. The surest lice indicator is the presence of tiny eggs or nits stuck to the individual hairs of the coat. The entire life cycle of the louse is completed on the body of the host—this is a help in ridding the house of any lice remnants, because they cannot live long without a host to feed on. Most sprays, dips and powders will do an effective job against lice, provided they are well and thoroughly applied and gotten well onto the skin. It is a job which should really be left to a veterinarian, because lice have a predilection for body openings and are often found clustered there, quite often around the eyes. As it is extremely inadvisable to get any sort of insecticide in the eyes, you should either be extraordinarily careful in application, or leave it to a professional, because it is important to get *all* the lice in the treatment. For effective disposal of the eggs stuck to your dog's hairs, in a severe infestation, he might have to be clipped quite close to the skin, but that is something to leave up to the vet.

TICKS

Handling ticks is an excellent example of the adage about an ounce of prevention, for with only a little care the tick problem is very easy to keep under control, but if it once gets out of hand, you are in for such a siege as you never imagined. The problem is that the tick lays its eggs off the dog, and that both young and old ticks can live for an incredible length of time—some authorities have estimated the period at two years—without feeding. There are numerous varieties of ticks, but most are what are known as three-host ticks, which means that within one life cycle, a tick will attach itself three separate times to hosts. The female attaches herself, feeds, and drops off to lay eggs. The eggs develop into larvae which attach themselves to another host, feed, then drop off to molt and become nymphs. The nymphs attach themselves to a host, then drop off to molt again and become adults, whereupon the whole cycle starts over again. The unpleasant part of all this is that a good part of the life cycle is spent off any host and thus immune to any direct action taken on the dog. Additionally, any one of the three host stages might be spent on you if you're available when the proper time comes. Even if you've never had a tick on you, you can easily imagine that it does not rate high in anybody's list of pleasant experiences.

Therefore, the only desirable tick control method is regular inspection of your dog and removal of individual ticks before they have a chance to start things along an undesirable course in your living quarters. Because any of the feeding stages will take about a week, weekly inspections are almost sure to catch any and all ticks your dog may have picked up. If yours is a city dog, he is not likely to pick up ticks in the course of his normal walks on the sidewalks, and you can logically do tick inspections only after he has had a chance to run in the country or in a park. In the country, inspection after every run in the woods or fields is obviously impractical, and in such cases the weekly schedule is best.

On a short-haired dog you may find ticks accidentally—in stroking the dog, you will feel a tiny lump under the hair, and nine times out of ten it will be a tick. But with any dog, examination consists of ruffling the hair against the "grain" so that all the skin is visible, a little at a time. A tick is instantly recognizable, being about the size and shape and coloring of a small watermelon seed, attached at the small end. Any tick you find on the skin will be attached, with its jaws buried in the skin, and requires some care in removal. If you simply pull it off, the head and jaws are very likely to break off and remain in the dog's skin where they may cause infection. The procedure is to anaesthetize the tick before removal, at least to the point where he relaxes his jaws and can be pulled off whole. (There is a folklore method of tick removal from humans which prescribes holding a burning match to or near a tick until it is persuaded that the neighborhood is unhealthy, or is killed; this is definitely not a practical method with dogs, for obvious reasons.)

Once you have found a tick, take a small wad of cotton, soak it with alcohol, and hold it directly on the tick and the surrounding skin for a few minutes. Ether is the best possible liquid to use for this purpose, but you aren't likely to have ether around the house, so any alcohol will do—preferably straight medical alcohol, but even rubbing alcohol or gin will do the trick. When you feel that the tick has had enough, take hold of him with a pair of broad-point tweezers. Grab him from top and bottom, slipping one blade of the tweezers between the dog's skin and the tick—don't try to grab the tick from the sides, because with his watermelon-seed shape you can't get a good grip that way. Then pull the tick slowly but firmly out of the skin. If you feel him snap off, you have probably broken the head off, but if he comes out more or less smoothly, albeit with effort, you have probably gotten him out whole. If you have broken him off, there's little you can do about it—give the area another dab with the alcohol to help prevent infection, and you probably won't have trouble.

Have a small bowl or a paper cup or a tissue ready to drop the tick into, and be careful during the tweezer trip from skin to receptacle. The tick is slippery in any case, and it is now wet with alcohol, and if you're at all nervous about it, you are quite likely to drop him on the rug, the floor, or back onto the dog. Burn all removed ticks as soon as you can, or flush them down the toilet—if even one healthy female tick gets away, she'll recover from the alcohol anaesthesia and lay her eggs somewhere and you're in for trouble.

When examining your dog, don't forget to look into his ears, a spot especially favored by ticks, in his "armpits," on his stomach, and on his feet and between his pads, another favorite spot.

If you have let ticks get out of control in your house, or if you live in a heavily tick-infested area, you may have to resort to chemical dips to keep your dog clean of the younger stages of the ticks—these dips are readily available as commercial preparations. If the ticks have become established in your house, you may have to call in the services of professional exterminators for a complete fumigation—it can be that serious.

In the drier sections of the southwestern United States, there is often trouble with a particular variety of tick called the spinose ear tick. The symptoms of such an infestation are very similar to those of ear mites—special irritation and sensitivity of the ears, shaking of the head, constant scratching and rubbing the ears. Because these ticks will penetrate into the ear canal and up against the ear drum, they can be treated only by introduction of a specific chemical into the ear, and this treatment, as with any serious ear infestation or problem, should be left strictly to a veterinarian.

DEMODECTIC MANGE

Also known as follicular mange, this is one of the least understood of skin conditions—the exact method of transmision is not known, nor is any sure and rapid treatment known at this time. Progress in veterinary research may yield one soon (there are several preparations being tested at this writing), and at least demodectic mange is no longer the bogey it once was. Not too many years ago, a dog with this type of mange was considered as good as dead, for nothing could be done to stop the spread over the entire body, unless it happened to be caught very early, in which case the only semi-positive cure was cauterization of the affected spots.

Demodex, as many veterinarians refer to it, is caused by a small mite which burrows inside the individual hair follicle, the tiny sac which contains the hair root. Inside the follicle, the mite destroys the hair, and causes considerable damage to the skin itself. For reasons no one fully understands, it is usually first seen on the head, and in a large proportion of cases the first sign is a small bare and reddening spot on the side of the nose. It may be simply that most dogs' hair is shortest in these spots, and that the nose and head are the areas most often seen by the owner, but even these considerations do not fully explain Demodex's apparent predilection for the face and head as a starting place.

From the head, if left untreated, it spreads rapidly over the body, usually first to the feet and legs and then to the body itself. Cases may go one of two ways—the skin in increasing areas may lose hair and become thickened, or the affected areas may ooze blood and serum and become infected by bacteria attacking the minute skin openings.

The curious aspect of demodectic mange is that its method of transmission is still open to wide dispute, some researchers maintaining that it spreads only by contact, others that it is transmitted from mother to puppies, and others that it is a combination of both. In any case, a badly infected dog may live in close contact with a healthy dog and never transmit Demodex, and on the other hand, one affected dog in a kennel may mean a dozen more cases in short order. Yet, to support the "hereditary" theory, occasionally three or four members of a litter, separated shortly after weaning and having had no contact since, will almost simultaneously develop this form of mange months after their separation.

Because of its resemblance to sarcoptic mange and, particularly in its early stages, to other skin conditions, positive diagnosis of Demodex can only be made by taking a skin scraping from a suspect area and observing the actual mites under a microscope. Therefore, do not suspect your vet of thoughtless cruelty if he scrapes your dog's skin quite deeply at the edge of a suspected mange lesion—he must get a good deep sample of the skin to be sure he has some mites, and it will bleed, and hurt the dog, but it is necessary.

There are several treatments, none of them certain to cure, and all of them far more likely to succeed if begun when there is only one lesion, or a few isolated areas. Therefore, early diagnosis is of the utmost importance—never ignore areas of your dog's skin which seem to be losing hair, even if these areas do not itch or bother him particularly. On short-haired dogs, the first lesion may be the size of a dime or even a quarter before it is noticed. Long-haired dogs may have quite a wide-spread infection before it is noticed—another excellent reason for regular grooming which would show up mange, and for regular skin inspections.

If only one or two lesions are found and identified, the treatment can often be limited to a thorough application of an anti-demodectic salve. This you will get from the vet. It should be rubbed thoroughly into the affected area, and for several inches around it, either with your fingers or with a *soft* brush, not a stiff brush such as a tooth or hair brush. Don't worry about coming into contact with the lesions—demodectic mange is not transmissible to humans.

In addition to salve, or if the lesions are more widespread, you may have to give your dog daily dips with a solution which will probably have a sulfur base and be quite evil-smelling. In both cases, be particularly careful about keeping either salve or dip out of your dog's eyes— you can help protect them with a few drops of mineral oil in each eye, or a bit of yellow Mercuric Oxide Ophthalmic ointment.

Long-haired dogs may have to be clipped quite close, to be sure that all Demodex lesions are discovered and treated. With hair of any length, it is a good idea, just before salve or dip treatment, to scrub the dog all over with pHisoHex or a similar germicidal liquid soap to combat the bacteria which can cause infection of lesions. Your veterinarian may also inject the dog regularly with a drug which has been successful in many cases—the drug in the system penetrates to the hair follicles from the inside, killing the mites buried deep below the surface. It is a treatment which is slightly expensive, but well worth it.

Don't be discouraged if in the early stages of treatment more hair falls out at the edges of the affected areas and the condition seems to be getting worse instead of better—it is a common phenomenon. The mites generally move outwards from the center of the lesion, and are working within the skin on follicles beneath apparently healthy hair. This hair has actually already been killed at the roots before treatment started— the hair now being removed by the mechanical action of your fingers or the brush. If the treatment is successful, the lesions appear to get slightly larger, and then, once the mites are all killed, a fine down will grow again over the area, slowly being replaced by normal hair. If the treatment was started too late, even though it does succeed in arresting the spread of the disease, the skin of the affected areas may darken and remain bald.

The treatment of demodectic mange can be a long and uphill fight, and a tedious one, what with daily salves, odorous dips and regular trips to the vet for injections, but a victory over this type of mange is an accomplishment to be proud of.

SARCOPTIC MANGE

Also known as "scabies," this type of mange is significantly different from demodectic in that it is relatively easily cured and can be transmitted from the dog to humans. Again, it is caused by a mite, but in this case the mite burrows into the skin and causes intense itching in the affected spots, along with reddening and thickening of the skin, and loss of hair. As with demodectic, diagnosis can only be made by identifying the distinctive sarcoptic mange mites under the microscope, and your vet will have to take a deep skin scraping to establish the identity of the condition. Sarcoptic mange also tends to start on the head or neck of the dog. It can be distinguished, though not accurately, by the fact that beginning sarcoptic lesions are usually redder and more raised than demodectic. It can and does spread much faster than Demodex, as the intense itching will cause the dog to scratch and rub at the affected spots, and the mites will be carried rapidly to other parts of the body on his feet and legs.

As sarcoptic mange progresses, it is characterized by drying and thickening of the skin, and scabs forming over the infected areas. As in Demodex, long-haired dogs may have to be thoroughly clipped so that all affected areas are discovered, and treatment then takes the form of scrubbing the affected areas with germicidal soap to soften and remove scabs and loosen dead skin, and to prevent secondary bacterial infection of the lesions. Then the dog is given a dip with one of a great number of possible chemical preparations which are antisarcoptic specifics—chlordane, benzyl benzoate, lime-sulfur and many others.

Although untreated dogs can die of sarcoptic mange, it is nowhere nearly as serious as Demodex, but it can be even more uncomfortable for the dog because of the severe itching involved, and should be watched for carefully because of the possibility of its being transmitted to humans, particularly children who may be in constant close contact with the dog.

RINGWORM

This curiously named skin problem does not involve a worm, but is a fungus infection of the skin, and derives its name from the fact that the lesions usually have a point source and then become small and then progressively larger circles as the fungus spreads outward quite evenly. The hair may not drop off immediately in a ringworm infestation, but becomes dry and brittle, and the skin becomes dry and scaly and somewhat greyish. Although it may be confused with one of the manges, generally, the retention of hair, and the manner of hair loss when it does occur—hairs break off and leave a small stubble, or split, rather than fall out—serves to identify it as ringworm. Your veterinarian may have among his equipment a light called Wood's Light. Ringworm lesions often show a distinctive greenish glow under this light.

Treatment of ringworm is at the same time simple and complicated— simple because a great many fungicides will destroy the fungus, but complicated because the fungus attacks the hair itself, and may be spread in hairs considerably beyond the apparently affected areas. Therefore, the hair around the lesion must be clipped carefully, with great care taken that the clipped hair falls on a sheet of paper for later burning. Otherwise, although the visible area may be cleared up, the fungi in the surrounding hairs will reinfect the skin very quickly. Additionally, ringworm quite happily attacks humans, so considerable care should be taken during its treatment.

ECZEMA

This has for years been a catch-all term covering almost any sort of skin eruption or disorder which is not easily diagnosed as something more specific. There are literally dozens of possible skin disorders, ranging from alopecia to urticaria, which may be diagnosed, generally, as "eczema," and these are too varied in their range and specific symptoms for any attempt at detailed coverage here. There is, however, one type of dermatitis, known as "moist eczema," which is usually thought of as being "the" eczema, if there is such a thing.

Moist eczema is characterized by a very sudden onset, and is most likely to occur in warm or hot weather. It usually strikes on the back or flanks or at the base of the tail, and may erupt so suddenly that where, only a few hours before, the hair and skin appeared perfectly normal, there are suddenly angry red or yellow, wet-looking patches of skin. The patches are very sensitive and painful, and the dog will scratch and rub at them in an attempt to relieve the pain. This aids its rapid spread, and complicates the already-present lesions.

For temporary relief, you can pat ordinary baby talcum powder onto the lesions, or coat them with calomine lotion—these will make the dog feel easier and will help prevent him from scratching at the areas. But successful treatment of moist eczema is something to be handled by a veterinarian. Getting this sort of eczema under control can be very difficult, for it tends to re-appear when you think you have at last gotten all the affected areas cleared up, and you may be months at it before it is settled.

The origins and causes of moist eczema are poorly understood, with possibilities that some cases may be due to food or other allergies, or that heat and humidity are largely at fault, or that Vitamin A and fat deficiencies in the diet are contributory. These latter are among the best prospects, for it has been found that well-nourished dogs who do have sufficient Vitamin A and fats in their diets very rarely are affected by eczema. If your dog suffers from this condition, give some serious consideration to his diet, and to supplementation of it with fats and vitamins.

If your dog itches constantly, and you find no evidence of skin parasites or visible eczema, the temptation is great to fall back on the simple and widespread belief that, "oh well, dogs just itch." Despite the fact that one of the most common mental pictures of the dog is that of scratching, constantly and at random, the belief that itching and scratching are somehow natural attributes of dogdom is totally untrue—itching and scratching are no more basic to dogs than they are to you.

Constant scratching, biting or chewing at the skin indicate that something is awry, and if you do not find evidence of parasites or eczema, the possibility is very good that the cause may be either insufficient fat in the diet or too-frequent bathing. These factors have been touched upon in other sections of this book, but they are presented again here because of the prevalence of the problem. Almost all commercial dog foods should be supplemented by addition of fat to the diet. (For a more complete discussion of fat in the diet, see Chapter II.) While a dog can exist quite well with a low fat level, his coat and skin will tend to be dry, which leads to scaling and itching. Supplementation of fats has cleared up many, many cases of constant general itching.

Bathing, also covered more thoroughly elsewhere, is a less frequent cause of generalized itching. But if a dog is bathed with regularity, and particularly if he is given several baths in close succession as an attempt to cure itching, the natural skin oils will be removed and the skin will again be dry—thus either starting or further complicating a case of itching. Rule: don't bathe a dog unless he really needs it. Subrule: he doesn't need it to stop itching, unless it is a specific anti-parasite bath given to combat specific parasites.

TWO MINOR PROBLEMS

Almost all dogs have calluses on their "elbows," resulting from lying on hard surfaces. These thickenings of the skin are normal and natural, and are formed as a protection, but occasionally they become harder and thicker than they ought to be, and in any case many owners find them unattractive. The best home treatment is regular applications of mineral oil, thoroughly rubbed into the calluses—nothing can prevent their formation, but this will soften them, and perhaps make life a little easier for the dog.

Many dogs of the short-haired, long-nosed varieties have a problem with infections at the point of the chin. This is seen as an irritated, pimply-looking area, and often results from infective material being driven into broken skin when the dog rubs his chin along the ground when sniffing or trailing. Another cause is liquid, particularly milk, dribbled onto the chin when the dog is drinking—this plus a little physical irritation will result in infection. If the infection is minor, which it almost always will be, you can clear it up very easily by daily scrubbings with pHisoHex or almost any other anti-bacterial solution.

INTERNAL PARASITES

Although worms and coccidia are largely puppy problems, adults do suffer infestations, particularly of hookworms, tapeworms, and whipworms. The general symptoms and courses of treatment have been described in the chapter on Puppy Care, and these symptoms and treatments are basically unchanged for the adult dog.

RE-VACCINATIONS

Although it has previously been discussed in the chapter on Puppy Care, the advisability of having periodic rabies inoculations for your dog is worth reiterating here. Constant work by public health authorities and veterinarians has been instrumental in cutting sharply the incidence of rabies, so much so that many large areas have been without a case of rabies for years. Nonetheless, any dog which bites a human is automatically suspect as a possible carrier of the disease. If your dog bites someone (and don't scoff at the idea, no matter how small he is—a lot of people are bitten by dogs every year, and very few were bitten by dogs whose owners believed beforehand that their little darlings would ever bite anybody), you may be in for an unpleasant time, with the dog confined for observation, and possible lawsuits for mental anguish on the part of the bitee, and general ill feeling all around. The chance of your dog actually being bitten by a rabid animal, and contracting rabies, is very small, but for more than his own protection, it is an excellent idea to have a periodic shot. Additionally, if you plan to travel with him, you will find that vaccination is a legal requirement for taking him across any international boundary, and that many American localities have laws about vaccinations—in which case a great deal of trouble can be saved if you are able to produce his vaccination certificate.

Veterinary thinking on distemper, hepatitis and leptospirosis booster shots for adults has undergone considerable change over the past few years. For many years it was thought that, with distemper particularly, one successful vaccination in puppyhood was enough to provide permanent protection. This belief was so firmly held that such shots were commonly referred to as "permanent" shots, and the new realization of their true temporary nature is so recent that many veterinarians, out of long habit, still refer to "permanent" shots.

The unfortunate fact is that, as recent research has shown, there is no such thing as a permanent shot for any of the three diseases. As one veterinarian has pointed out, "We know that shots for humans, such as smallpox inoculations, aren't permanent, so why should we expect that a distemper shot should give permanent protection to a dog?" It's an excellent point.

What the original vaccination for each of the diseases will do is to provide a puppy with good protection during his growing period, when he is most susceptible to infection or contagion. Having reached adulthood in good health, he is far less likely to get the diseases, even if his chemical immunity has worn off. Many thousands and millions of dogs have, in fact, lived without disease and without booster shots. But many haven't, which puts the decision squarely in your hands.

The immunity picture is far from clear and uncomplicated—there is the factor of "street immunity" discussed earlier in this book, and of course the factor of exposure. Dogs totally unprotected by vaccinations may get along quite well, for one reason or another. But current veterinary recommendation is a regular schedule of boosters for all three diseases— distemper, hepatitis and leptospirosis. For maximum safety, the best schedule would be once every six months, as indicated earlier under the discussion of leptospirosis. An annual series is next best, and will probably provide very high protection. It is, however, best to get direct advice from your veterinarian, who will be up to date on all the latest information on immunity periods and effectiveness of current vaccines— the field is still changing and new knowledge is gained every day.

It is possible to test a dog for immunity by an immunity check run on a blood sample. This can be used after vaccination to be sure of effectiveness, and is sometimes so used by people whose dogs are frequently in dog shows and thus subject to extra-high exposure to disease. But such an immunity check may cost at least as much as a booster, and if you are concerned about the possibility of your dog not having immunity, you might as well go ahead with a booster. There is an additional test, the "nomograph," which is valuable in determining the proper time for vaccine immunization of puppies—it is discussed in this light in Chapters VI and VII.

KENNELING

When you go on a trip or a vacation, you are faced with the problem of what to do with your dog while you are away. Leaving him with a friend or relative can be a good solution, but you must be sure in such a case to select the friend or relative with care. People who don't themselves have dogs are often entirely unaware of the problems involved in caring for a dog, and have little or no idea of what to do should an emergency arise.

The other, and generally better, alternative is a boarding kennel which will keep your dog at a flat rate per day which covers room and board. There are, of course, many varieties of kennels, ranging from those with little more than a fairly roomy cage for your dog to quite posh places with individual concrete runs, air-conditioning and every amenity. It is a good idea to look around for a kennel which suits your taste well in advance of your trip, asking dog-owning friends for recommendations, and, if you feel really concerned about it, taking a trip to the kennel beforehand to look it and its operators over for general impression. If the premises are clean, if the other dogs you see there seem healthy and happy, and the owners or managers seem to know and like dogs, the chances are you've found a good place.

In many areas the better kennels are so well patronized that you will have to have reservations beforehand to be sure that your dog gets into the place you want him to be, so check on this possibility with the kennel of your choice well beforehand. There are few things more distressing than running around on the day before your trip, frantically searching for a good kennel or for someone to take the dog off your hands at the last moment. Besides, you will probably be bothered on your trip by wondering whether the place you did get him into was the right one. Far better to have these things all planned and secure in advance.

When you sign a boarding contract with the kennel owner, you will probably find somewhere on the form a paragraph or so of small print which legally releases the owner from responsibility for a great number of things. Don't think because of this that you have walked into an undesirable place—a kennel owner will only accept dogs which appear to be healthy, but he has no way at all of knowing whether or not your dog or somebody else's may be harboring a latent communicable disease. Despite every reasonable precaution, a sick dog may enter the kennel—if he is yours, he may, despite treatment, at best be in very poor shape when he comes out. If it is another dog, and your dog catches something in the kennel, there is literally nothing the kennel owner can do about it. If he is a reputable owner, he will take all precautions, and in cases of sickness he will do everything he can in the way of isolation, sanitation, veterinary treatment and supervision, but epidemics sometimes break out in even the best-run kennels. Therefore, the owner must be legally protected from responsibility for things which are totally beyond his control.

What your dog is fed in the kennel will be the standard diet, which will probably be as good as or better than what you feed him at home. If yours is a problem eater, be sure to discuss this with the kennel beforehand, and if he requires special foods, either supply them or arrange for the kennel to supply them, along with your promise to reimburse the kennel, above and beyond their daily fee, for cost and trouble they incurred in this special feeding. It is not at all unusual for a devoted pet dog simply to stop eating when his owner leaves him, and if your dog has lost weight when you come to pick him up after the trip, don't assume he has been starved or mistreated. It may be his own fault.

When you put your dog in the kennel, have a perfectly clear understanding with the kennel owner or manager as to the length of stay, special foods or any special treatment you want. Some kennel people are quite abrupt and superior in their dealings with dog owners, and if you run into this kind, either straighten them out right then, or take your dog elsewhere—they may know more in general about caring for dogs, but this is a case of *your* dog and the way *you* want him treated. If a kennel man can't even be civil and courteous to a human, imagine how your dog will be treated.

TRAVELLING WITH A DOG

One of the most difficult problems of taking a dog along with you on a trip is, not health, but simply finding a motel or hotel which will take dogs. If you are on the road and just start looking for signs, or stopping to ask, it can be difficult. Fortunately, there is an excellent booklet out which neatly solves the problem—"Touring With Towser," compiled and distributed by the Gaines Dog Research Center, 250 Park Avenue, New York 17, New York. Send 25c in coin, and the Gaines people will send you a copy—the money helps cover their handling and mailing costs.

"Touring With Towser" lists several thousand hotels and motels in literally every part of the country which accept dogs, and it is periodically revised to include new places, so the copy you get will be as up-to-date a list as it is possible to have. If you have a definite itinerary, you can write ahead for reservations to places listed, or you can just keep the booklet in the glove compartment, and whenever you decide to stop you'll almost always find at least one dog-accepting place very near.

In preparation for the trip, it is a good idea to have a rabies shot for your dog, and be sure you have the vet's certificate and the rabies tag. Get a certificate of general good health from the vet while you're at it— it never hurts, and might save you some difficulties.

For the trip itself, make up a regular kit of supplies for your dog—you can pack them in a separate flight bag, small suitcase or a shopping bag. Include enough of his regular food to last for a few days, in cans or boxes or however it normally comes—many brands of dog food are not nationally distributed, and being sure to have a supply of his regular food will help him out in those areas where it is unavailable. Many dogs get nervous and excited about trips anyway, and adding strange food to his problems will only complicate matters. Take along a feeding dish for him, and a water bowl, and cans of evaporated milk if he gets milk in the mornings. Include a thermos for cool water to give him during the day, when you stop to exercise him briefly. Take along a familiar toy for him to play with. It's not necessary, but it's a good idea to have along a spare leash and a spare collar, just in case something happens to the regular ones. And arrange some regular place in the car for his leash when it's off—there is nothing more frustrating than scrounging around the floor, under suitcases and clothes, and down the backs of seats for a leash, while your dog is leaping and yowling about in his excitement and anxiety to get out for a walk.

However unlikely you may think it that he could run or wander off, you should have an identifying tag on his collar, because it does happen. A stamped metal tag is best and most durable, but you can make a good tag from one of the imitation-leather luggage tags with a slip of cardboard showing through a glassine window. Put your name, address and phone number on it, legibly, and be sure to include the state, because surprisingly few people know which state good old Center City happens to be in. In large letters put, "If Found, Please Telephone or Telegraph Collect. REWARD." If you are on a long trip, give, instead of yours, the name, address and phone of a relative or friend at either end of the journey—someone who'll be home most of the time. That way, whoever finds the dog can get in touch with somebody right away, and you can check periodically to see if he has been located while you're still in the area.

Insist on at least a modicum of discipline in the car, and don't let him play the old "locomotive engineer" game, with his head sticking out the window to catch all the lovely smells and breezes. This is dangerous on several counts: he can very easily get irritating dust or plain harmful objects in his eyes that way, he just might jump out (it does happen, and nobody ever believes beforehand that it could), and he may get into the habit of putting his head out of the car window, which could lead to nipping of innocent pedestrians who happen to brush up against your car at some parking place. Be particularly sure to restrain this habit at toll booths and such places—you have no idea how testy a toll-booth attendant can get if he sticks out his hand and gets several teeth instead of a coin.

Car sickness is of course the genuine curse of travelling with some dogs. If your dog has any tendency at all to car-sickness, refer back to the section on the subject in the Puppy Care chapter, and take a few days to get your dog over it. Never feed him within six hours of starting the trip, and there will be less chance of trouble. As a final resort, see your vet about special dog tranquilizers and use them—don't try aspirins, human tranquilizers or sea-sick remedies. Have readily available a roll of paper towels, and spread an old blanket or sheet over the seat where the dog sits, just to hold down the damage when and if it does happen. And above all, do not under any circumstances get mad at him if he does vomit in the car. It happens because he's upset in the first place, and your hollering at him will only compound the problem. Sympathize, and be gentle, and he may get over it.

As long as it is kept in the car, nobody much minds what you carry in or through their communities, but outside the car, you'll find that many localities have surprisingly strict regulations about dog control. Keep your dog strictly on leash, and don't take him into any store unless and until you're sure there are no laws against it—many communities will not allow dogs in restaurants, lunch counters and groceries, and some even keep them out of other establishments. There are leash laws almost everywhere these days, so don't let him off for a run until you've inquired.

With a little sensible caution, and a bit of planning, you'll be surprised at how successful a trip with a dog can be.

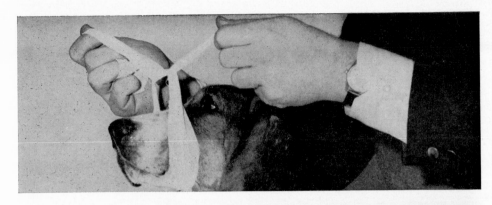

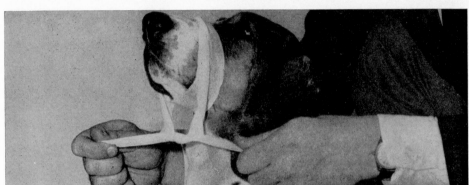

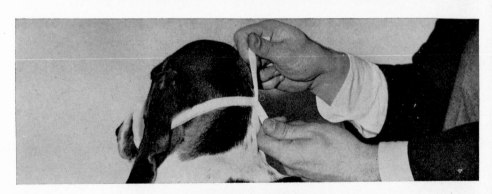

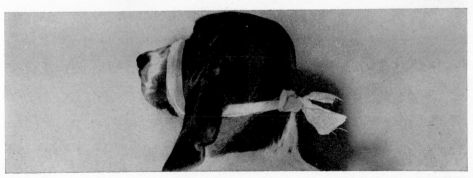

Four steps in applying the gauze muzzle

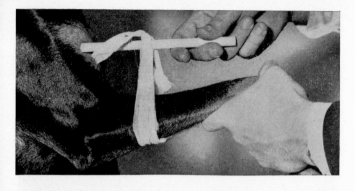

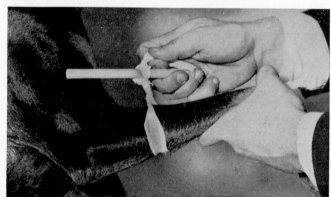

In applying a tourniquet, a stick is placed through a loop of cloth around the leg, then twisted like a wheel spoke until the cloth is tight enough to stop the bleeding.

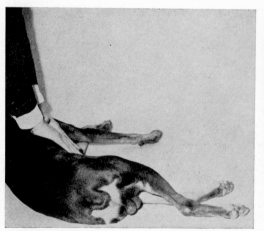

Artificial respiration: Hands press on the rib cage to force air out of the lungs, and release to draw air in.

Optional leg-lift to help lungs expand "release" phase of respiration.

Splint: A stick or other support is placed alongside the leg (the black mark indicates the point of the break), then tied firmly to the leg above the break. With the leg pulled straight, the splint is tied again below the break to immobilize the leg and broken ends of bone.

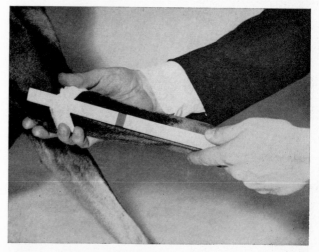

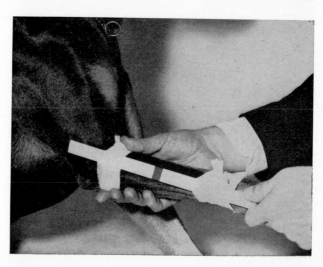

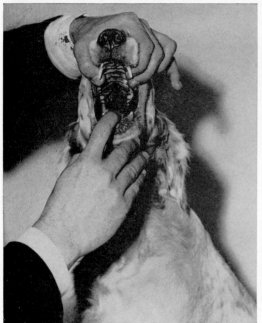

Opening the mouth

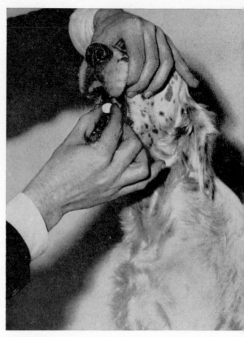

Administering a pill

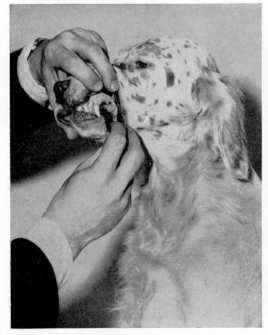

Making a lip pouch

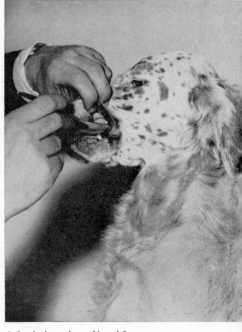

Administering liquids

CHAPTER V

FIRST AID AND HOME NURSING

DOGS, like people, often get themselves involved in mishaps and accidents. They may be bitten, burned, struck by cars, poisoned, cut, they may be half-drowned or electrocuted. They may be heat-prostrated or suffer convulsions. Blood, pain, vomiting, torn tissues—all these are violently unpleasant to some people. They are of course pleasant to nobody, but it is well to accept in advance that you may have to deal with them sometime, in emergency treatment to preserve your dog's life until you are able to get him to a veterinarian, or a vet to him.

It is worthwhile pointing out here that this is just what "first aid" means—the first aid or assistance you can give to a victim of an accident or mishap. It is strictly a temporary and emergency measure, given to save life and prevent further damage until you are able to get professional help. First aid is not meant as a permanent solution or cure for anything, and you should not treat it as such.

Of all the factors in an accident or other emergency, your dog's worst enemy is panic. Not his panic, but yours. The sight of a much-loved dog writhing in pain is a frightful thing, but if you lose your head, rush around aimlessly and apply wrong treatments or none at all, you will have killed your dog more certainly than the original circumstances. Therefore, the first step in any first aid treatment of your dog is one long, deep breath. It may sound curious, but it is the best possible thing you can do. Try timing a long breath—you'll get a figure of about ten seconds. But that ten seconds might save your dog's life. There's no situation in the world where a ten-second delay in treatment will push your dog over the line of recovery. But you will have a vital moment to collect your thoughts, look at what has happened, begin to decide what to do about it, and then do it, calmly and properly.

Read the first aid sections of this chapter through with close attention—you may never anticipate having to use any of them, but surprisingly few accidents happen to dogs whose owners are aware that an accident is going to happen. If you have to apply emergency first aid measures, you're not going to have time to go back and read calmly over these sections—you must know and remember what to do. Study these sections as though you were going to have a test on them. Someday you might.

APPROACH AND EVALUATION

Let us assume that something has happened to your dog—what, we don't yet know. Whatever it is, your first general approach is vitally important, for what you discover in your examination will obviously dictate what emergency measures you will take to save his life and prevent further injury until you are able to get professional help. Once you've taken the prescribed deep breath, take a close look at the dog to determine the major factors. First, is he breathing? If so, how well? Is the breathing normal, rapid, shallow, slow, weak, or what? Assuming he is breathing more or less normally, always allowing for shock, then check for bleeding. If there is excessive bleeding, that is obviously the first thing you will notice, but make a general check for wounds and bleeding anyway. If he is conscious, watch for any particular area that may be giving him pain—if none is immediately apparent, probe very gently with your fingers (after applying a gauze muzzle, of which more in a moment) along his legs, along his abdomen, his sides and back, along his neck and around his head. This test is mainly for broken bones, and if he is conscious, you will find out very quickly if there are any breaks.

If he is breathing well, if there is no severe bleeding, and if there seem to be no symptoms of poisoning, now is the time to arrange for help. Send someone for a vet, or to make arrangements to get the dog to the vet as soon as you have applied whatever emergency treatments may be necessary. Although it is an extremely safe bet that you don't even have your own doctor's name and phone number on you in case of emergencies, you should have a note somewhere of your vet's name and telephone. If you just shout at somebody, "Get a vet!" it may help very little indeed, particularly if that somebody is a neighbor or stranger who doesn't know any vets or even how to find one. And however well you may remember your vet's name and phone number, have it written down somewhere—people have been known to forget their own names in the shock and tension of an accident situation, even an accident not to themselves but to a dog.

Up to this point, *you haven't moved the dog!* This is important, and very much so. Many people's first reaction to an injured dog, particularly a small one, is to lift him to cradle him comfortingly in their arms. It is the worst possible thing you can do until you know what is wrong. If there are broken bones, you may aggravate the injury severely by moving the dog carelessly. If the injury should be to the back, or an internal injury in which broken bones are poking into or about to poke into his organs, your moving him may literally kill him. Only if the dog is in a roadway where he is likely to be hit should you move him immediately —here it is simply a choice of the lesser of two evils.

When you have completed your evaluation, and your emergency treatments, then you can turn your thoughts to moving the dog. As outlined later under treatment of broken bones, the best method of transport is to slide him gently onto a piece of wood, a screen door, or anything rigid which will allow you to get him from one place to another with a minimum of internal motion. The next best bet is to get a coat or blanket under him and use this as a carrier. It isn't good, but at worst it is better than picking him up in your hands or arms. But first and most important, don't move him until and unless you have to.

As to his own movement, limit yourself to the most gentle restraint if he wants to and is able to move. If he badly wants to sit or stand, let him. Try with a very gentle and soothing touch to keep him down and quiet, but any forceful restraint will only aggravate the situation—he will resent it and in an injury situation he will not be himself mentally, and may become violently frightened because he is being restrained, all of which will at best contribute to shock, and at worst may aggravate already serious injury through his thrashing around trying to escape from the restraint. If he has any injuries that would be aggravated by his own motions, there will almost always be enough pain associated with them that he will stop trying as soon as his movement causes more pain.

One final word in general approach—don't give him anything to eat or drink, except in the obvious case of poisoning when you must give him something to induce vomiting and later as an antidote. In cases of physical injury, you must always suspect that there are internal injuries—rips or dislocations of his internal organs. If you give him water, for example, it might leak out through a tear in his stomach or digestive system, into the peritoneum, and cause severe complications or death. Also, in shock, panic or a semi-conscious state, liquids may enter his windpipe, with unpleasant results. So give him absolutely nothing until you are told by your veterinarian that it is all right to do so.

RESTRAINT

In accident cases, the first problem you will have to face is that of restraint. If your dog has been severely injured, as in an automobile accident, a serious fall, a fight, or as a result of any circumstances which leave him in pain but conscious, your first step is to apply a gauze muzzle or its equivalent—the only exceptions are when there is copious bleeding which requires such immediate attention that the minute taken to arrange a gauze muzzle might result in so much loss of blood that death would ensue, and when the dog is vomiting or appears about to vomit.

The name "gauze muzzle" derives from the gauze strips veterinarians use as a temporary aid during the treatment of any dog which might bite. As you are not likely to have a roll of gauze handy outside your house, a necktie, woman's stocking, light rope, or a strip torn from a skirt or shirt will serve very handily. (For one reason or another, many people in emergency situations will run about aimlessly looking for cloth, without stopping to think that they are carrying quite a bit of it around on them. There is, too, a natural reluctance in people to rip up perfectly good clothing, but if cloth is needed for a muzzle, tourniquet, bandage or splint, the clothes you're wearing may not be the most sterile and sanitary answer, but are at least better than none.)

For the gauze or emergency muzzle, make a loop of your strip of material with a half knot (the first half of a square or granny knot). Slip this over the dog's nose, the half-knot at the top or bridge of his nose, to about half-way between the eyes and the tip of the nose. You will find, if you examine your dog's nose beforehand, that just forward of this point the actual nose bone ends and slightly softer cartilage begins—be careful that the muzzle is over bone, not cartilage. Then tighten the loop until it is holding his jaws snugly closed—don't tighten it too much—and bring the ends around under his lower jaw to make another half knot. From there take the ends back and *under* his ears and tie a bow knot at the back of his neck. With a small dog, you can even make this emergency muzzle of a piece of string or a shoelace, but if you use anything this thin, be very careful about not doing it tight enough to cut into him.

With the emergency muzzle in place, the dog may be uncomfortable, but it will not harm him, and he will be unable to open his jaws to bite. Don't think all this is unnecessary or cruel, that your own dog wouldn't bite you, no matter what. A dog who is in severe pain may slash at anything that moves near him, and particularly at the hands that are attempting to move and aid him. Don't take that chance, for it is difficult enough to treat an injured dog, and considerably more so if you are bitten and bleeding yourself. No matter how docile he may appear, use the muzzle—it also serves as a handy reminder that you shouldn't give him anything to drink.

In almost all accident cases, the original shock will be such that the dog will be quiet enough to allow you to put an emergency muzzle on. In the rare cases where the dog is actively thrashing and snapping at any approach, you should have someone to help you with the muzzle—have your assistant take hold of the dog by the scruff of the neck, and hold firmly while you slip a large loop over the nose and then tighten it in the first step of the muzzle. If you are alone, you can attempt to hold the scruff by one hand while you maneuver the loop with the other, then once you have it on, tighten it by holding one end in your free hand and the other in your teeth. It's difficult, but you may be able to do it. Do not, however, attempt anything like holding him down with your foot or knee on his body or neck while you're getting a muzzle on—you could cause further injury that way.

If you simply can't manage to get a muzzle on, the situation will be so bad that you shouldn't attempt to treat him at all except to stop copious bleeding which threatens his life within minutes. In such a case, which you are very unlikely to encounter, and if you are alone, then simply put a knee or a foot on his neck, or even get a loop of something around his neck—anything that will enable you to make a try at stopping the bleeding. Your harsh restraint measures may injure him, but if you don't restrain him, he'll die of loss of blood, so it is again a choice of the lesser of two evils.

One further note on the emergency muzzle—because of shock, or for other reasons, the dog may vomit before or during treatment. Keep a close eye on this possibility, and if you see him beginning to gag or heave, get the muzzle off as quickly as possible—this is one of the reasons for tying a bow knot at the back of the neck, rather than something more permanent. Then when it is over, put the muzzle back on gently, and proceed with the first aid.

If you are able to get a vet to come to the scene, take the muzzle off when you have finished your first aid treatments, as it will make the dog a little more comfortable while you're waiting. But if you are going to have to transport the dog, leave the muzzle on, as moving him may cause further pain and attempts at biting in panic.

CONTROLLING BLEEDING

The control of bleeding in a dog is very much the same as in a human. Most bleeding you encounter will be mild, and can be controlled by either a simple bandage or a pressure bandage. If the bleeding is non-severe, clean the wound as well as you can with flowing water, or sponge as much dirt and debris away as you can, gently, with a wet cloth. Then apply a simple bandage by wrapping gauze or any other cloth several times around the leg or body and over the wound to control bleeding at the point of injury. Moderate bleeding which continues to soak through a simple bandage can be controlled by a pressure bandage—fold several layers of cloth into a pad slightly larger than the injured area, place it over the wound, and then proceed to wrap a simple bandage over that, snugly but not so tight that it becomes a tourniquet. The extra thicknesses of material at the site of the wound will give more pressure directly on the spot than a simple bandage, and although it may become soaked with blood, it will generally stop any but the most severe bleeding.

If no amount of direct pressure will avail, or if you see immediately that the bleeding is copious—especially if the blood is coming in spurts, which indicates that an artery has been torn—you will have to resort to a tourniquet. That phrase, "resort to," is used advisedly, for a tourniquet should only be used when absolutely nothing else will stop bleeding.

The tourniquet is an item which everyone has heard about, but very few have ever had to use. In theory it is simple. If there is severe bleeding in any extermity, loop a strip of cloth around the leg above the wound, making the loop about twice as large as the circumference of the leg at that point. Then knot the loop firmly (don't tighten it onto the leg, but make a knot in the loop leaving it still twice as big around as the leg), put a stick or even something like a pencil into the loop and begin turning the stick like the spoke of a wheel. As you will see, the loop must be large enough at the beginning to allow the stick to take up a turn or so of material before it begins tightening the loop around the leg. Continue twisting the stick to tighten the tourniquet until the bleeding stops.

Holding onto the stick to keep the tourniquet in place will be tiring if you have to maintain it for long, and if you are alone the necessity to hold onto it will prevent you from taking such other first aid measures as may be required. You can keep the stick from unwinding by lining it up parallel to the leg, then making a loose loop around one end of the stick and the leg under it, only tight enough to hold the end of the stick in place.

Despite the fact that you are not likely ever to have to use a tourniquet, it is a good idea to practice making and tightening one—use the leg of a chair as a substitute for the dog's leg. It's really simple, but if you've just read a description and have never actually made a tourniquet, you can fumble it and use up precious minutes when and if you ever have to use one actually.

One thing about tourniquets not realized by people who have never had to use one is that they hurt—it is obvious enough, when you think of it, that anything twisted that tightly around a leg is bound to hurt. So if you ever have to use one, don't be surprised if the dog doesn't like it, which is another reason for the precaution of the emergency muzzle. It may be, of course, that there will already be so much pain associated with the area that the extra hurt won't be felt, or that shock will numb the pain, but if there are also broken or smashed bones, it might be severe. Don't hesitate, incidentally, to use a tourniquet where needed, even if there are broken bones. Try to put the tourniquet on above or below the actual break, but if you have to put it right over a break, go ahead. Your pressure on the tourniquet will complicate the bone situation, but it would do precious little good to worry about the broken bones and let the dog die of loss of blood.

The most important point of all about a tourniquet is that *it must not be kept twisted tight for longer than ten minutes at a time.* A tourniquet, to be effective, cuts off all flow of blood to the leg below it. If all blood is cut off for much longer than ten minutes, gangrene will develop, and the very least result of gangrene is amputation of the limb. Therefore, and this is vitally important, note the time you put the tourniquet on. After ten minutes, loosen it until blood flows a little from the wound, and leave it just loose enough to allow a slight flow for about a minute. Then tighten it for another ten minutes, loosen it again, and so on for as long as necessary. Don't be concerned when the injured area starts bleeding again when you loosen the tourniquet (loosen it only enough to allow a mild flow of blood—don't take it off completely). That means that blood is also getting to the rest of the limb.

When there is severe bleeding from the body, neck or head, the only good answer is direct pressure. If you can apply a pressure bandage wrapped under a simple bandage to stop the bleeding, fine. But you may have to fold a bandage pad and simply hold it hard on the wound with your fingers or hand. It is tiring, but if you switch hands occasionally, you'll be able to keep good pressure on, and with any luck at all, the blood will soak into the bandage and form a clot that will stop the bleeding of itself. Don't worry about the bleeding starting up again when the bandage has to be removed—the vet can handle that.

Watch carefully, of course, if you are pressing on the lung area or the neck, that you are not interfering with his breathing, but aside from that, press for all you are worth, always keeping in mind, particularly with a small dog, not to put enough weight on to cause internal injuries. It is something you will have to judge for yourself, if you ever find yourself in such a situation.

ARTIFICIAL RESPIRATION

In various accident situations, breathing may stop although the heart still functions and the blood still circulates, however feebly. The dog can live for five or six minutes in this condition, but if air is cut off for only two or three minutes damage to the brain results. The idea of artificial respiration is to keep air moving in and out of the lungs and available for circulation in the blood, until the dog recovers sufficiently to resume his normal automatic breathing. As long as the heart is going, the body can survive on artificially pumped air for long periods, but once the heart action has stopped, the body is dead—artificial respiration does not bring any dog "back to life," but simply substitutes for normal breathing to *maintain* life until normal breathing is restored. Do not, however, attempt to determine for yourself whether the heart is still working if you are giving artificial respiration, or assume that it has stopped—it may be still working feebly, too feebly for you as a layman to detect its action. Always continue respiration until you are able to get veterinary attention, or until the dog grows cold under your hands.

Breathing may stop temporarily for a number of reasons, drowning being the principal one. Electrocution, shock and severe blows to the head can also interrupt breathing. The preliminary steps in each of these circumstances will be treated in later sections, but the essential part of the treatment is, not surprisingly, almost identical with that employed on human victims.

Depending on the cause of the stopped breathing, the dog's tongue may have been pulled down into his throat, and must be pulled out before air can be taken in. The easiest way to do this is with a piece of gauze or any sort of cloth, to give your fingers a better grip on the slippery tongue. Simply reach in as well as you can and pull the tongue out into normal position. Be gentle, of course, but don't worry about injuries to his tongue. That will always heal. Then probe with your finger as deep into the throat as you can get to clean out any saliva or anything else that may have collected there. Then, with the dog on his side, begin a rhythmic pressure on his chest to force the air to move in and out.

A dog's normal breathing rate is about fifteen times a minute (this is an average—the rate varies from 30 per minute in tiny dogs to 10 in giant breeds—but it will serve very well in artificial respiration), so your forced breaths should be timed at about four seconds each. Press down firmly on the chest to force the air out, hold it for about two seconds, then release and wait two seconds, then press again. The best method of counting seconds is the old familiar one of saying, "One thousand one, one thousand two, one thousand three, one thousand four," slowly and deliberately. Press down as you say "four," release as you say "two." Your pressure will force air out of the lungs, and normal expansion of the chest will draw it in again, but you can aid the "in" cycle slightly by lifting the top front leg (as he lies on his side) as far as it will go without strain during the "release" part of the cycle. This helps a bit in expanding the chest and lungs. Using this technique, the cycle would go—press, one, two, release, lift the leg, three, lower the leg, four, press. Make the rhythm as steady as you can.

If you are moving air, you should be able to hear it going in and out. If you don't, check the tongue again and make sure his throat is clear of fluid or other obstructions, then begin again. Keep working until he either begins to breathe by himself, or you are sure there is no further chance. Steady, tireless artificial respiration has brought many a dog back from the edge of death after he seemed certainly dead, so keep it up. Remember that a doctor is required to pronounce a human dead, not because it provides more work for doctors, but because untrained laymen can and do make mistakes about it. An hour of artificial respiration is not beyond reason, so keep at it.

When there is any reason to suspect a broken rib, or severe internal injuries, the pumping method should not be used, for obvious reasons. In such cases, a very good technique is that of forcing your own breath into his lungs. To do this, first check his tongue and throat as before, then cover his lips with one hand to keep air from leaking out his mouth, place your mouth over his nose and blow gently into his nostrils. If you can make a reasonably airtight tube of the other hand, put that over his nose and blow that way, but it will do no good at all to blow from a little distance away—there must be a closed pressure system to force the air to expand his lungs. Therefore, either your mouth must be closed over his nose, or your hand as a tube must be reasonably airtight.

The oxygen from your breath going into his lungs will help revive him, and the carbon dioxide, far from being harmful, will help stimulate his breathing, even as the carbon dioxide in your own lungs helps stimulate your own breathing.

Blow into his nose, then remove your mouth, take a breath, and blow again, with the same rhythm as in pumping respiration, about fifteen times a minute. This method is in many cases even more efficient than the basic pumping treatment, but as it is a procedure not particularly appealing to many people, it is listed as a second choice. Additionally, although mouth-to-mouth respiration is fairly simple when reviving a human because it is easy to provide an airtight seal between the two mouths, an inexperienced person will have difficulty in maintaining an airtight condition with a dog.

DROWNING

Before applying artificial respiration in the emergency treatment of drowning, it is important to get as much water out of the dog's lungs as possible. Do not, however, let this procedure delay the beginning of artificial respiration more than a few seconds—in many drowning cases there is very little actual water in the lungs, and if you wait for quantities to drain out that aren't there, you may delay the start of respiration to the point where it will be of no use. Quickly check to see that the tongue is out of the throat—in drowning, the convulsive gasps for air often draw it into the throat. Then lift the dog by the hind legs as nearly vertical as you can and hold him that way for perhaps ten seconds. Then put him down on his side and start immediately with respiration, whether or not you have been able to drain any water out of him.

ELECTROCUTION

Here the danger is mainly to yourself. You must be very careful that you do not get, at best, a bad electrical shock or a burn. Dogs most commonly get themselves electrocuted when, as puppies, they chew through the insulation of a household light cord or similar power supply, although severe consequence here is, fortunately, rare. Even more rarely, they may stumble over, or have fall on them, live outside power lines. In either case, approach the situation carefully. Inside the house, either get the main power switch turned off quickly, or poke the wire off him before you touch him. Outside, poke the wire off—in either case, *do not touch it with your hand* or with anything of metal. You can poke it away with a dry stick, with the rubber heel of your shoe (held in your hand by the toe), or pull it off with a loop of dry cloth, with your belt, or with whatever is handy. Generally, inside the house, the accident will have blown the fuse, but don't take a chance on it. Also be exceptionally careful if the ground or floor is wet. It is not uncommon for the shock of an electrical contact to cause the victim to release the contents of his bladder, which may make the surrounding area electrically dangerous for you. So be very careful. Once you have removed the wire and dragged the dog to a safe area, examine the dog for condition and injuries. Listen and watch very closely for breathing—if he is breathing at all, no matter how faintly, do not interfere with it. Your attempts, out of timing with his own, might cause breathing to stop. Treat him for shock (see below). If breathing is not present, then attempt to start it again by artificial respiration, and keep it up until you get results or obviously can do no more.

SHOCK

Almost any serious injury will be accompanied by traumatic shock, here again just as with humans. The most notable symptoms of shock are general collapse or weakness and listlessness, pale to nearly white gums, irregular shallow breathing punctuated by gasps, a weak or barely discernible heartbeat. Very frequently there is dilation of the pupils, and subnormal temperature which can be felt in a cool skin. The degree of shock varies greatly, from a mild condition which does not last long, to such severe shock that death may result. Look for shock symptoms in any mishaps, and suspect it in all accidents.

After taking any of the more immediate emergency measures, such as restoring breathing or controlling bleeding, the first aid treatment for shock consists of simply keeping the dog warm and keeping him as quiet and comfortable as possible. To keep him warm, wrap him in a coat or blanket, but don't use any artificial sources of heat such as hot-water bottles or electric pads or blankets. Simply wrap him so that he is able to conserve his body heat better. You may have heard that in the treatment of human shock cases, the idea is to keep the head low, lower than the feet, and this is a good rule, but don't worry about this with a dog. If he is lying on his side, he will be in the optimum anti-shock position— don't try to lower his head, but if you have put a pillow of folded coat or anything under his head to make him more comfortable, remove it so that his head lies on the ground or floor.

Once you get the dog to a vet, there are a good many things that can be done to counteract shock, including transfusions, administration of oxygen, and injections. But you can do a great deal for the moment if you will simply keep the dog warm and quiet.

Be on the lookout for secondary shock, which may show up hours later, even if the dog has seemed perfectly okay immediately after the accident. If a dog has been struck by a car, or dragged by one, or had a severe fall, or an electric shock—in fact any sort of mishap or accident—he may seem perfectly normal for several hours afterward and show no signs of injury or effects of the accident. Then secondary shock may set in. Keep an eye on him until the next day, by which time the danger of secondary shock will be effectively gone. The symptoms of secondary shock are the same as those of primary traumatic shock, and it should be treated as if it were primary shock. If it seems mild, then rest and quiet are the best treatments, but secondary shock is often severe, and should have veterinary attention as soon as possible.

BROKEN BONES

There is very little you can do about broken ribs, back or other bones of the body except to make sure that the injured dog is transported as gently as possible to the vet's office. Most important, keep internal movement— changes of position, twisting and turning—down to a minimum, for such motions will move the jagged ends of broken bones about within the body, tearing tissues and possibly causing further internal injury and bleeding.

If you suspect such broken bones, try to slide any rigid flat object under the dog and carry him on that. A piece of plywood would do, a door, a heavy screen or anything of that nature. The next best procedure is to move him gently onto a blanket or a coat, and then pick him up by holding the ends of his support as an improvised litter and keeping the material as taut as possible. It is best done by two people, but in extremis, if he is a small dog, you can do it by yourself. Once he is in any position in or on a carrying device, do your best to keep that position unchanged. It is best of course not to move him at all.

You can do a great deal for broken long bones of the legs by splinting to immobilize them until you get professional help. Remember when you use a splint that it is not within your province to try to set a dog's leg—this is first aid, and all you are doing is keeping things still so that, again, the broken and jagged ends of the bones will not move about causing further damage to themselves and the surrounding tissues.

You can use almost anything for a splint. The traditional stick or board is best, but a rolled-up newspaper or magazine will do, or even several layers of heavy corrugated cardboard. Remember that the function of a splint is simply to immobilize the broken ends of the bone and hold the leg in more or less straight position. You could do it by just taking the paw and pulling gently away from the break and holding it that way, but you are unlikely to be able to maintain a smooth and even pressure for long, particularly during a car ride to a vet.

In splinting, the emergency muzzle is a must, no matter how trusting and grateful his big brown eyes look. Having a broken leg splinted is no fun, and can hurt like the seven furies, and the pain may be sudden, so prevent any possibility of being bitten. Then, to splint the leg, wrap a few turns of your splinting cloth (the old familiar gauze or torn strips of shirt or skirt again) gently around the leg, from above to below the break. Place the splint alongside the leg, or half-way around it if you are using a rolled newspaper or magazine. Wrap several turns of the cloth firmly (not tight enough to cut off circulation, though) around the leg and splint *above* the break so that they are firmly tied together, and make a knot. Then pull *very gently* on the leg below the break to straighten it, wrap the cloth around the leg and splint *below* the break, tightly enough so that the leg is held extended as you pulled it. *Do not* wrap at the point of the break!

This sort of splint will be enough to keep the leg in tolerable condition until you can get the dog to a vet for treatment.

POISONING

There are two general poison situations: that in which you know your dog has eaten a specific poison, and that in which you believe you see general poisoning symptoms without having any way of knowing what poison caused them. In the first case, the emergency procedure is inducing of vomiting, followed by administration of an antidote; in the second, you may be able only to administer a general antidote.

If you know that your dog has taken in a specific poison, you will very likely find the antidote listed somewhere on the container's label. If so, and if you have the antidote in the house, get the dog to vomit, administer the antidote and rush him to a vet. In many cases, however, an antidote may not be listed, but you may be able to get the information by a phone call. Call your vet, a local hospital, a pharmacist, or a Poison Control Center. Some large cities have these Centers, staffed by people who know a great deal about poisons, and in their files they have lists of ingredients and antidotes for almost every possible poisonous substance. They are open 24 hours a day and ready to give telephone advice on poison cases. Although they are maintained for cases of poisoning in humans, they will probably be glad to help you—the Poison Control Center in New York City, for example, says that it often gets requests for antidotes in cases of poisoning in dogs, and that they don't mind at all. Find out in advance the phone number of the Center in the city nearest you, and call long distance if you need an antidote in a hurry. They are usually listed under the local Department of Health.

Assuming the dog has definitely ingested a poison, the first step is induction of vomiting. There are several good ways. Among the best are doses of mustard water, or peroxide. The mustard water is made by mixing a teaspoonful of powdered mustard with about a quarter of a glass of warm water. Mix well and force it down his throat until he vomits. The peroxide solution is made with ordinary 3% hydrogen peroxide, the standard drugstore strength. Mix this with an equal amount of water and administer it until vomiting occurs. For lack of either of these, soapy water or even warm salt water will often work. With any of them, get the dog's mouth open (see the later section on administration of medicines) and pour it into his mouth, immediately closing his mouth and holding his muzzle up to make him swallow it.

Be prepared for a hard and messy job. He will probably already be in some pain if the poison is a quick-acting one, and it is going to be no fun getting anything as unpleasant as mustard water, peroxide solution or soapy water down him in sufficient quantities to cause vomiting. When he finally does vomit, the efforts may cause prostration. But it may be necessary to save his life.

There is one definite exception to the vomiting rule—he shouldn't be made to vomit if he has taken in either a corrosive acid or an alkali such as a sink drain cleaner. In such cases, vomiting is not recommended because the caustic material would cause even more damage to the throat and mouth as it came out. Your best bet in these cases is rapid neutralization. For acids, administer baking soda solution (four teaspoonsful to a glass of water) or Milk of Magnesia. Get in as much as possible, but be careful with the soda solution, as it may nauseate him and cause vomiting. For alkalies, give vinegar or lemon juice. In either case, follow the "antidote" with milk, olive oil or raw egg white, as much as you can get into him. Fortunately, you are very unlikely ever to encounter such poisoning in a dog.

In all other cases, once the dog has vomited, give him the specific antidote if you have one, and follow this with as much milk as he will take to soothe his stomach. Then treat him as in traumatic shock by keeping him as warm and quiet as you can until you are able to get a vet to him or him to a vet—remember that this treatment is only emergency first aid and that the dog needs a vet's attention—it is not meant as a "cure" for poisoning.

If you do not know the specific antidote, or can't get hold of it, you should have in your dog's medicine cabinet something known as Universal Antidote, which you should have made up in advance by a pharmacist. The formula is: two parts activated charcoal, one part light magnesium oxide, one part kaolin, one part tannic acid. Universal Antidote is a dark grey powder which is inert and can be stored for long periods of time—a pharmacist may not have it on hand, so don't think you can rush out and grab a bottle. But he will make it up for you if you give him the formula above, and will probably charge you very little. The ingredients are very inexpensive, and most of the cost will be the pharmacist's time.

After the dog has vomited, mix four heaping tablespoonsful of Universal Antidote with a standard glass of warm water, stir well, and get as much of it as you can into the dog. It is not really a *universal* antidote, but it is the closest thing to it—the charcoal and kaolin adsorb poisons and keep them from entering the system, the tannic acid reacts with alkiline types of poisons (and is a specific for strychnine), and the magnesium oxide reacts with stomach fluids to help evacuate the stomach, thus getting everything harmful on its way out.

If you haven't had Universal Antidote prepared in advance, you can make up a partial home substitute for it, in a very few minutes. The formula is: two parts crumbled, heavily burnt toast (for the charcoal), one part strong tea (for the tannic acid) and one part Milk of Magnesia (for the magnesium oxide). Mix about half a cupful of tea with half a cup of Milk of Magnesia, and stir in a cupful of the crumbled burnt toast to make a paste, and force as much of this into the dog as he will take. It isn't as effective as real Universal Antidote, but it will at least do some good.

Lacking even this, give the dog as much milk as he will take, and raw egg white, which will help tie up mineral poisons and prevent them from being absorbed into the system. Then treat as before for shock.

Suspicion of poisoning is a tricky problem. The general symptoms of poisoning are elusive, but the most common are: manifestations of severe pain in the abdomen, labored breathing, trembling, general nausea, prostration, vomiting. It usually takes an expert's eye to be sure that a dog has been poisoned and that his difficulty is not something else with similar symptoms. In any case, by the time you see such symptoms as the above, any poison will have entered the system in such quantity that trying to eliminate the remainder in the stomach would not be too much help— and the dog will probably be so close to full prostration that attempts to make him vomit would do him more harm than good.

Because of the great variety of possible poisons, it is impossible to describe any specific picture of symptoms without getting into a table of poisons and accompanying symptoms which is simply not practical for a layman. Even veterinarians have trouble identifying specific poisons from symptoms—the veterinary text *Canine Medicine* says to its veterinary student readers, "Since every poison acts in a different fashion, it is not possible to tabulate causes and effects in such a way that absolute certainty of diagnosis can be assured." So don't spend your time on amateur diagnosis of which poison it might be. This includes trying to use such standard detective-story symptoms as the characteristic bitter almond odor in cyanide poisoning—it is a fairly safe bet that you don't know what bitter almonds smell like in the first place, and so would have trouble thus diagnosing cyanide.

If you believe from his symptoms that your dog has been poisoned, and he is conscious enough to take it, get Universal Antidote into him, which can't do him any harm even if it isn't poisoning. Or use any of the substitutes, such as milk and raw egg white or olive oil. Then get help immediately. If he is far enough gone to be prostrate or semi-conscious, it will be next to impossible to get anything at all into him, either to induce vomiting or as an antidote, and all you can do is treat for shock and try to get to a vet in a hurry.

SNAKE BITE

Fortunately, most snake-bite wounds in dogs occur on the legs. Emergency treatment needs to be fast and drastic, but even a dog injected with a massive dose of poisonous venom can be saved if you take the proper steps in time. You may actually see the bite occur, or your dog may display snakebite symptoms. If the bite is from one of the pit vipers— rattlesnake, cottonmouth or copperhead—there will be intense pain and dramatic swelling at the site of the bite, sometimes with blood oozing from the actual point of the strike. The bite of a coral snake sometimes shows relatively little swelling, but is accompanied by pain at the site.

Assuming your dog has been bitten on the leg, the first step is to apply a modified tourniquet above the bite. The word "modified" is used here because, ideally, you should tighten the tourniquet only enough to cut off the return flow of blood towards the body—in the vessels which are nearer the surface of the skin—and not the arterial flow which supplies blood to the leg. If you can guage this, all well and good, but better to cut off all blood flow than too little, for the idea is to prevent the bloodstream from carrying the venom to the heart and other parts of the body. If swelling has already progressed above the bite, apply the tourniquet about an inch above the top of the swelling.

Once the tourniquet is in place, and if you can bring yourself to it, find as nearly as you can the original point of the bite and cut it open to drain as much blood and venom as you can. If you are able to find the two fang marks, cut a small X through each mark. The cuts should be small, one cut of each X along the line of the leg, and the other across it—make each cut about a quarter of an inch long (for average sized dogs; slightly smaller for small dogs). The lengthwise cut can be about a quarter of an inch deep, but the crosswise cut should be shallow so as not to sever any muscles or tendons. This is all very precise, and in such an emergency situation you won't have time to worry about whether a cut is exactly one-quarter of an inch long, but it at least gives you a guide to the ideal.

If you are unable to find the actual fang marks (and don't waste time looking for them if you don't find them right away), cut one or two small X's at the point of worst swelling and reddening, treating this as the probable point of the bite. This all assumes, of course, that you have something to cut with. If you live in snake country, you should make a habit of carrying with you, particularly if you go walking much with your dog, a small pen-knife, with the smallest blade honed as nearly as possible to a razor edge. There are available quite small two-blade knives, not toys, which have good blades, and they are small enough to carry on a keychain. If you don't have a knife with you, there's nothing you can do but put on the tourniquet and hope to find a knife and a vet as quickly as possible.

Once the cuts are made, squeeze out as much blood as you can. The best method is to take hold of the leg just below the tourniquet, squeezing it hard, and bring your hand down firmly towards the cuts, milking the blood out, as you might get toothpaste out of a tube. Work from both above and below the bite, but mostly above. Don't worry about loss of blood—a dog can easily stand to lose the amount of blood in a leg, and you're not likely to get even that much out. In the unlikely event you have a suction cup handy, draw the blood out with that, but it is not a good idea to try the traditional human-treatment method of sucking the blood and venom out with your mouth. If there are any cuts or sores in your mouth or on your lips, or if you have infected gums, the poison you draw out is quite likely to enter your own blood stream. But if you want to try this method, it is up to you—if you are careful to spit everything out after each mouth suction, and rinse your mouth thoroughly as soon as possible, you'll probably not get enough poison into your system to make you more than mildly sick.

When you have drained as much blood and venom from the wound as possible (or after putting on the tourniquet, if you can't make the cuts), apply ice packs to the swelling and above it. If there is no ice available, even a cloth soaked in cold water will do a little good, although nowhere nearly as much as ice—the effect of the cold treatment is two-fold, reducing the pain, and slowing physiological processes and as a result slowing the spread of the venom.

Don't forget the emergency muzzle in snakebite treatment. Even with it, you are going to have a hard enough time treating a snakebite, for the entire procedure is painful in the extreme. The bite itself hurts like fury, and by the time you get through putting on a tourniquet, making cuts in the skin, and squeezing the leg in an already painfully swollen area, the pain will be ferocious.

If you are sure you will be able to get your dog to a vet and have him shot with antivenin within an hour, it is all right to leave the tourniquet on without release for that length of time. But if you don't know how soon you will be able to get help, loosen the tourniquet every twenty minutes to let blood flow to the leg, for about a minute, then retighten it. This seems a contradiction of the rule for controlling accidental bleeding, but here control of the venom within his system is of greater importance than the risk of gangrene—but still the tourniquet must be released at intervals. Once you have released it, reapply it a little farther up the leg. In any case, if the swelling seems to be passing the tourniquet, move it up the leg, for the idea is to keep the tourniquet between the swelling and the heart.

If the snakebite is on the body, your chances of saving your dog drop sharply, as you obviously cannot use the tourniquet. Here, the only procedure is careful x-cuts at the wound's site, squeezing out as much blood as possible, and application of ice-packs or some other source of cold. If the bite is on the head or neck, don't even try to make cuts, for there is a possibility that the amount of venom injected was a sub-lethal dose and that the dog might survive, whereas any cutting you do in these areas might just kill him. Apply cold, if possible, and keep the dog as quiet as possible until you can get professional help.

BURNS

There are two major causes of burns in dogs—hot liquids or corrosive chemicals, and direct fire or contact with a hot surface. If your dog should knock over a pan of boiling water or, say, soup, the first step in treatment is to flush the area with cold water in considerable quantities. Particularly for a dog with a heavy coat, drench the area with continued applications of cold water to wash away the hot liquid, to keep it from burning any deeper than it has. The same treatment applies for corrosive chemicals, to dilute their effect and wash them away.

For direct fire and heat burns, go directly to the second step, which is bathing the area with a solution of baking soda and water. Make a solution with four heaping tablespoonsful of ordinary household baking soda in a quart of water, and flush the burned area with it. *Do not* scrub the burned area—simply soak a sponge or cloth with the solution and let it pour over the burn. Then, if the burn is severe, or the area large, soak gauze or a clean pad of cloth in the solution, place it gently over the burn, and bandage it lightly in place with strips of gauze or other cloth around the body or leg. If it is going to be some time before you can get a vet, pour more of the solution on this pad every fifteen minutes or so, to keep it wet.

No matter how bad the burn may seem, and even if it has become fouled with dirt or matted and singed hair, don't attempt to put any antiseptic, such as iodine or mercurochrome, on a burn—it will do considerable harm. Also, never put cotton onto a burn, for it will stick to the burned surface and seriously impede later treatment and healing. It is best, if possible, that the cloth you use be clean and sterile—fresh gauze or a freshly laundered sheet or other cloth will do the job.

For immediate treatment of less severe burns which you believe will not need a veterinarian's attention, flush the area as before and then smear the area gently with Unguentine or plain Vaseline, which excludes air and reduces the pain in the burned area. Then cover the area with a gauze pad if possible, to prevent the dog's licking at it. For larger burns, this treatment is not advisable, as the presence of the greasy material may hinder professional cleaning and treatment of the area.

Burns on the legs will respond very well to a relatively new treatment— put the leg into a tub of ice water as quickly as possible, and keep it there for fifteen to twenty minutes. The quickest method is simply to put the leg into as cold water as you can run from the faucet, then add ice to the water. This treatment will rapidly reduce the pain of the burn and will promote healing with a minimum of scar formation. After the period in the ice water, remove the leg and give it no further treatment, unless the burn is severe or widespread enough that it appears veterinary attention will be needed.

In severe burn cases, shock is a danger, so after you have given the immediate burn treatment, wrap the dog in a blanket or other covering to keep him warm, and keep him as quiet as possible. And of course use the emergency muzzle from the first.

HEAT STROKE

The symptoms of heat stroke are easy to identify—quite often the dog will appear to be in a state of collapse, his breathing will be heavy and panting, and he may drool. Together with the weather, these will point to heat exhaustion. It may seem a bit obvious to say that the problem is simply too much heat in the body, but it does point to the best and most direct relief. First, pour cold water over him in quantity, in the meantime filling your bathtub or a washtub with cold water. When there is enough water in the tub, plunge him into it, keeping only his head out, and sponge or splash water over his head. This will rapidly reduce the heat in his body, and quite possibly save his life. If there is no tub handy, then simply keep pouring cold water over him, and if possible place a fan so that it blows on him all the while and speeds evaporation. Feel his body from time to time to see if it is still hot to the touch. When the skin is reasonably cool and his breathing and general condition seem better, you can stop the treatment. After that, let him rest as he sees fit and he will recover quite rapidly. In the future, watch his activities, and don't let him run around in the sun during the hotter hours of the day. Do not, however, as a heat stroke preventive, shave him. It may make him look cooler, and may in fact make him a little cooler when he is out of the direct heat, but it robs him of his natural protection against the sun.

The breeds known as brachycephalic, or "apple-headed," such as bull-dogs, Boston terriers, pugs, Pekingese and boxers, are more susceptible to heat stroke than others. The construction of their noses and throats leads to minor or major difficulties in breathing under normal circumstances, and thus interferes with their normal dissipation of heat through the breath. If your dog is of any of these breeds, keep a close eye on him during the summer, and try not to let him get exposed to too much heat for too long a period.

INSECT BITES AND STINGS

It is very rare that the bite of an insect (other than black widow spiders or scorpions, of course) is serious or fatal. Except in the case of a very small dog, or massive multiple stings in a large dog, the worst result is local pain and swelling. Insect bites and stings, including those of hornets and bees, can be somewhat relieved by making a paste of baking soda and water and applying it liberally to the site, and covering with a small bandage if the dog attempts to lick the paste off. Or a paste made with baking soda and cold cream is even better for relief, but less desirable if the dog attempts to lick it. Otherwise, calamine lotion will help.

There is little or no first aid for black-widow or scorpion stings. Cuts and suction at the site do no good at all, but ice-packs directly on the site will help relieve the pain and slightly slow the absorption of the poison. Otherwise, a vet's attention is the only help.

CONVULSIONS

Convulsions, or fits, in a dog are frightening things. Depending on their cause, the dog may writhe on the floor, spin around violently, stiffen with legs extended, howl, bark incessantly, moan, froth at the mouth. Whatever the exact symptoms, you will never mistake a convulsion for anything else. The general progress of the most common type is this—he will sit or stand with a wild and frightened look in his eyes, then begin foaming slightly at the mouth and begin champing his jaws. This is followed by jerking and writhing movements of the body, quite often lying on the side and making leg movements of running. Later, as the convulsion has begun to run its course, the dog will be able to stand weakly, but will appear to be dazed, and will wander sometimes aimlessly, sometimes on what seems to be a definite course which leads him to an obstacle, then turn and walk or lope in another direction.

Heartbreaking though it is simply to stay out of the way, there is absolutely nothing you can do to help your dog in such a situation. If he is seized by a convulsion at the edge of a drop, as at the head of the stairs or at the edge of a porch, you can put something in the way to keep him from falling off. If he is thrashing in an area where there are sharp objects, such as wrought-iron furniture legs, you can try to cover these or block them to keep him from hurting himself. But do not approach him, touch him or try to handle him. During a convulsion, the dog is so completely out of his mind that he does not feel any pain, but he is almost always terrified of what is happening to him, if he realizes it at all; and he is particularly terrified of anything and everything around him during the early stages. It is a blind, unreasoning and total terror, and you will only make it harder for him if you attempt to touch him or comfort him. In fact, in the very early stages of the "common" convulsion, if you try to help him by wiping the drool or foam away from his mouth (which, incidentally, you strictly should not do), you will see that he is frightened of the approach of your hand. There are other causes of foaming at the mouth and drooling (including rabies, but this is rare—a foaming mouth does *not* inevitably mean "mad dog"), but if you ever see drool and foam, combined with wide and frightened eyes and jerky retreat from approach, draw back yourself, for a convulsion is coming.

Let the convulsion run its course until he is over the dazed condition and you can see some recognition in his eyes and he responds to your voice. Then you can comfort him and clean up both him and the area. A dog in convulsions characteristically urinates and defecates, losing all control of his bodily functions, and he will very likely have smeared himself considerably with both urine and feces.

Convulsions can result from a number of conditions. Epilepsy, brain tumors, kidney disease and congenital brain malformations are among them, but the majority of convulsions are due to brain damage caused by distemper, particularly in young puppies. It was once commonly believed that worms caused many cases of convulsions, but this causation is actually rare. There is no way you can make any judgment from a convulsion, although an accurate description of the course of the convulsion, including the total time elapsed, is the best thing you can give your vet when you get your dog there for treatment.

If your dog goes into a convulsion, foams at the mouth, or behaves in an erratic manner, with a dazed or wild look in his eyes, there is a slight possibility that he might be rabid—which is one of the many reasons you shouldn't approach a convulsing dog. However, if he recovers from the convulsion and appears afterwards to have little or no after-effects, then he definitely is not rabid. A rabid dog does not foam and then recover, but continues a straight course of decline which ends in death. So don't be afraid to approach your dog to comfort and clean him, and transport him for treatment, once a convulsion has run its course.

GENERAL WOUNDS

Wounds break down into three classifications: incisions, lacerations and punctures. An incision is a "clean" wound made by a sharp instrument, a laceration is one in which the area is torn and bruised by a ragged surface, and a puncture is simply that—quite often made by a single tooth in a dog fight, a wound such as would be made by an ice pick.

Incisions quite often keep themselves relatively clean by spontaneous bleeding. In emergency treatment, unless the bleeding is so copious that you see it should be stopped as soon as possible and has obviously already carried any dirt out of the wound, let it bleed for a moment to wash out infective material. Then place the edges of the wound together as well as you can, just like closing a zipper. If the incision is not a large one, wash the skin around it with tincture of green soap with one hand while holding the incision closed with the other—don't use antiseptics such as iodine or Merthiolate. Then put a sterile gauze bandage on top of the wound and bind it down just tightly enough to keep the incision closed. If the incision is much over an inch long, you will probably want to have the vet clean and stitch it—otherwise, for small incisions, leave the bandage binding on for a day to allow the skin to start knitting together, then take it off and apply Vitamin A & D Ointment (available in drugstores) twice a day to promote healing.

Lacerations are generally more difficult to treat, because of their greater area and the bruised condition of the flesh around the wound. Unless it is necessary to stop bleeding, your best course with a laceration is not to bandage it, except for a general loose bandage of gauze or cloth strips covering the area, just to keep further dirt out. Do not apply any antiseptic such as iodine to a lacerated area. If it is a mild laceration which does not seem serious enough to bring to a vet's attention, simply scrub the area gently with tincture of green soap, and leave it open to the air for healing. After two days, apply a light coating of Vitamin A & D Ointment twice a day until you can see that healing is well progressed.

For more serious lacerations, if you know you are not going to be able to get to a vet for some time, again scrub with tincture of green soap (or with any mild soap and water, lacking green soap) and cover with the loose gauze bandage until you get to the vet.

Puncture wounds are the most difficult of all to treat. Whatever instrument causes the puncture quite often drives infective material well under the skin and into the puncture. When the instrument is withdrawn the skin usually closes over the puncture hole and prevents bleeding. Thus the infective material remains inside, and serious infections can result. Don't be fooled by the generally innocent appearance of a puncture—often all you will see is a small bruised area centered around the point of entrance of the puncturing instrument. You can scrub the area with tincture of green soap, or treat it with iodine or other antiseptic to clean the surface, but there's nothing you can do to get at the material below the skin. The best course is to keep a close eye on minor puncture wounds, and if you see any reddening of the area, take the dog to a vet for an injection of penicillin or whatever other antibiotic he may wish to use.

Wounds sustained in dog fights are usually combinations of lacerations and punctures, and the best treatment is washing with green soap. If any of the wounds are serious—as in flaps of skin lifted or dangling, or ears torn and lacerated—it is best to leave them alone, unless you know it is going to be some time before you can get to a vet for stitching. Attempts to clean such wounds will be extremely painful for the dog. But if treatment will be delayed, use a gauze muzzle and then simply flush the wounds first with luke-warm water in quantity, then flush with peroxide solution, and leave them alone—but try to prevent the dog from licking or chewing at them—until you get help.

FIRST AID KIT

As you will have seen in this chapter, there are a number of items you ought to have around the house, for use both in first aid and in general treatment of your dog. It is a good idea to assemble the following in a sort of first aid and nursing kit, ready at hand for emergencies.

Peroxide, 3% solution—standard drugstore peroxide, useful as a general antiseptic in wound treatment, and for inducing vomiting.

2-inch or 3-inch gauze rolls, standard sizes—handy for making bandage pads, for general bandaging, for tourniquets and gauze muzzles.

Sterile cotton—useful for soaking ticks for removal, for ear care, and other purposes.

Mustard powder—for inducing vomiting.

Kaopectate—for control of diarrhea.

Witch hazel—for cleaning the coat without bathing.

Burn ointment, any good commercial product—for treatment of minor burns.

Vaseline—for burn treatment, and for lubricating thermometers.

Rectal thermometer—different from the standard oral thermometer in its construction: rectal thermometers have a bigger bulb for the mercury and are generally sturdier.

Baking soda—for burn treatment and poison neutralization.

Universal Antidote—for poisoning.

Germicidal soap—pHisoHex is excellent and widely available, as is tincture of green soap.

Vitamin A & D Ointment—to promote skin healing.

Yellow Mercuric oxide ophthalmic ointment—for minor irritations of the eye and for use when bathing or dipping.

Mineral oil—for eyes, and as a mild laxative.

Milk of Magnesia—as a laxative.

Rubbing alcohol—for tick removal.

This all seems like a formidable list, and if you are like most people you will read it, nod, and promptly forget all about it. Most people won't even take the trouble to keep a first aid kit around for themselves in case of accident. But you should compile one. You might have the kit on hand throughout the life of your dog and never use it, except for such minor items as tick control, but a good first aid kit is something like insurance—it is a blessing if you never have cause to collect on your insurance, but you'd be foolish not to have any.

DRUGS AND MEDICINES

There are warnings scattered in other spots throughout this book on the dangers of giving your dog medicines designed for humans. With very few exceptions, you should never, repeat never, dose your dog with the various potions, pills and panaceas you may have in your own medicine cabinet. Only when a human medicine is directly prescribed or authorized by your veterinarian should you even consider using it. Just as one example, consider strychnine sulfate. This poisonous drug is used in various small quantities in some human tonics and occasionally in cathartics. In the recommended amounts it doesn't hurt people, but in even the smallest quantities it will be poisonous to your dog, and possibly fatal. There are other drugs which act in much the same way, so, in short, don't!

Old medicines for your dog are another thing to be avoided. This same warning is given periodically to humans about the odds and ends of pills, powders and liquids that hang on in the medicine cabinet after their use, but few people pay much attention. It is doubly important, however, that you throw out old pills and medicines you have been given for your dog—you are considerably less likely to know that the same thing is wrong again with your dog, and even if you do have it diagnosed correctly, there may be some good reason, such as deterioration of the drugs or complicating conditions in the dog, which dictate that you shouldn't dose him with the same stuff again. So, as soon as you have given your dog a prescribed course of pills or any medicine, throw out what's left over. True, the pills may have been expensive, but keeping them in the medicine cabinet won't recover your investment.

As to the medicines prescribed by the veterinarian, there is one major caution—give them in the amounts and at the times he tells you. This may seem superfluous advice, but it is very much to the point, for it is easy to forget a regular dosage schedule, skip a time, and then simply take up the schedule again, or worse, give him a double dose to "make up" for having missed one time.

When a certain amount of a drug is prescribed at certain intervals, it is arranged that way so that a definite level of the drug can be maintained, as nearly as possible, in the bloodstream throughout the course of the treatment. Look at the mechanics of it—you give a pill, or two pills, or a dose of liquid, and the drug quickly enters the bloodstream in a certain concentration. As time goes on, this concentration declines as the drug is absorbed or eliminated. Then, when you give another dose, the concentration shoots up again and subsequently begins to decline again. When a dosage is calculated for treatment of any condition, it is calculated so that the initial surge of concentration won't be too high, yet high enough so that the concentration will not have fallen below the minimum effective level before the next dose is due. When you look at it this way, you can see that if you miss a dose, the concentration will have fallen way below the minimum effective level during the time between the missed dose and the next one. During that time, the original condition will either not improve, or may get worse. Then, if you give more than a standard dose to "make up," you will likely give too much—above the safety level.

Keep all this in mind when dosing your dog, and stick as closely to the prescribed amounts and schedule as possible. If the illness is a serious one, and your dog is due to get medicine on, say, a three-hour or a four-hour schedule, don't hesitate to ask your veterinarian if it is worth while getting up in the night to keep the schedule. If he tells you not, then obviously don't bother. But if you convince him that you are willing to disturb your sleep for the health of your dog, and it will help, he'll tell you so. And if he does, do it.

ADMINISTERING PILLS

The secret of giving pills successfully is largely in the approach. While it may be a bit late at this point to tell you that you should start giving pills the right way when your dog is a puppy, nonetheless, that is the best way to do it. The writer's dogs, who have been of many and various temperaments, have always taken pills without fuss or bother, from puppyhood, largely because pills were always presented to them calmly and without fuss or fighting—so much so that they often eat them from the open hand.

Assuming that this is the first time you've had to give your dog a pill, remember in your approach to the situation that there is nothing to worry about. That may seem a surprising first step, but your own attitude about things is transmitted to your dog with astonishing speed and accuracy, as you no doubt know by now. If you are nervous about the whole thing and look on it as a coming ordeal, he'll get the clue in short order. But if you simply sit down with him as if it were one more normal part of life, you'll find that he responds much better.

As to the technique itself, first arrange it so that he stays in one spot. If he is accustomed to your handling him and believes that no harm will come to him, he'll probably sit still and wait to see what happens next. If he is uncooperative, you'll have to put on a collar and leash, and then sit on the leash to keep him localized. Once he is set, take hold of his muzzle with your left hand, either from above or below, but preferably from above, and squeeze his lips against his teeth, on both sides, with your thumb on one side and your fingers on the other. Squeeze just forward of the corners of his mouth, and you'll find that he will open his mouth. Try it on yourself once and you'll see why—it hurts to keep your teeth closed, and he feels much the same way about it, so the mouth will come open. If he is really set against the idea, you may have to squeeze hard, but don't worry about doing him any real damage—and don't worry about your being cruel to him, as he can stop the hurting any time he wants to by simply opening up like a good little soldier. All the while, incidentally, you should be praising him and telling him what a good dog he is—don't shout at him, curse him, or anything of that nature. That will only complicate matters. Be calm, and persistent.

When he does open up, slip the thumb and fingers of your left hand inward so that they carry a little of the lips over the teeth on each side— it's a little hard to describe, but you'll get the hang of it quickly enough. The lips over the teeth are to prevent his biting down on your fingers, so don't forget this point. Pieces of finger are nowhere nearly as good for him as the proper pills.

With the mouth successfully opened, take the pill in the thumb and forefinger of your right hand, or better, between the forefinger and middle finger, and put it well back on his tongue, and just set it there. Don't try to flick it in, or toss it in, as you may get it into his windpipe instead of his throat. Then close the mouth firmly and lift his muzzle up and stroke his throat. If you've gotten the pill far enough back on his tongue, and you lift the muzzle and stroke the throat to promote swallowing, there's nothing in the world he can do about it—the pill will go down.

There is one alternate way if you simply aren't up to the above method, and this is to hide the pills or capsules in food, preferably hamburger. It might work, but don't be surprised if you find all the food gone and the pills resting neatly on the bottom of the bowl. Or if you are giving him capsules and can't get them down any other way, ask the vet about the advisability of opening the gelatin covering of the capsules and stirring the powder into milk or mixing it with food—but check first with the vet, for some medicines are very bitter to the taste, and this is one of the reasons they are in gelatin capsules.

GIVING LIQUID MEDICINES

There are three ways of administering liquids, largely depending on your control of the dog and your relations with him. First, if it is an innocuous liquid, you may be able to mix it with milk or some other liquid he likes, and get him to drink it all up, thus solving the problem neatly. This is not likely to work, because dogs are not easily fooled this way, but if you have more of the liquid medicine than you need, it won't hurt to try. Direct administration is better, however.

If he will sit quietly and allow you to open his mouth without much fuss (and he should), then you can simply have him open up and can pour the medicine towards the back of his tongue. As with pills, don't pitch it down, as the danger of getting it in his windpipe is considerably increased with liquids. Then do as before, holding his muzzle up, and stroking his throat to promote swallowing.

If you have difficulties, the lip-pouch method is nearly infallible. First, measure out the dose of medicine in a spoon or some small container like a whisky shot glass. Then get your dog to sit still in one place. If he is obstinate about this sort of thing, it helps indeed to have someone else holding his head in one position, for in the lip-pouch method you really need a third hand to hold the head still, whereas in giving pills, the hand that forces the mouth open also forces the head to stay put. But even without help, you can get it done. Simply take hold of his lower lip, just forward of the corner of his mouth, with thumb and forefinger, and pull out gently to form a little pouch, or pocket. Pour the medicine into this pocket, a little at a time, and after each partial dose, close the "pouch," lift the muzzle and stroke. The medicine will trickle through the most firmly closed teeth, and into his mouth, from which point it will conveniently trickle down his throat when you hold his muzzle up. It may take two or three smaller doses to get as little as a teaspoonful into him, but it works marvelously.

Liquid measures, for medicines and other purposes, are sometimes given in teaspoons, tablespoons, ounces, or more rarely, fluid drams or cubic centimeters (c.c.). The table below will help you make conversions from one measure to another.

	Cubic Centimeters	Ounces
Fluid Dram	4	⅛ approx.
Teaspoon	4-5	⅙-⅛ approx.
Tablespoon	15	½
Ounce	30	1
Cup	120	4
Av. water glass	240	8
Pint	480	16

FEEDING A SICK OR INJURED DOG

Sick and injured dogs must sometimes be persuaded to eat, and because of the importance of nourishment during such a period, you should devote your attention to making sure that your dog gets at least a little something into him. If he has been put on a liquid diet by your vet, you can feed him soup, milk or whatever it is by the open mouth or lip-pouch method described for giving liquid medicines. It is a tedious process, especially if you are trying to get a cupful of soup into him one teaspoonful at a time via the lip, but at least you can force him to take it this way.

As to solid or mushy food, personal attention and coaxing will solve many problems of feeding the sick or post-operative dog. Although it is generally inadvisable in other circumstances to feed your dog by hand, during sickness it is recommended if he won't take his food any other way. Don't worry about establishing bad habits—maintaining his health is more important now. Rub some of the food on your finger and hold it up to his nose to let him smell. He may take a lick of it from your finger and then get interested enough to begin eating by himself. Even if not, he may then consent to eat bits of it you put in his mouth, or hold in the palm of your hand. Tempt him, of course, with whatever goodies your vet will allow under the circumstances of the dog's condition.

If he absolutely refuses to take anything, then you may have to force-feed him for a brief time. The method depends on the consistency of the food. If it is of a more or less hamburger consistency, you can make little "sausages" of it about the size and shape of your thumb, or smaller if your dog is a puppy or a small breed. Force his mouth open as in pill administration, shove the pellet deep into his throat, close the mouth, lift the muzzle and stroke. Repeat as often as necessary to get the requisite amount of food into him. If he gags on it, or vomits, desist, and turn your attention to getting some broth into him.

If the food is of a mushy and semi-liquid nature, again open the mouth and spoon it onto the back of the tongue, and proceed as before to get him to swallow it. And remember, whatever you are force-feeding him with, to approach it calmly and matter-of-factly as with pills and medicines. Don't shout, don't hit, don't make a big fuss over it. Just get it done.

For difficult eaters, you can make an excellent broth by warming a can of beef bouillon without diluting it—just warm it, don't cook it. Put in a few drops of a good multi-vitamin supplement and then feed it to him either straight or by force-feeding. Or you can warm a can of chicken soup, or make your own beef or chicken broth to feed him. But be sure to add the supplement to make sure he is getting the proper vitamins. Some sick dogs can also be fed kibbled biscuit, one chunk at a time, if the biscuit is soaked in warm milk or warm broth until it is spongy.

You may find that a sick dog, after having eaten either voluntarily or by force, will vomit his food and suddenly become interested in eating what he vomited. To a human, this sort of thing may be repellent, but the best thing you can do about it is just not watch. It is an entirely natural thing for a dog to do—puppies are sometimes given their first solid food by their mothers just this way, and the trace of stomach acid which comes up with the vomited food makes it more appealing and tasty to the puppy or sick dog. If he does it repeatedly, of course, it is an indication that something is more out of whack than was originally diagnosed, but a few times means nothing.

IN GENERAL

There are only two general cautions and advices about the treatment of a sick or injured dog—do what the vet tells you, exactly, and be calm. It is difficult to say it too often.

First, as to post-treatment, or post-operative care, be absolutely sure you know exactly what the vet has told you to do. Don't hesitate to ask him to write it down, or write down yourself everything he tells you— how many and what kind of pills, or what amount of liquid medicine to give and on what schedule. It is very easy to nod and understand when he hands you the pills or medicines, and then five minutes later have forgotten what it was he said. So write it down.

Second, keep calm. This is very easy to write about, and to think about before the fact and decide upon. It may be more difficult to do, but your dog's life may just depend on it. Keep in your mind a large sign, like IBM's "THINK," yours saying "CALM." One hint in the way of human treatment, for yourself—if you find yourself getting shaky or panicky, and especially if you are confronted with an ugly situation in the way of an accident or injury to your dog, aside from the one deep breath to collect yourself, breathe fast and heavily through your nose. Strange though it sounds, it will sometimes work wonders both in maintaining calm and in preventing the rush of bile at the back of your throat from causing you to throw up. Just drop your arms to your sides, sit down if possible, close your mouth, and breathe in and out as deeply and quickly as you can, through your nose.

If you keep your head, you'll be likely to keep your dog.

CHAPTER VI

SEX AND MATING

Mating and whelping are moderately complex procedures, although to the average dog owner, it seems that they should be simplicity itself. The vision of thousands of years of natural, uncomplicated mating and whelping presents itself, along with that of the apparent present ease with which wild animals, stray dogs and even pet dogs mate and bear their young. Here again the human analogy is instructive—it is true that the human race managed to survive and prosper through thousands of years without obstetricians, pediatricians and delivery rooms. It all seems very easy and natural, but what must be kept in mind is that what we are dealing with are the survivors—in earlier days, and in the present-day backward areas of the world, there was, and is, enormously high infant mortality, childbirth death of mothers, and other complications which are almost entirely eliminated by modern science and care.

The same applies to animals. What you see are the survivors, whether they be wild animals or stray dogs—for every living animal there are others who died young or were never even born alive. It is true that under normal conditions of health and care, domestic dogs may mate and bear their puppies without complications up to 90% of the time, without any help or supervision. But it is, first of all, the other 10% which concerns you and your dog, for he or she may easily be in that group; and secondly the fact that even without complications, in the normal course of affairs, you are likely to end up with a healthier mother and healthier, stronger pups if some care and attention are given.

Finally, there is the philosophical point of survival of the fittest, and natural selection. The accusation has been made, and with some justification, that one ought not to interfere in natural processes because such interference, by aiding and abetting the survival of weaker individuals, will slowly weaken the entire race, breed or strain. If mating, whelping, raising or weaning need any human interference, says this theory, then the individuals shouldn't have been bred in the first place, and the pups oughtn't to be helped to survive. Taking the long view, this theory has much to recommend it, however cold and callous it may be, and would probably result, in the long run, in sturdier stock through natural selection. You have only one dog, however, and one litter of puppies, and the long view will have little appeal to you. Your concern is the survival of the one dog, and the one litter, and therefore it behooves you to know something about breeding and whelping, and raising just-born puppies.

THE MALE

The male dog is so constituted as to be generally interested in sex at all times, and this will be apparent in most dogs from puppyhood. Male puppies when quite young will begin to display "practice" mounting activity, on fellow puppies if available, on blankets or rolls of bedding, and on the legs of their owners and sundry other humans. It must be emphasized that this is no indication whatsoever of depravity or degeneracy on the part of the male dog. When it is discouraged, it should be done firmly and unequivocally, but with understanding and without harshness. Almost all of the play activities of puppies are instinctive preparation for adult activity—playful fighting among puppies is practice in serious fighting skills, playful mounting is instinctive practice in mating behavior.

As the male puppy grows older and begins to have extensive contacts with other dogs, he will often engage in apparent sex activity with them, whether they be male or female. The extent of it depends entirely on the individual dog—some are almost totally indifferent to it, some seem obsessed with sex, and there is every range of attitude in between these two extremes. Depending on the acquiescence of the other dog, a male will engage in extensive sniffing of the other dog's rear, licking this area, licking the ears and face, and attempting to mount. Because of inexperience, the young male will often get into mounting position almost anywhere on the other dog, front, back or side, and begin a pumping action which simulates genuine mating. Again, it must be noted that there is absolutely nothing abnormal about this sort of activity—even if it is practiced on another male. Inexperienced males are sometimes undiscriminating, and do not fully learn the difference between males and females until they have been actually mated.

Owners, particularly those of the dog which is on the receiving end of this mock-sex activity, sometimes react with considerable disgust and will frighten one or both dogs out of their wits by shouting, screeching and swinging in order to put a stop to it. The reasons for this sort of over-reaction to dog sex-play lie outside the realm of this book, but suffice it to say that such sex-play can be discouraged firmly and gently, without rancor, and all will be well.

On the whole, it is a good idea to hold down your dog's participation in this sort of thing, for it is possible for him to be injured as a result. Younger males often show little choice as to the sex of their play-objects, and the mock-sex activity will often irritate a male, and also often irritate a female. The other dog may snap suddenly, or even start a serious fight if it is a male, and your own dog is quite likely to come out on the short end of it.

As he grows older, and insofar as you are able to prevent it, keep him well away from bitches who are in heat, unless, of course, you plan a mating. There are a number of reasons for this—if he hangs around a house or yard where there is an in-heat bitch, he may get involved in fights with other males who are there, he may injure himself attempting to climb or jump over fences and walls, he may get to the bitch and be injured in the act of mating, or may be slashed by her if she is not totally receptive. Finally, he may become a serious annoyance to a neighbor, what with roaming, howling, scratching and urinating around the house.

Ordinarily, it is up to the owner of the female to handle mating arrangements, but you may have a nice male whose looks, temperament or whatever you like well enough to want a pup sired by him. In such a case, start early making inquiries around the neighborhood among the owners of females you would like to breed him to. It may be four or five months before the female you have in mind comes into season, but it is well to have a firm arrangement of mating made well in advance. As the owner of the male, the mating will in all likelihood take place on your premises, for reasons given later in a section on arranging and handling the mating.

MONORCHIDS AND CRYPTORCHIDS

These two terms describe the not uncommon conditions in a male dog, in which one or both testicles are retained within the body and are not apparent in the scrotum. There are differing opinions on the causes of these conditions, but veterinary research has led to a very strong suspicion that they are hereditary. There is no question about the mating of a cryptorchid (no visible testicles) because this condition causes sterility, due to atrophy of the testicles within the body, or if they remain healthy, to the fact that the body heat will kill or render inactive any sperm produced.

The monorchid (one visible testicle) usually retains his full sexual ability and is able to sire puppies about as easily as an "entire" dog. However, a monorchid should not be mated if you have any concern about the possibility of monorchids or cryptorchids among the resultant puppies—genetic transmission hasn't yet been definitely proven, largely because of the extreme difficulty of gathering information and isolating the factor, but much of the available evidence points in that direction. Therefore, if you own a monorchid male, lovable and beautiful though he may be, it is best not to attempt to breed him for a pup. To the owner of a female, the advice is redoubled—don't breed your bitch to a monorchid dog, for there is an excellent chance that the litter will consist at least partially of monorchid males—plus females who can transmit the defect to their pups in turn.

THE FEMALE

Quite opposite the male pattern, the female is interested in sex only twice a year, during her "season" or heat period. The average female first comes into heat at about nine months of age, and thereafter at fairly regular six month intervals. There are exceptions and deviations from this norm—some females may come into their first heat several months earlier or later than nine months, and may have irregular heats. The heat period lasts 20 to 21 days on the average, and during the middle week of this period she will accept males for copulation. At other times of the year, females will either be generally indifferent to males, or will actively and snappishly repel them, or may simply accept them as fellow dogs and enjoy playing and romping with them in a friendly way. There are some few bitches who seem to suffer from a form of year-round nymphomania, but this condition is rare, and you are very unlikely to encounter it.

The very young female puppy will quite often show much the same sexual play pattern as the young male, to the point of going through practice mounting, but as she grows older she will abandon this sort of activity. Later in puppyhood, and in early adult life, she may show friendly interest in males, to the point of investigative sniffing and occasional licking of genitals, but in nowhere as aggressive a pattern as the male. If your female is in constant contact with other dogs, you may be surprised to see that, even if she is a very small bitch, the largest and most ferocious males will respect her when she snaps at them to warn them off if they bother her too much. You need never have any fear of her being hurt, for there is a rigid code among dogs about male-female relationships, which dictates that males never harm females, no matter how abusive they get. There are some few males who would just as soon bite a bitch as look at her, but these are usually of such a sour temper at all times that you are not likely ever to allow your bitch loose with them.

The heat period itself may or may not be bothersome, depending on where you live, the breed and size of your bitch, and on her as an individual. The first signs of heat are an increased appetite and a swelling of the vulva—the general area of the vagina. This progresses for about five days, and then the first few drops of   bloody discharge appear. Here is where breed, size and individual will determine just how much trouble you will have with the heat. Some bitches will have very little vaginal discharge of blood, and of these, many lick themselves clean so efficiently that you may never see more than a tiny bit of blood. Some bleed quite copiously and will leave stains all over the floor, rugs and furniture.

The obvious warning that a heat is coming or in early progress is a sudden access of interest on the part of male dogs in the neighborhood. Dogs have an incredible sense of smell to begin with, but the ability of males to smell a female in heat sometimes defies belief. You might even have male visitors who have been apprised of the situation by so seemingly remote a method as catching her in-season smell carried away on the feet of another dog, and following that track right back to the source. If you live in a city apartment and walk your female on leash, other on-leash males will start straining frantically at their leashes as they go by, and males in other apartments of the building may catch the smell and set up howlings all over the building at all hours of the day and night. In the suburbs or country, you will find your premises besieged by more dogs than you knew existed, and life just might get a little bothersome.

An additional sign is coyness on her part towards humans. Many pet bitches will be exceptionally receptive to attention and patting as the heat begins and progresses, and will often seem to be attempting to seduce you or your guests, particularly if the guests have the smell of a male dog about them. She may back up to them quite seductively, and "flag" her tail (lifting it) just as she would in invitation to a male. This, fortunately, is one of those situations which have within them their own solutions and probably will never cause you any embarrassment. Experienced dog owners will recognize the activity for what it is and think nothing of it, while people who have had no dog experience won't know what she's doing, and therefore won't have a chance to get fidgety and fluttery as they would with a male's mounting behavior.

If it happens that your bitch's discharge is small and that she cleans it up fairly efficiently herself, you may not have to bother at all with her during the heat, except for making sure that she is protected from males. This, by the way, may take more doing than you would think. Don't leave her out in a yard alone for any length of time, even if there is a secure fence around the yard. Amorous males can perform marvels of climbing and jumping to get at a receptive female, and even a small male may climb over as much as a six-foot fence. So you must keep her inside, or when outside, have her under fairly steady observation.

If you don't have the facilities for confining her, or if she makes considerable mess, you can board her at a vet's or boarding kennel during the three weeks of heat. Many people do it as a matter of course and hold down the expense by getting a flat rate from the kennel as good and steady customers. Even at that, though, six weeks of kennel expenses a year can be something of a drain on the budget.

If her discharge is considerable and you don't want to board her, you will have to confine her in a spare room, or in the kitchen at home. The best procedure is to put down several layers of newspaper on the floor of the room you select, and then just make that her home during the time she will be spotting and staining. There are, incidentally, commercial pads and harnesses on the market for bitches in heat, and although they may be a bother to you and her—and to some people quite ridiculous—they will do the job.

After about three weeks, however you handle it, the heat will be over, and that will be that for another six months. It is a good idea to mark down on your calendar the dates of her heat, with a note made six months ahead (from the beginning) to be on the lookout for the next time—otherwise you might miss the beginning signs until she starts messing up the house, or have her caught outside by a male.

SPAYING

The above description of the trials and tribulations of handling the bitch in heat may make it sound as though spaying (sometimes erroneously called "spading") is the only way out. It isn't, really. Many people will automatically have a bitch spayed and never think anything of it, but many people who have "entire" bitches have very little trouble with the heat.

The question requires some examination and thought, for there are good points on both sides. For spaying, there are the following arguments: first, the direct and obvious one that there will be no trouble with "heat" messes, boarding, confinement, unwanted male attentions and unwanted puppies of indeterminate ancestry; second, there is the fact that unspayed bitches are often afflicted with false pregnancies, cystic ovaries, infections of the uterus, and breast tumors. Spaying is almost a guarantee that she will never have any of these problems as she gets older.

Against spaying there are two major arguments. First and most important is the possibility that some time later in your female's life you may decide that you want to mate her—particularly if she has become so dear to you that you want to have one of her own puppies to replace her when the sad but inevitable day of her death arrives. If she has been spayed, you're out of luck. Second, you may find that caring for her during her heats isn't really that much trouble after all—you'll never know until you've been through one with her. There is also a third and minor consideration, in the case of pure-bred dogs, that a spayed bitch is ineligible for the show ring, and you might just possibly, later, want to try her as a show or obedience dog.

One thing which should definitely not be a factor in spaying is the possibility that she will be fat, ugly or temperamental as a result of the operation. There is a considerable body of folklore about the effects of spaying, most of it erroneous. Many of the stories you will undoubtedly hear about the effects of spaying, at whatever age, spring from the easy error of assigning cause-and-effect where it does not exist. True, a spayed bitch may become fat, or timid, or snappish, or shy, or aggressive, or whatever, but the chances are excellent that she would have become what she became in any case. There are uncounted unspayed bitches who have also turned fat, timid, vicious, or shy as they grew older, for quite other reasons—but if any of these happens to a spayed bitch, it is easy to make an assumption which may have no foundation. The next time you hear about the unfortunate results of spaying a bitch, ask your informant how he knows it wouldn't have happened if the bitch hadn't been spayed.

Therefore, to spay or not to spay can only be answered by balancing the above considerations. If yours is a borderline decision, in which you think you just might want to breed her in the future but think it may not be worth the troubles with heats and the possible health dangers, there is unfortunately very little hard and fast counsel which can be given.

If, when you first get a female puppy, you make a definite decision in favor of spaying, the age recommended by many veterinarians (including the very highly regarded ASPCA Clinic in New York City) is at six months. At this age the operation is relatively simple and inexpensive, and the danger to the bitch is slight. It is not as simple as is thought by some people, who are wont to bring a bitch to a veterinarian and say, "I'd like to have her spayed, doc. Shall I wait?", but in the young bitch it is not a too-serious operation. As the bitch grows older the operation becomes more serious and difficult, but this should not be taken as a major argument against waiting until after the first heat, if the trouble you have with heat messes is going to be a factor in your decision.

Spaying is still not all that difficult or dangerous in a bitch up to, say, a year and a half, if she is in good condition. It is when a bitch gets much older than two or three and/or is obese that the matter becomes a really serious one. At that point, spaying becomes major and difficult surgery.

A knotty problem? It can be, but fortunately it will or should be a much easier decision if your bitch is a mongrel. In that case, the consideration of getting pups like her will be almost entirely eliminated, for you won't be able to, and it is probably far better to have her spayed. She will be just as good and delightful a life-long companion, she may in fact live longer, you will be spared all the female problems, and you will be able to find another appealing puppy to replace her at the end of her life. This is not, mind you, an underhanded espousal of spaying all mongrels in the hope of eliminating the species—there always have been and always will be mongrels aplenty, and more power to them, for many people prefer them to pure-breds. It is simply that you are very unlikely to undertake a deliberate program of breeding a mongrel bitch, and thus the health and convenience factors of spaying become very strong arguments.

MATING FALLACIES

As with feeding, there are a number of wild and curious notions about mating, some of which have surprisingly wide acceptance. Probably the foremost among them is the theory that dogs should be bred because it makes them happier. This one has a logical ring to it, because it is certain that animals are driven to mating by instinct and pleasure-gratification reactions built into them to insure that they will in fact mate and that the race will be perpetuated. But in the wild state, a considerable number of animals live without ever mating, and domestic dogs by the millions have lived and died with never a brush with sex. It has never been shown that they were any the unhappier for it. True, nobody has been able to have a heart-to-heart talk with an older dog who never had a chance to mate, but automatic assumption that lack of mating makes a dog unhappy is one of the many traps of anthropomorphism—assuming that dogs think and react like people. They don't. But if you remain convinced that a sexless life is bad for your dog's psyche, and want to mate him for morale reasons, there's nothing to be said against it.

This leads directly to the opposite belief, that a male, once mated, will turn nasty or vicious or aggressive or whatever. This one has a partial basis in fact, but can generally be considered untrue. The partial basis is the fact that a mated male, particularly a stud dog who is often used for breeding, will often become more aggressive towards other males, because he apparently comes to look on all males as possible rivals for the affections of some unspecified bitch. But in other aspects, stud dogs who are used frequently by professional breeders remain, if they were that way before, perfectly gentle, friendly and lovable. One particularly large and fearsome male Doberman comes to mind in this light—as one of the country's top show dogs, he is constantly being used as a stud. He is hard as nails, tough as a timberwolf and would happily kill any adult male dog he could get at. An excellent watchdog and protector of the house, he is with his owners and their friends the world's biggest and most lovable patsy—nuzzling any and all comers for protracted petting, and wiggling on his back in the hope that someone will rub his stomach. With females he is gentle and considerate, and so worried about the possibility of accidentally hurting even the tiniest puppy that he jumps up on a couch to stay out of the way whenever a puppy comes into the room. Don't worry about your male becoming nasty because of having been mated—he won't unless he has a faulty temperament and probably would have gotten surly about things anyway.

One notion, once widespread but now reduced to a few pockets of scattered resistance, is the one scientifically called "telegony." This is usually stated, "If a purebred bitch ever has a litter by a mongrel, then she's ruined forever after for breeding," with some sort of conclusion that she will never be able to have purebred puppies. It is a patently non-sensical idea, but surprisingly durable—the mere fact that it has such a resounding and scientific name shows how well accepted it was at one time.

When a bitch conceives, she releases ova which meet semen from the male, develop and eventually become puppies of whatever nature. Then everything is over until the next heat, at which time more ova are released. To assume that a previous mating could affect a later one, one would either have to postulate that some of the first-mating sperm had managed to survive the interval, that some of the fertilized ova had been lurking about all that time, or that in some mysterious way the new ova were aware of what had happened to the ones that went before. There is, in short, absolutely no truth to the idea. A purebred bitch can have a litter sired by a Dachshund, then one sired by a Great Dane, then one sired by a mongrel, and finally one sired by a male of her own breed—the puppies resulting from the last mating will be totally pure specimens of her own breed.

You will also, though more rarely, run into the theory that acquired characteristics can affect the heredity of puppies—this gets into an internationally hotly disputed area of Lysenkoism versus Darwinism, as to whether acquired characteristics can be passed along to the offspring. Rather than get into an involved discussion, it is safe to say that no accidental damage to either the female or the male will affect the puppies in any way—with the obvious exceptions of physical damage to the bitch which would mechanically interfere with carrying or delivery of the pups, or directly injure them during pregnancy.

It is really surprising how this one pops up, even in modern books. In one massive and authoritative reference work on dogs, one of the contributing authors discusses a breed (which shall here be mercifully nameless) which is tail-docked and has been for centuries. At one point, he says, ". . . the shortening of the tail has been going on for so long now that many puppies are born, to all intents and purposes, tailless." This, like telegony, is simple and thoughtless nonsense, for to believe it you would have to believe that the ova of a docked female, or the semen of a docked male, knew that the tail had been cut off, and somehow magically altered their chromosomes so that the puppies would be born with shorter tails. If you say, sure, but after hundreds of generations, mightn't it affect them somehow, you still have to pin down the start of the change to shorter tails somewhere, and those ova still have to find out about it, and change their chromosomes, even if just a little.

It is believed that mange mites may be passed from mother to puppies, and it is definite that a female infested with certain types of worms will transmit them to her pups, and it is true that a bitch who is badly nourished may well have sick and weakly pups. But these things have nothing whatever to do with hereditary or genetic characteristics—they are physical parasites, or nutritional weaknesses, which affect the pups well after their inherited characteristics are determined in the first moment of the meeting of the sperm and the ovum. Take anything you hear about transmissible acquired characteristics with several pounds of salt.

AGES FOR MATING

The outside limits of age for both males and females are pretty well set by an American Kennel Club regulation regarding eligibility of puppies for registration:

> "No dog or litter out of a dam under eight months or over twelve years of age at the time of mating, or by a sire under seven months or over twelve years of age at the time of mating, will be registered unless the application for registration shall be accompanied by an affidavit or evidence which shall prove the fact to the satisfaction of the American Kennel Club."

In short, they doubt it. You aren't likely to try to mate either a male or a female that young or that old, but people obviously have, or at least tell the A.K.C. they have and that there are puppies as a result, or the regulation wouldn't be in force.

Although males are capable of siring litters before they are one year old, this is about the minimum age at which you should mate a male, and ten years is probably the oldest. After that age, there is a good possibility that the dog will not be potent, and that the mating will be wasted. Some dogs have sired litters when older, but it is fairly uncommon.

For females, it is best not to mate them until the second heat. At her first heat a female is still a puppy. Her body is still getting itself organized, and there are good chances of failure of the mating. In addition, when and if the litter is born, she will still be less than a year old, and whatever her instincts to mothering, will still be a puppy at heart and possibly not up to the responsibilities of caring for her pups. At the other end of the scale, ten years is again about the oldest a bitch should ever be mated, with six years a much better top age—many bitches are old at the age of eight, and the strain of pregnancy and whelping might easily be fatal.

Among the "first heat" arguments you may hear is one concerning those breeds which habitually encounter difficulties in whelping because of head size. Bulldogs are prominent among them, but you may hear the same story about other large-headed breeds, or about any of the toy breeds which often encounter such difficulties. This theory holds that a bitch of any of these breeds should be mated at her first heat, because then she will have puppies while she is still young and her bones are still pliable—that, in effect, the whelping of big-headed pups while she is still young will enlarge her pelvic girdle and thus make any later whelpings that much easier. This theory is false, for whelping a litter will have no effect on the pelvic structure of the bitch—while it is just barely possible that younger and springier bones will make a first-heat whelping slightly easier, it is certain that the momentary displacements, if any, of the emerging puppies will not cause her pelvic girdle to enlarge permanently.

ARRANGING THE MATING

In the normal course of affairs, it is the owner of the bitch who takes the initiative in arranging for a mating, although a male's owner wanting to mate his dog may have made inquiries as to general availability. If you own a bitch, it will be up to you to select the male you want to sire her pups; arrange with that male's owner to have the dog available at that time your female will be in heat and receptive, and, of course, have all this taken care of well in advance of the predicted time of her season.

There are any number of ways of handling the arrangements once preliminary agreement has been reached. Almost always, the actual mating will take place where the male lives—one reason is that males perform better when they are in familiar surroundings, and another is that in the case of a much-used stud, it would simply be impractical for the owner to drag him around, or send him around, to bitch after bitch. If yours is to be a neighborhood mating, establish with the male's owner some place on his premises for the actual mating—his garage, a spare room, or even a secluded back yard.

If yours is a pure-bred bitch, and you are planning to mate her to an established, professional stud dog, the preliminary arrangements become slightly more complicated. First, there is the fact that some owners will allow their studs to be bred to "approved bitches only." This simply means that, to safeguard their dog's reputation as a producer of top-quality puppies, the owners reserve the right to examine the bloodlines and appearance of your bitch before they will agree to a mating. Therefore, if you are contacting the owners of such a stud, be sure to have her pedigree in hand, or a copy of it to be mailed, and be prepared to present the bitch herself if the distance is small, or at least a good picture of her. If you are not familiar with this sort of proceeding it may all seem a bit ridiculous and refined to you, but to professional and semi-pro breeders it is a matter of deadly seriousness, and rightly so. But don't think you are likely to be turned down cavalierly. If yours is indeed an attractive pure-bred bitch, of decent parentage, you will be accepted and there will be no trouble at all.

Professional breeding by an established stud is always done at the home of the stud, and the mating itself is supervised and handled by the stud's owners, which takes that matter and its attendant problems entirely out of your hands. You either deliver the bitch directly, and then call for her later that day or several days later, or ship her and then get her back some days later. If you want badly enough to have her mated to a stud distant enough to require shipping, the stud's owners will give you all the necessary advice and instructions on routes, crating and all other details. If you get into this, don't worry about your bitch—in professional breeding, hundreds of bitches are shipped across the country every day, some by air coast-to-coast, and the incidence of un-pleasant consequences is so tiny as to be totally insignificant.

For such an arrangement, you must be thoroughly familiar with the signs of the heat and how to recognize the proper time for mating—if you send your bitch a week too early she will just have to wait at the stud's premises for the right time to arrive, and the stud's owners would be fully within their rights to charge you board. And, of course, if you send her too late, you are just out of luck for six months.

Professional breeding calls for hard and fast agreements on what it will cost you as the owner of the bitch. The normal practice is to charge a stud fee, which may be anything from a few dollars to well over a hundred in the case of an outstanding stud. Quite often, the stud's owners will take "pick of the litter"—their choice of the best puppy in the litter, the choice generally being made at six to eight weeks of age, depending on the breed—in lieu of money. This is a widely accepted practice, and once the agreement is made, it is binding unless the other parties want to be soft-hearted about it. You can't change your mind once the litter is born and decide you want to give them the money after all. If they've agreed to accept a pup instead of money, it means they think the breeding has possibilities of producing some very good specimens; it is not uncommon for a pick-of-litter puppy to be sold to a third party, sight unseen, possibly even before the litter is born, and occasionally even before the mating is completed, simply on the strength of the combined pedigrees of the sire and dam.

The pup may just have been sold for a great deal more than what the stud fee would have been, so don't expect to be able to make a switch in arrangements once they've been settled—this business of selling a puppy for more than the stud fee would have been, incidentally, is completely ethical and a common practice, so don't think you have fallen into a den of thieves if you hear about it happening in your case. Don't be unhappy because *you* could have pocketed that money for the best puppy —you couldn't have. The professional breeder earns his money by his knowledge of breeding, and by his contacts.

A contract with a professional stud usually calls for a repeat breeding if the first time doesn't take, and without any additional charge or change in the arrangements, but rarely will it cover more than one repeat. There is no question that a proven sire is fertile and potent, and his owners will be experienced and capable breeders. It may be accidental if it doesn't take the first time, but if nothing happens the second time around, the chances are very good that your bitch cannot, for one reason or another, conceive. If your arrangement was pick-of-litter and nothing happens on two breedings, then everything is called off, no hard feelings—it is one of the chances professional breeders take when they agree to such terms (and another reason you shouldn't feel resentful about them getting a higher price for "your" puppy, for in pick-of-litter arrangements the breeder gambles a sure stud fee against the possibility of an outstanding puppy).

But if you have paid cash for the breeding, it is nonreturnable. The stud's time and services are literally valuable, the owners have bred him in good faith, and the times he was bred to your bitch meant times he couldn't be used on others, so they are entitled to the money. A very soft-hearted professional might return part of the fee, but you shouldn't ask for it, and he is entitled to keep it all.

Finally, in a professional arrangement of pick-of-litter, the one case in which the agreement will be changed is if your bitch produces only one living puppy. In the case of the one puppy, the stud's owners are still legally entitled to that one pup, but almost any breeder in the world will allow you to keep it after all you have been through in the way of care of the bitch and the whelping. They may or may not ask for a stud fee in lieu of the pup in such a case, but probably they won't.

Amateur arrangements with a neighbor or friend, are, of course, entirely up to the two of you. There is hardly ever a stud fee in cash in such informal cases, and often the male's owner may not even want to have a puppy, but just to mate his dog, to see what kind of puppies he produces, or simply as a service. A common arrangement, though, is for one puppy of the litter to go to the male's owner, and sometimes more than one, up to relatively uncommon arrangements such as splitting the litter evenly. But it's entirely up to you.

As the owner of the bitch, there is one major responsibility you have, and that is having her in good health for the mating, and this includes a thorough worming if a fecal examination shows that worms are present. Because puppies acquire certain worms from their dams, every bitch mated should be as free from worms as possible. There is a distinct possibility that a litter of puppies born of a worm-free dam may never have worms in their entire lives, and never have to go through the process of being de-wormed themselves. There is nothing at all to the old folktale about every puppy having worms and needing a routine worming—many pups never have a worm in their lives.

This worming should ideally be carried out within two weeks before the beginning of the bitch's heat, but it can be done up to two weeks after the mating. After that it becomes dangerous, both to the bitch and to the unborn litter, and shouldn't be done. If for one reason or another you've let it go until then, you'll just have to leave it be, and face the high probability of having worming problems with her puppies.

WHEN TO MATE

The exact timing of the mating for sure conception is of very considerable importance. The progress of the average heat period is this:

Five to seven days for preliminary vaginal swelling, then:

First day: discharge of bright red blood begins, marking the beginning of the true heat period.

Fifth to ninth days: discharge changes gradually to light pink or becomes almost colorless. Bitch begins to become playful and submissive to males.

Tenth day (approximately): bitch will accept males for copulation. This is ordinarily the first day of possible conception.

Eleventh day: ovulation begins.

Eleventh to fifteenth days: bitch eager to accept males for copulation. Conception is very likely during this period. Opinions vary on the optimum day for mating, but the consensus is the 12th or 13th day.

Sixteenth day: bitch may begin to reject males, but conception may still be possible. It is advisable to mate well before this time.

Seventeenth day onward: bitch may be quite vicious and violent about rejection of males, although they are still interested in her. Conception is still barely possible if the bitch should happen to be mounted by a particularly strong and aggressive male.

Twentieth or twenty-first day: the heat is over, and conception is totally impossible.

Because of the inevitable individual variations, this schedule may be off by two or three days in either direction, which is one very good reason for guarding the bitch well from the moment she first comes into heat, and until she is well and truly out of it. The optimum days, however, are normally the eleventh through fourteenth, with the twelfth and thirteenth being the top choice of most practical breeders.

It is possible, incidentally, for a bitch to have a litter of puppies sired by more than one dog, if more than one has mated her during her fertile period. Therefore don't think all is safe once you've had her successfully mated with the sire of your choice. A later copulation may produce even more pups, or at least a higher percentage of the litter, and you might end up with seven mutts and one pure-bred in the litter.

It is all well and good to specify the eleventh through fourteenth days after the beginning of the heat, but there is a very good possibility you will miss noticing the first day, and may in fact miss the first several days. If you do, the most reliable indicator to use is the change in color of her discharge. Once it has become pink or nearly colorless, she will be ready for fruitful copulation for about the next five days to a week. The best time is square in the middle of that period, the same days specified before. The best way to determine the color of her discharge is to take a small wad of absorbent cotton and wipe a bit of the discharge from her vulva.

Lacking any of these signs, the obvious general rule is that she is likely to conceive if she accepts a male. This won't do you much good for planning a mating in advance, but at least it might get it done at more or less the right time. If you are somehow able to observe the time she first is willing to copulate, the best mating days are those beginning about two or three days after her first willingness. If, for whatever reasons, you have not been able to observe even this, then simply mate her when she will accept a male, and hope for the best.

HANDLING THE MATING

The standard amateur method of handling a mating is simply to lock a male and a female together in a spare room, a garage or an enclosed yard for up to 24 hours during the apparently proper period of heat, then separate the dogs and wait for the puppies to come. This may work, and certainly has on innumerable occasions, but as often as not it doesn't, and the owners are mystified because there is no conception. It is all very well to drag in at this point the argument about stray dogs seeming to have no trouble, which is what these amateur owners usually do. What they forget is the fact that an in-heat stray bitch, during her acceptance period, is willing to copulate continually and repeatedly with any and all males. Her odor attracts large numbers of males, and a dozen or so may attempt to mount her during this time. Some of them will be experienced males and will achieve copulation, some will be novices who accidentally get it right the first time, and some will simply have no luck at all. But out of the volume of attempts, some fertilization will be successful.

The trouble with the inexperienced male is that he simply doesn't know how to go about copulation. He has all the right instincts for mounting and pumping, but it takes more than that, and the techniques he learns only by trial and error. An amateur garage mating may be successful because a certain percentage of males happen to have success the first time, or possibly the male is, unknown to his owner, quite an old hand at such things. But there is the eminent possibility that nothing will happen at all. Additionally, there is a very good possibility the male may be injured, for during the mating "tie" (see below) the bitch may try to lunge away and thus injure his genitals, or snap repeatedly at him before or during the actual tie.

It is best for all parties concerned, therefore, that the mating be supervised and aided in every way possible, to insure successful copulation and to prevent injury to the dogs involved. The best course is to have someone experienced help you supervise your first attempt at mating dogs, and this means someone *really* experienced, not just a neighbor who has happened to have luck with a leave-them-alone-in-the-garage mating. If no experienced person is available, then follow the procedures outlined here. Helping dogs copulate strikes numerous people as a curious way to pass the time of day, but if you want puppies, it is the only proper way to go about it.

First, a brief anatomical outline of mating. There are two very unusual features of the construction of the male dog's genitalia—within the penis itself there is a bone which aids in the original insertion, and at the base of the penis there is a "bulb" which during copulation enlarges considerably. In the female, there is a muscular ring at the opening of the vagina. Once the male has attained insertion and the bulb has passed this muscular ring into the vagina, the ring presses on an extremely sensitive plexus of nerves at the base of the penis. This causes a violent reflex thrust forward and closes a blood outlet valve, at which time the true erection begins as the penis becomes engorged with trapped blood, and the bulb swells to many times its original size. This swelling creates the "tie," and the dogs are unable to separate until the male's ejaculation is complete, and usually for a considerable time after that. This mechanism is designed to insure fertalization.

The length of the tie varies widely, and may be only a few minutes, or as much as several hours in extreme cases, with the average time being fifteen to twenty minutes. No attempt should ever be made to interfere with or release this tie, as severe damage could result to one or both dogs. Even a very long tie is not in itself injurious to the dogs involved, although it may cause them irritation through simply having to stand still for that length of time.

Now, assuming the bitch is at the proper time of heat, prepare both male and female by not feeding them anything on the day of mating. Take the bitch to the mating area, keeping the male well away until you are ready, and take the precautionary step of putting a gauze muzzle on her (see Chapter V for details). This will prevent her from snapping and biting at the male. Even experienced bitches may snap, and young and inexperienced ones who are a little upset and frightened by the whole business are quite likely to. Nothing is better guaranteed to end the attempts of an inexperienced male, and may in fact ruin him for all future attempts at mating. A fully experienced stud will ignore this sort of thing, and may give her a good snap right back to show her who's boss, but it is best to prevent it happening in the first place.

With the gauze muzzle in place on the bitch, bring the male to her and allow him to sniff around her, and she around him, until he is aroused enough to begin attempts to mount. She will show her willingness by standing quietly as he attempts to mount, carefully pulling her tail out of the way. If she is at all nervous and snappish, but otherwise obviously receptive, hold her head, soothe her, pet her and talk to her in a gentle tone, and she will almost always calm down and stand ready to accept the male. If she will simply not put up with it, but vigorously repels his every attempt, you have somehow made a mistake about timing her heat, and the best course is to separate them and wait a day before trying again. But there is a wide and very easily recognizable difference between absolute rejection on her part, and simple coyness, teasing or nervous snappishness—you are unlikely to confuse them.

Assuming she is standing patiently, allow the male to try to mount her without assistance, always providing he is at least working in the right area. Some inexperienced males are so excited and/or poor at it that they will try to mount the bitch from the side, and in such a case it is easy to guide him gently to her rear. Then allow him to try again to make entrance without assistance. Although matings should be supervised, always give only as much assistance as may be absolutely necessary—the less you have to interfere, the better and easier it will be. Too much handling and assistance may put the male off completely, so let him have a good try himself before you decide to help him along.

If the male has worked away for a few minutes without obvious success, and is panting heavily and frantically, take him away into another room until he is calmed down, and then bring him back. A male who is overexcited is unlikely to have any success at all.

One of the most common difficulties is difference in size, even between pure-bred dogs of the same breed. The bitch may be either too tall or short, and this you can help remedy by putting her hind feet on a rolled-up rug or a shallow box, or his hind feet on something, depending on which one needs raising. To prevent the bitch sitting or moving forward once the male gets into approximately proper position, with his forefeet on her back, or with his stomach on her back and his forelegs holding her, it is a good idea to kneel beside her and hold her up with your hand under her stomach, or even your knee braced under her if she is of a large breed.

There are infinite ways in which the male may fail to make connection, and the only advice is that you may have to help him. The male's owner may take him by the hindquarters and gently help guide him if he is consistently missing—if the male is on target and the penis touching or sliding slightly into the vagina but failing to enter fully, the male's owner may even have to give him a push forward along the back of the bitch. It is generally better to handle only the bitch, if raising or lowering is needed, to give *her* the push in the right direction if it is at all possible, for the bitch will not mind the extra handling whereas it just might dampen a male's ardor. Exactly how to help best can only be learned by experience, but the major point for you to realize is that you just may have to help actively.

With a novice dog, be prepared to spend hours of sweaty, hard work trying to get them together. Always gentle, never lose your patience.

Don't work for more than an hour at it—then take the male away for at least an hour to allow him to rest and gather his strength again. And don't give either the male or female water during this rest period. You may not even make it that day. If so, take the bitch home and bring her back the next day to try again. With gentle and understanding assistance, and the male's growing experience, you should always be able to effect mating.

Once the male has achieved insertion, you will see the reflex thrust that locks him in, and he will begin pumping in ejaculation. This pumping soon subsides, and both dogs will stand quietly, the male on the female's back, waiting for the tie to release itself. The male may himself lift a foreleg over her back so that his forelegs rest on the floor beside her. If he doesn't do so within a few minutes after the pumping has subsided, do it for him—all the while, be sure that someone is controlling her head so that she cannot lunge away in an attempt to escape the tie, thus injuring the male's genitals, or reach around to snap at him (although this should be prevented by the gauze muzzle). Throughout the length of the tie, stay with both the male and female, particularly being sure that the heads are under control so that neither can snap at the other, and that neither is able to try to pull away—a sudden pull by either could seriously injure the male, as could the female by suddenly lying down or sitting. If necessary, support her.

Then there is nothing to do but wait for the mating tie to subside. It will be obvious when it does, as the dog's penis is released and the two attempt to move apart. Then lead the male away, and take the muzzle off the bitch. It's all over.

Some breeders have curious and personal superstitions about what to do with the female immediately after the tie is released, all aimed at insuring conception. One of the major practices is holding the bitch up by her hind legs, like a wheelbarrow, to make sure the semen does not run out. Although this practice is harmless enough, it accomplishes nothing, except possibly to confuse the bitch. The origin of it is probably in the fact that exactly this practice is followed by veterinarians who have artificially inseminated a bitch, for in such cases the semen is inserted into the bitch via a glass tube, and there is no lengthy tie with the male. But in a normal mating, by the time the tie is released, the bitch is either pregnant, or she isn't, and nothing that happens afterwards will make any difference.

It is, incidentally, even possible for conception to occur without a mating tie having happened, if the male has managed to achieve any sort of insertion and ejaculation. Under these circumstances, give some thought to the possibility, and don't automatically assume that nothing has happened.

To insure fertilization, even assuming a firm and positive tie has taken place on the first mating, it is a good idea to bring the male and female together again in two or three days for another try. If you have attained mating the first time, and have been careful that no damage occurred to the male, everything will be much easier the second time, and mating may be accomplished right away without any fuss or bother. This second mating after two days will insure that she is mated at least once on a "good" day, if you have been even partially accurate about your calculations of her heat.

After the planned mating or matings, be absolutely sure that the bitch is confined or otherwise securely protected against other males. As indicated earlier, the bitch may be receptive to males for several more days after the optimum mating time, and it is possible to have a multiple-sire litter. But once the twentieth or twenty-first day has passed (from the beginning of the true heat) she will no longer be especially attractive to males, nor they to her.

CHAPTER VII

FROM PREGNANCY TO WEANING

THE CARE of a bitch in pregnancy and in whelping, and the care and raising of newly-born puppies are major endeavors, but they are well within the average, intelligent owner's ability. With a little fore-thought, some instruction and a dash of common sense, you can see your bitch through and have a healthy litter of puppies to show for it. Both normal and difficult pregnancy, whelping and raising are treated here in some detail, for this is *the* major area of care which you can handle by yourself—things can go wrong, but they are not likely to if you follow the recommendations and procedures of this chapter. It is at times hard work, but there are few satisfactions greater than having seen it through with her, and it will draw you closer together than you have ever been before.

THE PREGNANT BITCH

The first step in the care of a bitch you presume to be pregnant is to be sure she has been checked for worms. If you have overlooked this, take care of it as soon as possible after the mating—within the first weeks. If she is free of worms, it is not a guarantee that the puppies will be worm-free, as worm larvae migrating through her tissues may infect the pups, but it gives at least a good chance that the litter will have less likelihood of developing worms.

The second step is to be sure she has been inoculated against dis-temper. If she has already had a successful inoculation, or has recovered from a bout with distemper, there may be no need to give her a "booster" shot. It is vitally important, however, that she have acquired immunity from one source or another, and not only for her own protection during pregnancy and whelping. The primary, overpowering consideration is that a protected bitch will transmit vitally important temporary immunity to her pups in the colostrum—first milk—they receive from her just after they are born. An unprotected bitch will provide little or none of this colostral protection, and the puppies will be wide open to distemper infection for weeks until they can have their shots.

For the fullest protection of the puppies, you might look into the possibility of the distemper nomograph—a test made from a sample of the bitch's blood, through which her "titer", or level of immunity, can be determined with considerable accuracy. By determining the antibody level in her blood, a properly equipped laboratory can tell quite closely just how much immunity she will be able to transfer to her pups. A bitch with a very low titer may transfer almost no immunity, or only enough to hold the pups until, say, two weeks of age. A bitch with a very high titer might give them immunity until they are well over nine weeks old. From the nomograph, a veterinarian can determine the exact age at which the puppies should get vaccine distemper shots. Also, he will be definitely able to tell whether she herself is immune. The techniques at this writing are still not widely known, but your veterinarian will be able to tell you whether or not he is able to arrange for such a test, and to interpret the findings. The nomograph is, however, a refinement with which a great many professional and semi-professional breeders don't bother, and so it may be of little interest to you.

Aside from worming and disease protection, you should try to be sure that the bitch is free of the major skin parasites. But beyond this there is no need to take any other special care of her, at least during the first four weeks of pregnancy. In particular, it is important *not* to coddle her and treat her like a delicate little mother. Many pet bitches have considerable trouble with the late stages of pregnancy and with whelping because their owners have, with only the best will in the world, overfed them and restricted their exercise, thus allowing them to become fat and flabby. Let her eat, play, run and sleep as always, for it is important that she keep up her muscle tone and general condition. While maintaining about the same amount of food, it is a good idea to increase the proportion of good-quality animal protein in her diet—plain meat. A daily ration of vitamin supplement at this time is an excellent idea, as well as a cooked egg or so a day (depending on size, of course) and a bit of raw liver daily.

The average gestation period of the dog is just nine weeks, or 63 days from the time of fertilization. It is important to note that this period is counted from the time of fertilization, and not necessarily from the day of mating—this common error has caused many amateur breeders days of unnecessary anxiety, when they expect whelping several days too soon. If the bitch was mated early in her acceptance period, fertilization might not have taken place until two or even three days later.

If you have kept close track of the bitch's heat, start counting from about the thirteenth day of heat, even if the mating took place earlier. If it took place later, or if you have no idea of the exact days of the heat, then there is no other way than to count 63 from the day of mating. Remember that even if you know the days of the heat exactly, 63 days is an *average* figure, with all that word implies. It is not at all uncommon for a normal bitch's gestation period to vary a day or two on either side of that figure.

After the first month, she may want more food. Give her whatever she wants, and definitely at this point make the ration a high-protein one. Starting about now, you should give her a calcium supplement, probably calcium gluconate or calcium lactate in the dosages recommended for her weight. The general vitamin-mineral supplement can be continued, along with the cooked eggs and daily bit of raw liver.

The first physical signs of pregnancy occur at about the end of the fourth week. If you are really anxious to know whether or not the mating has "taken," take her to your vet. A man with sensitive fingers may at this early date be able to feel the very small enlargements within her abdomen, but don't expect to be able to feel them yourself. It is a good idea, in fact, to keep your hand off her abdomen—any amateur poking and prying may injure her.

Many quite normal bitches who have not actually conceived, and in fact quite a few who have not even been mated, go into false pregnancy and show absolutely every other sign of being pregnant except for the presence of the uterine lumps—they will show abdominal enlargement, and as the false pregnancy progresses, will engage in every action and show every symptom of true pregnancy—even to the point of making a "nest" and showing all the signs of approaching whelping at the proper time. In properly mated bitches it is of course far less common than true pregnancy, but prepare yourself at least for the possibility.

At about the end of the fifth week, there is usually the beginning of visible enlargement of the abdomen, and from the end of the fifth week on, the abdomen will continue to grow heavier. During this time, she will probably be eating more, and it is a good idea to give her her food in two meals rather than in one large meal. This helps, among other things, to prevent constipation. A diet very high in animal proteins also helps prevent constipation, as well as nourishing the bitch. The prevention of constipation is very important at this point, and even more so as whelping approaches. If she does seem constipated, small doses of mineral oil can be mixed with her food to relieve the condition. If the constipation does not yield to this mild treatment and continues for more than two days, she should have veterinary attention.

As to exercise, she should still be allowed to take as much as she wants to. Don't force her to exercise, and do prevent her from unusually strenuous activity, such as jumping, running wildly up and down stairs, or anything else which might result in a fall. Otherwise let her do pretty much as she pleases, and, again, avoid coddling her.

About the sixth week is a good time to prepare a whelping box for her. This should be a square box, about 50% longer on a side than her length lying down. Make the sides about eight inches high on three sides (slightly larger for the large and giant breeds), with the fourth side about half as high as the other three. This lower fourth side is to allow her to get in and out of the box easily, before and especially after whelping, while preventing the pups from getting out. It is a good idea to put the box up on short (3 to 4 inches) legs to keep it off the colder floor, but it isn't a necessity. One optional feature is a bumper rail around the four sides of the box on the inside. Some breeders swear by this, while about as many more say it is totally unnecessary. A bumper rail is a board, preferably a 2 x 2, on the inside of each of the four walls, about as far from the floor of the box as half the height of the bitch's body when she is lying down. The idea of this rail is to prevent her accidentally squashing a puppy in the angle of the box when she lies down. It doesn't happen often, but it has occurred—whether to add this refinement is up to you.

Once the box is built, cover the floor of it with many layers of news-papers, and put in an inch or so of shredded newspaper so she can nest in it. Don't use rags, old clothing or blankets for the whelping box, for although it might please her, there is a very good possibility that one of the pups might get lost under cloth and be suffocated—something which can't very well happen with shredded newspaper.

During the last week or two of her pregnancy, it is a good idea to try to make the box her home. She may not take to it right away, but if you keep leading her back to it, and can persuade her to sleep there, she will soon adopt it.

ECLAMPSIA

Although eclampsia, variously called "nursing fits," "milk fever" and other similar names, is almost always associated with the weeks following whelping, it can occur during the week or two prior to delivery, and is therefore included at this point.

The condition itself is directly due to the calcium drain made on the bitch, first by the puppies growing inside her, and then by the production of milk. However cruel it may seem, it is a part of the grand design of nature, which considers the welfare of the mother entirely secondary to the welfare of the offspring—if puppies need calcium, it will be drained from the bitch's body, even from her bones and teeth, to supply the pups. If, therefore, she does not have an adequate amount of calicum present in her body, she will reach a certain low level and be prostrated by calcium deficiency shock, or eclampsia.

If she has been eating a fully balanced diet high in calcium, she is not likely to suffer an attack of eclampsia, and calcium supplementation is almost a guarantee that it won't happen to her. Calcium lactate or cal-cium gluconate are excellent supplements for pregnant bitches; lacking these, she can be given dried skimmed milk mixed with her food during the last month of pregnancy.

An attack of eclampsia can frighten you right out of your wits if it happens to your bitch, for with the usual physical symptoms of preg-nancy, or in most cases with nursing, you will almost always miss the early symptoms of nervousness, restlessness, unsteady gait and elevation of temperature. The actual onset is sudden—the bitch falls to the ground and lies there stiffly extended, either rapidly twitching or simply rigid.

She usually retains consciousness, and her eyes will probably be open and wild-looking. If she is not twitching and mildly convulsing, she may be so rigid as to appear dead.

There is unfortunately no home treatment for eclampsia, the only relief coming with a quick injection of calcium by a veterinarian. Get the vet to her as quickly as possible, and once he has made the proper injections, recovery is almost always rapid and dramatic. After recovery, should the attack occur after whelping, the bitch should ordinarily be isolated from her puppies for about one day, during which time you will have to take over their feeding. If it occurs before whelping, the only course is a crash program of very high calcium supplementation to protect her during whelping and nursing—feeding her high levels of supplement will do little good at this point, as calcium can only be absorbed into the body at a certain rate from the intestine. It will probably require calcium injections if she is to live through whelping.

The possibility of eclampsia is, incidentally, one very good reason for not breeding a bitch at her first heat. That young, she will not be finished with growing her own bones, and the calcium drain on her smaller supplies may well stunt her growth, even if it doesn't lead to eclampsia.

The incidence of eclampsia seems to vary in reverse proportion to the size of the bitch. It is most common in small breeds, less so in the medium-sized, and relatively uncommon among the giant breeds. This is apparently because, although puppies of small breeds are smaller than those of larger breeds, they are proportionately larger when compared with the bitch. There is, however, no other known predisposition to eclampsia, despite scattered folklore to the contrary. It is not higher among pure-breds than among mongrels, or vice-versa, nor higher among house pets than among working outside dogs, or vice-versa, nor yet higher among nervous, timid, shy or pampered dogs as opposed to more normal and outgoing specimens. Temperament and/or purity of breeding have nothing at all to do with the calcium level in the body, and calcium level is the only factor that has anything to do with eclampsia.

CAESARIANS AND DIFFICULT DELIVERIES

As with humans, the necessity sometimes arises with dogs of a Caesarian delivery, in which the abdomen is surgically opened just before the expected whelping date, and the puppies removed through the incision.

In normal breeding of mongrels or of most pure breeds, you are not likely ever to encounter the necessity of a Caesarian, but the possibility definitely exists with such large-headed breeds as Bulldogs and Bostons, and often with any of the toy breeds. Therefore, if you are breeding any of these, consult with your veterinarian well beforehand on the possibility, and plan to have him either in attendance or on call for an emergency Caesarian if the bitch is unable to pass her pups normally.

A Caesarian is a serious operation, and is nothing to be taken lightly. It requires the cutting of the abdomen and of the uterine horns, the reclosure of these tissues, and subsequent healing. Many, many thousands of successful Caesarians have been done on dogs without any after effects, and some bitches have even had more than one Caesarian, but there is inevitably somewhat more danger in such a procedure than in a normal whelping. If, however, a bitch is pregnant and cannot deliver her pups normally, there is no other recourse.

Even if a Caesarian is not necessary, there may be delivery problems with the above-mentioned breeds—difficulties in passing the pups which require forceps assistance on the part of a veterinarian. Therefore, even if you have reason to expect a reasonably normal delivery, have your vet on quick call for such professional assistance in case the need arises.

THE ONSET OF LABOR

Assuming that all has gone well and normally during the bitch's pregnancy, you should start watching for the first signs of labor at about the 60th day after mating. The great majority of bitches will not begin this soon, but some will, so it is well to keep an eye cocked at her behavior. Careful and anxious waiting for a bitch to begin labor could easily give rise to a slight alteration of the old maxim, to the effect that "a watched bitch never whelps," for it seems like that at times. So be prepared for day and nights of waiting.

A preliminary step is to arm yourself with the home phone number (and prior agreement to be on call) of your veterinarian. Many vets don't like to give out their home phone numbers, because they dislike being called at four in the morning by nervous dog owners whose pets are displaying minor and unimportant symptoms. Whelping is something else again, and you should have arrangements made well in advance.

If you happen to have a bitch of one of the relatively large-headed breeds, such as Bulldogs or Boston Terriers, as indicated earlier, you really should have the veterinarian on hand at the delivery in any case. If you are simply nervous and unsure about things in general, have your vet there to assist in the delivery—the great majority of bitches deliver and nurse their pups without any difficulty whatever, but it never hurts to have experienced help on hand. Otherwise, simply arrange to have the vet on call if anything goes wrong.

Depending on the breed, you may have to clip the hair around her breasts and vulva. Take a look at these areas—if she has shed the hair, then all is well. If she hasn't, and the hair is long enough to get matted and in the way during delivery, or the hair around the nipples might interfere with the pups' suckling, clip it away with clippers, *not* scissors.

If you have lacked either the time or the inclination to build her a whelping box, now is the time to arrange some sort of makeshift place for her—she really needs some small, somewhat enclosed area to call her own. If you have a dry, warm cellar, or a spare room, partition off a corner some way, with low boxes or anything, and put down many layers of newspaper and cover these with an inch or two of shredded newspaper—then let her know that is her area. Don't, however, make a whelping area of a cellar or spare room if it is cold and drafty. This is one of the surest ways in the world to imperil her health, and to guarantee the deaths of at least some of the pups. Minimum whelping-area temperature is a draftless 70°, and 90° is optimum.

You may see either physical or temperamental changes first as labor looms near. Between three and two days before delivery, the bitch's abdomen may sag considerably, changing from generally round and heavy to almost barrel-shaped. At about this time, she will begin to show signs of anxiety and restlessness. She may stop eating, whine a little, and generally act as though she didn't know what was happening to her, which is just about exactly true with a bitch having her first litter—although she is heavily laden with instinctive drives forcing her to do various things in preparation, she literally doesn't know what is about to happen, and she is confused. To understand her better, try to imagine a human female, approaching labor, who has never heard or read about, seen, or even imagined what birth is all about, and in fact believes that children come from watermelon seeds. The dog is a little better off, largely because of stronger instinctive drives, but it is a fairly apt analogy.

The bitch may wander aimlessly about the house, hide under things, and she will almost always scratch and tear at her bedding, the couch, chairs and rugs as she tries to make a nest for delivery. If she is at all normal, she won't want to have anything to do with your carefully prepared whelping box, but will want to be close to you all the time, receiving consoling attention. The best solution for this is to guide her to the box, and sit with her there until she accepts it. One of the things that will influence her acceptance will be the plain and shredded newspapers, for she can dig and scratch at them and worry them into a real nest, which somehow partially satisfies her instinctive nest-making drives.

This sort of activity reaches a peak within about 12 to 24 hours before the actual beginning of labor. The first sure sign of approaching labor is a drop in her temperature, and you should start taking it regularly as soon as she begins to show the pre-labor anxieties (and keep a record of the temperature readings). If the temperature is near 102° (about normal—but you should have checked her normal temperature before this), you still have a little time to wait. When the temperature drops sharply —it may be as low as 98° in normal cases, in some extreme cases as low as 96°—her time is approaching rapidly. Now is the time to call the vet if he is going to be there to help. The labor may begin within minutes, or at most within a few hours.

True labor begins when the bitch is lying on her side, straining purposefully and unmistakably to expel the puppies.

NORMAL DELIVERY

The mechanism of birth is this: the fetuses have developed and grown in a somewhat Y-shaped structure (the uterine horns), the joint of which is the cervix (outward point of the uterus, leading into the vagina). The bottom bar of the Y is the vagina, which opens through the vulva to the outside. At the time of delivery, each of the puppies is contained within an individual, closely-fitting amniotic sac, or fetal envelope. This is attached to him at the navel where it joins the umbilical cord. It is through these structures that he has been receiving all his nourishment up to the point of delivery. Within the amniotic sac the puppy's heart is already beating, but his lungs and trachea are filled with fluid, for he is not breathing yet. The puppies are distributed within both horns of the uterus, in line, and normally one comes out of one horn, then one out of the other, and one again out of the first horn, alternately until all the pups are out.

As labor begins, the cervix relaxes and waves of muscular pressure begin forcing the first puppy in line, from either horn of the uterus, through the cervix, into and through the vagina, and out through the vulva. As the muscular pressure forces the puppy out, the resultant pull on the umbilical cord pulls the placenta loose from the wall of the uterus, and this follows the puppy out. The same pull on the cord stimulates the first breathing reflex in the puppy, and if the amniotic sac bursts as he emerges, he may start breathing before his body is completely de-livered. Or if it remains intact, and the bitch pulls it off him herself, and bites through the umbilical cord, this pressure will stimulate the reflex.

Finally, with one puppy out, followed by the placenta (or "after-birth"), there is normally a period of rest before delivery of the next. Sometimes the first puppy in the other horn of the uterus is delivered quite quickly and there is a longer period before the first of the next pair emerges.

The first things that must be noted about attending a whelping is that there is nothing neat and clean about it. It is plain and simply messy— people of decidedly delicate sensibilities would do well to avoid even watching a delivery. The average person, however, will have no trouble, and delivery is, in fact, a marvelous and wonderful thing either to watch or participate in.

As you will witness it, the perfectly normal delivery proceeds as fol-lows. After some minutes of straining, or even after an hour or two, the first puppy will emerge from the vulva. The bitch will almost always be straining around with her head near the vulva, and this is normal— in fact, her straining around often helps expel the pup. There is often a small discharge of amniotic fluid preceding the first puppy, and she will lick this, and may even lick at the puppy as it emerges. Once the puppy is out, she will tear the sac from the puppy (this sac looks very much like clouded cellophane), and if the placenta has emerged natur-ally with or after the puppy, she will bite or tear through the umbilical cord close to his navel. This clearing of the sac and biting of the cord starts the puppy breathing, and the bitch may first eat the sac and placenta before turning her attention to licking and drying the puppy.

There is a school of opinion which dictates that the bitch shouldn't eat this material. It may be upsetting to watch for aesthetic reasons—the placenta looks like nothing in the world so much as a thin bit of raw liver —but there is no reason she shouldn't. It does, in fact, provide her with nourishment, and the instincts which direct her to eat placenta and sac are apparently based in the wild bitch's needs for nutrition during and following whelping. Additionally, there seems to be a factor in the placenta which stimulates contraction of the uterus, to help with the delivery, so at least let her eat the first one and then remove the later ones.

Ingestion of the placenta sometimes causes vomiting—don't be alarmed if it does—and may also cause mild diarrhea for a day or two following whelping. Otherwise it is apparently harmless.

In even the most normal-appearing delivery, a careful count should be kept of the placentas. There is one placenta per puppy, and it should emerge with the puppy or immediately afterward. Don't rely on memory for this, but make a note—one puppy, one placenta; another puppy, another placenta. A retained placenta may be pushed out ahead of the next puppy, but it is often the cause of complications in delivery—one way of helping avoid this is treated later in this chapter.

Before or after eating the placenta and sac (or if she just ignores them), the bitch will begin licking and nuzzling the just-born puppy until it is warm and dry, and then nudge it onto a nipple so it can begin to nurse. Then, before long, the next puppy will come along, and she will go through the procedure again, and again, until the entire litter is delivered.

Just before and during whelping, give her nothing to eat or drink. She may be panting heavily and look as though she desperately needs at least a small drink, but the best policy is to give her nothing until the delivery is completed. The placentas are the exception, of course, but if you did feed her, and the delivery was a long one, there exists the possibility that the food would, after digestion, cause a constipated mass in her lower bowel, and mechanically interfere with delivery.

Normal, healthy puppies are perfectly blissful, quiet and at peace with the world—continual crying, squirming and crawling about are indications that something is wrong with them. But assuming that the delivery has gone as outlined above, and the puppies appear to be in good condition, the best thing you can do is to watch what goes on, staying near at all times to comfort and console the bitch. Resist the temptation to handle or examine the puppies for a while. They may vary considerably in size, and they look totally unimpressive, but this doesn't mean there is anything wrong—there will be time enough later to look them over to determine sex, and to check for deformities. And above all, don't make an exhibition of either the whelping or the puppies just after whelping. The bitch will accept you and your family, and the vet or other helper who is there, but too many strangers will make her upset and nervous.

Be especially firm about keeping strangers out once she has completed delivery—there is plenty of time later for friends and neighbors to see and handle the cute little puppies. Even the friendliest, nicest, sweetest, most timid bitch can be a death-dealing fury if she thinks her pups are being mistreated or stolen from her. She will almost always trust you, but she is very likely to try to tear a stranger into small pieces if he gets anywhere near the whelping box. It is one of her strongest instincts, so be very careful about it. In some cases, she may even snarl at her owners —if this happens to you, don't think she has gone mad. Simply be very slow and cautious and gentle about approaching her or the puppies, but be firm about it all the while. Remember, it's not a matter of forcing her to let you near, it is a matter of convincing her everything is okay. She is, after all, your pet, and you shouldn't have much trouble, even if she does resent it at first.

There is some belief among professional breeders that, if the bitch is predisposed to eclampsia, the condition may be triggered by sudden loud noises or disturbances, particularly during the early nursing of puppies. This theory has neither been proven nor disproven, but the possibility is another good reason for keeping strangers away during delivery and nursing.

The rule about keeping people away also applies to other animals— in particular the father of the puppies. It's not that he runs any greater

danger from the nursing bitch than any other dog, but many people are
prone to "bring daddy in to see his puppies," and, lo, daddy is sliced into
small and quivering bits before their eyes. There is significantly little
recognition of paternity among dogs, and neither the bitch nor her pups
will now or ever recognize the sire as such—he or any other dog is likely
to be attacked with even more ferocity than a human coming near those
precious puppies.

DIFFICULT OR IRREGULAR DELIVERY

The operative general rule for whelping is: don't interfere. The greatest percentage of deliveries go along quite nicely without any human interference, and your getting in the way would only complicate things.
There are, however, major and minor difficulties and irregularities which
may arise, some of which you can handle very well by yourself, and
others which may require the assistance of a veterinarian. Whether or
not you will really be able to handle any such situation yourself depends
largely on you. If you are a calm sort who takes most things in stride, and
have a gentle touch, you can be a very effective midwife for your bitch. If,
on the other hand, you have any tendency to panic, lose your head or get
frantic and jittery about emergencies, your best course is to have a veterinarian or experienced breeder in attendance at any whelping, or at
least ready and available for a quick trip. This is no time for bravado
and self-deception, because you won't be able to bluff the puppies out
alive and healthy in case of difficulties.

In normal delivery, a bitch may work for an hour or even two hours
of purposeful straining before she is able to produce the first pup, but
anything much beyond that becomes a major problem, and one which
can only be solved by a vet. Be sure you are reckoning from the beginning of true labor—the time the bitch lay on her side and began straining,
not just acting nervous and making nests. Watch her overall attitude—if
she seems seriously depressed and apathetic about her lack of success, or
labors with her head thrown back and her mouth open, you've got
troubles. Something is keeping that first puppy from coming out, and even
something as relatively drastic as a Caesarian may be required to save
both the bitch and the pups. So call the vet, and get professional help
at once if the labor goes on for longer than two hours with no results.

The next category of problem is difficult actual delivery of one or more puppies. In the largest percentage of deliveries, the puppy's head will emerge first, and he will proceed out slowly but smoothly, with umbilical cord intact, followed by the placenta. Contrary to considerable amateur opinion, it is not at all uncommon for puppies to emerge hind-end first, and although this "breech presentation" is considerably undesirable in human births, veterinarians estimate that as many as 30 to 40% of all puppies are born in this fashion. This may cause problems, but if the puppy proceeds out slowly and smoothly, breech presentation causes no more trouble than head-first.

Whichever end appears first, the puppy may be stuck in the canal for a bit. If the head appears first, and then nothing more happens for two or three minutes, clear away the cloudy membranous sac covering his head and face, if the passage and straining have not cleared it away naturally. Even before he has completely emerged, his umbilical cord may be pinched or severed within the bitch, and if it is, he may have to begin breathing—a puppy can breathe while still only halfway out.

Don't interfere with the birth of any puppy (other than clearing away the sac) until the bitch has been trying for at least five minutes to get him out herself. Then, if she has either stopped straining, or continues with no results, you can help if you are very, very, careful. Assuming that the head has come out, take hold of it near the neck, with rough towelling or gauze around your fingers to afford a hold on the slippery, wet surface. Then, apply only very gentle pressure in the direction of her hind feet to hold as much of the puppy as she has managed to push out. DO NOT TURN OR TWIST THE HEAD! In the quiet words of veterinary texts, this will cause "disarticulation of the atlanto-occipital joint," which means, more bluntly, you'll break his neck.

Simply hold the head close to the neck and apply a gentle pull, as delicately as though you were trying to pull on a fragile egg. The idea here is that the pup may have been slipping back slightly after every pressure wave the bitch has been able to apply—you are not, repeat NOT, pulling him out, but simply holding what ground she has been able to gain. If you actively pull, you will be working against her, and considerable harm may result.

If your combined efforts have gotten the puppy out as far as his hind legs, then you can take gentle hold of his body and apply very slightly more pressure, again in the direction of her hind legs, to help get the rest of the puppy out. A firm, gentle touch is required, to avoid injury to the pup, and to help ease the placenta out at the end of the umbilical cord. The cord may have broken, leaving the placenta inside, but don't worry about that for the moment.

Once the puppy is out, offer him to the bitch for her natural care. If she begins cleaning and licking him, all well and good. But if she is a poor mother, you will have to get the puppy going yourself. If he is breathing, all you will have to do is wipe him dry with your towelling —give him a good, vigorous drying—and place him on a nipple to start feeding. If his breathing hasn't started, some fast and sure work is called for.

First, make sure the sac is cleared away from his head and face. Then wipe his mouth and nose clean with towelling. Next, hold him in the towelling, with his back in the palm of your hand—upside down, to drain whatever fluid may be left in his respiratory system. If this is draining readily, let it drain. If not, shake him vigorously (still head down and tail up), or with a firm grip, swing him head down to apply centrifugal force to the fluid. However, as you swing, don't snap him like a whip, but swing him vigorously and smoothly. If he still has not begun breathing, rub him vigorously with a towel, particularly over the ribs. Always remember not to press in on him in such a way as to injure bones, but still rub vigorously.

As a final step, if nothing else will start the breathing, hold him head down, his back in the palm of your left hand, and take hold of his umbilical cord close to the body with your right thumb and forefinger. Now, alternately, pull gently on the cord, and press down gently on his chest with the three remaining fingers of your right hand. This provides both direct artificial respiration and the normally-required stimulus to the cord which helps spark the breathing reflex. Keep this up for a few minutes, then revert to rubbing, and then back to the artificial respiration. It will be the rare case where you will have to go this far in getting life breathed into a puppy, and once having had to go this far, rarer still when you will not be able to start him breathing by this method.

The most important thing to remember in all this is that, in the words of one vet, "no puppy is dead until he begins to smell." Keep at it, keep at it, and keep at it still more. Puppies have been worked on and then thrown aside in despair, and have then managed to start their own breathing going. If you have to abandon working on one pup to help the bitch produce the next one, either give the first pup to an assistant with instructions for continuing, or simply put it aside until the next pup is out and breathing. Then return to the first one and keep working at it.

In the case of a rearwards or "breech" presentation, where the puppy is coming out backwards and is stuck in the canal, again wait for at least five minutes before you attempt to help get him out. There is a danger here of the puppy suffocating if his umbilical cord is pinched, but the danger is less than that of your causing injury through clumsy help. But after five minutes, if the bitch has stopped straining or continues with no progress, take hold of the pup's body and again apply gentle pressure in the direction of the bitch's hind legs. Do not twist or turn the body, but pull straight. You may apply very slightly more pressure in a breech presentation, but very little more. As soon as the head has emerged, give the puppy to the bitch to see if she will take care of it. If not, clear away the sac yourself as before, and proceed to get him breathing.

Whether the puppy has been born normally, or with difficulty, and the umbilical cord has broken, the placental end may still be hanging out of the bitch's vulva. If so, grasp this delicate cord with towel or gauze, and ease the placenta out very gently and discard it. If the cord breaks again as you are pulling, or if none is left protruding, leave it alone—it may come out ahead of the next puppy.

Although most puppies, however born, will get immediate attention from the bitch, there are cases where the bitch absolutely refuses to give them any attention at all. If this happens, proceed as above for difficult delivery, gently tearing off the membranous sac, get the breathing started, and towel the puppy dry and warm. Then, if the umbilical cord is intact, sever it about an inch (for puppies of small breeds) or two inches (for puppies of medium and large breeds) from the abdomen. This can be done with your fingers, thoroughly cleaned, or with blunt scissors— preferably blunt, for the squeezing action of the blunt edges tends to close the umbilical opening. Sterilize the scissors by dipping them into alcohol first. *Never* cut the cord shorter than one inch!

There is no need to tie the umbilicus off—in the normal course of affairs it will dry up in two or three days and fall off of its own accord. In fact, if you do put thread or anything on the stump, the bitch will very likely lick or chew it off, with considerable danger to the puppy, as she does not like anything foreign on her puppy's body. There may be a drop or two of blood when you cut the cord, which is normal. If there is more than this, you may have tie it off to save his life. Simply put a piece of thread around the cord, as near to the cut end as possible, and draw it tight and make a knot. In such a case, keep a close eye on this pup when you return him to the bitch. If she leaves it alone, fine, but if she persists in trying to get the thread off, you'll have to take him from her for a day or two and feed him as an orphan puppy. If this happens, though, be sure that he gets a first feeding from her for the colostral anti-distemper protection.

There are relatively rare cases in which, due to some complete mal-presentation—bad angle of the puppy coming through the vagina—forceps delivery by a veterinarian will be necessary. There is nothing whatever you can do about this, and you shouldn't attempt to help, for putting your fingers or anything else into her vagina is extremely dangerous for her. Simply get the vet over as quickly as possible, giving him full information first so that he can bring with him the necessary forceps. If he cannot come, bundle her up and rush her to his office. If some pups are already born and alive, simply be sure they are huddled together somewhere warm, and then rush her off. If you bundle them up care-fully, you can even take the puppies along, for examination and in case the bitch has to remain at the vet's for the completion of whelping.

It is difficult to estimate the average duration of whelping, because of individual bitches and, of course, individual sizes of litters. Some bitches many deliver eight puppies within two hours, and others may take several hours to get three or four out. Litters of only one puppy have been recorded, as well as fantastically large litters numbering fourteen or sixteen or even more puppies. Observe the average interval between puppies. Then, after several have been born, wait until about twice this time has passed after the last one before you begin to calculate that she is through. When this much time has passed, take one of the delivered pups in your hand to get the feel of it, and then probe her abdomen very gently to see if there are any lumps of this size remaining anywhere below her ribs. If you find none, then whelping is probably completed. If you have accounted for all the placentas, and delivery is complete, then simply let the bitch have her puppies to nurse. It's all over for the moment.

If, however, there is a placenta missing, or you feel a suspiciously puppy-sized lump remaining in her abdomen, and she has not produced either after an hour or two, get veterinary attention. Retention of a puppy or a placenta can cause her very severe damage, and must be taken care of by a professional as soon as possible. This is one of the reasons for keeping an accurate, written account of the number of placentas produced, for a mistaken guess might cost her life.

After either normal or difficult delivery, there remain several minor problems you may have to take care of. One of them is slight difficulty on the part of one or more puppies in finding and using a nipple. In most cases, the bitch will take care of nudging the puppy onto the nipple, but an indifferent bitch—particularly in the cases where you have done the work of cleaning the puppy and starting his breathing—may just ignore the whole affair. In this case, hold the puppy up to a nipple, and if he still doesn't get the idea, open his mouth gently with a finger-tip and put him directly onto the nipple. If for any reason he still doesn't start feeding, then you may have to revert to the orphan-feeding directions given later, but devote some attention to trying to get him to take at least his first meal from the bitch, so that he will get his colostral immunities.

Another, fairly uncommon problem is that in which the bitch has delivered a very large litter of puppies. The bitch has only eight or ten nipples for feeding, and so after each of the puppies has had its first colostral feeding, you will have to work out a system of supervised rotation to make sure that all the pups get the same amount of nourishment from her. This might just take care of itself, but it is more likely not to, for puppies are not at all considerate about such things as getting food into themselves. It is survival of the fittest, and a slightly weaker puppy just may be closed out if you don't enforce a rotation system.

Feeding more than eight puppies will probably put considerable strain on the bitch, and you should prepare some orphan-puppy formula to take some of the load off her and insure that all the pups are as thoroughly fed and nourished as possible. Let them all feed off her for the first time, and then a few hours later, prepare bottles (see Orphan Puppies) for them and try to give each of them a good bottle-feeding. Then let her feed them the next time, and you take over the next feeding. The arrangement will have to be altered in line with the number of the puppies and the amount of milk the bitch is able to provide, and only you and the circumstances can decide exactly how many meals she should provide as against how many you provide. But don't try to set up a system in which you exclusively feed one or more pups and the remainder are left to her. You'll have difficulty telling them apart, and, in any case, the more of the natural bitch's milk all the puppies get, the better.

Don't let all this discussion of difficulties and irregularities frighten you off—it's really not as bad as all that. Remember that perhaps 90% of all puppies are born quite normally, and are taken care of very successfully by their dam, and that nothing at all goes wrong which will require your attention. But the possibilities of difficulties have to be discussed, as they do occur, and just might occur to you.

POST-NATAL CARE OF PUPPIES

As soon as whelping has been completed, and all the puppies have had their first feeding, wait about half an hour and then take the bitch out to let her relieve herself (up to now it won't have bothered her much, even during a long delivery, for the pressures in her abdomen are being relieved by the whelping). While she is out, or at least away from the pups for a few minutes, clean up the whelping box and its area. Remove enough papers from the box to get down to a clean level—to do this neatly, put the pups gently into another box (a small cardboard box will do, provided it's big enough not to pile them one on the other) while you are cleaning. You may not have had enough papers down in the first place, so make sure there are enough now. During this brief separation from her pups, take a moment to sponge the bitch off and then towel her dry. Then let her return to resume care of the puppies.

Newborn puppies look like nothing so much as small blind, wet rats. Most of them have no teeth, although you may be able to see the deciduous or milk teeth under the gums. Their eyes are tightly sealed and will remain so for some days. Although it isn't apparent to you, their ears are closed and they don't hear anything. Thus for over a week, to nearly two weeks, a puppy is a little bundle of nothing, unable to see or hear, and seeking only food, sleep and warmth. At this point puppies hardly even feel much, for their nervous systems aren't well organized yet.

Once the bitch is back to resume her care, you can take care of several items. First, if you are interested, weigh the puppies. For this, a kitchen scale that reads in ounces is excellent—don't try to use a scale that reads only in pounds if you want to keep anything like accurate records of their weight and growth. And when you put a puppy on the scale platform, cover the platform with a layer or two of cloth, such as a folded towel, so he doesn't hit a cold metal surface. Just subtract the weight of the cloth. With some breeds it may be difficult to keep accurate records at first, for there is very little in the way of color or marking differences by which to tell the pups apart. Do not, however, attempt to identify them by tying different-colored ribbons on, or putting tags around their necks. This will make the bitch very unhappy, and she will spend some time chewing or licking the identifying ribbons or tags off, and you won't have gained anything.

With the weighing accomplished, you will be able to spot any runts in the litter that you may not have noticed before in just looking at them. Keep a close eye on any runts, and watch their growth carefully, for you may have to supplement their diet—not only do they start out small, but they tend to get pushed around by the bigger puppies, even at this age, and may not get fully fed at the nipple. If you need to supplement, use the formula you will find in the later "Orphan Puppies" section of this chapter.

This is a good time to check, too, for deformities or birth injuries. The most common deformities you might spot are cleft palate and hare lip. You can feel a cleft palate by putting your little finger (clean!) very gently into the puppy's mouth to see if the roof of the mouth has completely closed over. Hare lip will be visible, as an incomplete closure of the upper lip. Ordinarily, you will notice the results of these before you find them—pups with these deformities very often have trouble suckling successfully, even if carefully put onto and held onto the nipple, and may show milk draining from the nostrils as they suckle. Do not, however, jump to the conclusion that a pup is deformed, particularly in the cleft palate and hare lip area. If you are unfamiliar with these conditions, you may very easily misdiagnose something which is a normal condition of a very young puppy. So, if you suspect deformities, get the advice of an experienced breeder, or of your vet.

This first day is a good time, also, to introduce your immediate family to the bitch and her puppies. Bring in your children, and anyone else in the house who may have occasion to care for the bitch or puppies, and have each of them pick up a puppy (one individual and one puppy at a time) and hold it for a moment, under the watchful eye of both you and the bitch. Stay right there with her and talk to her and reassure her that everything is all right. Don't encourage handling of the pups, just have each individual pick one up and hold it for a moment, and then return it. If the bitch growls or snaps or attempts to attack, restrain her firmly—this is one area in which you can stand for no nonsense, although you shouldn't be harsh. You can help overcome resentment by picking up a pup yourself, then handing it carefully to the child or other family member to hold briefly, thus bypassing the moment she resents most—when a stranger reaches into the litter and takes a puppy.

Don't let this introduction become an invitation to your children or anyone else in the household to make free with the puppies. In particular, lay down the law firmly and unmistakably to children about taking puppies and playing with them. A child can injure a puppy very easily —and the main danger here is not to the pups, but to the children. If a puppy is hurt, or if the bitch thinks one is hurt, she may attack even a small child, and viciously. There are few things stronger in this world than the bitch's instincts to protect her newborn puppies—she will trust you a long way, and if properly introduced, will trust your household, but be careful. Don't let accidents happen, either way.

Aside from necessary introductions and any obvious care, the major rule with newborn puppies is: leave them alone. The less handling they get, the better. The characteristics of a healthy newborn pup are warmth, quiet and sleepiness. Puppies which constantly cry and wander about the whelping box are those to watch for. The normal puppy has an unmistakably healthy appearance, plump and solid, and when picked up feels firm and warm. A thin or limp puppy, with wrinkled or cold skin, which squirms a great deal, is a puppy with troubles. Check such puppies over carefully to be sure they are getting enough natural feeding. If they're not, supplement their diets with orphan formula, and if this does not rapidly solve the problem, get veterinary help.

Two to three days is about the proper age for having dewclaws removed and tails docked, if you are going to have either or both these operations done. At this point the bones involved are extremely soft, and removing dewclaws and docking tails causes little or no pain to a puppy. It is an excellent idea to remove dewclaws to avoid minor troubles later in life—whether or not to dock the puppy's tail is a matter between you and the breed standards in the case of a purebred puppy. In either case, the operation should only be done by a veterinarian. When the puppies are brought back after such an operation, or if it is done at home by your vet, keep an eye on them for a few days. Dewclaws or tails may bleed a little, and the bitch may lick constantly at the wound. This licking may prevent healing, and the pup will have a constant, although invisible (because the bitch keeps licking it away) loss of blood. If she constantly licks at the tails or dewclaws of one or more puppies, the best course is to remove them from her for a day or so, keeping them in a small warm box, and returning them to her only at about four-hour intervals for their nursing.

At about this time, two to three days of age, the umbilical cord normally has dried up and will drop off. If it is retained for a few days longer, though, there is normally nothing to worry about.

Between ten and twenty days of age (the average is the 13th day) the puppies' eyes will begin to open, although they will be unable to focus on anything for several days yet. Keep a watch on the eyes around this period, and if any one puppy has swellings under the eyelids instead of normally opening eyes, consult your vet. At about the age the eyes open, do the first clipping of just the very tips of the puppies' toenails. This can be done with a standard clipper, or with blunt scissors. Take off only the tiny sharp tip of each nail. This accomplishes two things—when the puppies nurse, they often work their front feet against the bitch, and if the toenails are left sharp, they may irritate her abdomen to the point of bleeding and infection. Additionally, as they begin to be aware of their surroundings and play with each other, they can very easily damage each others' eyes with sharp nails. So clip them, and then keep clipping them on a weekly schedule.

Shortly after the eyes open—it may be up to a week later, with the 21st day of life surprisingly often the exact day—the ears open too, and the puppy will begin to hear the noises of the world about him. Within this time (between 18 and 22 days) most puppies will have begun to stand by themselves and begin walking, however unsteadily. Check at this time to be sure the sides of the whelping box are high enough to restrain them, particularly the relatively low fourth side the bitch uses to come and go.

At about fifteen to eighteen days, the normal puppy will have doubled his birth weight. This of course varies with breeds and with individuals, but any really sharply underweight situation at this point should be a warning that something is probably wrong with the pup in question. He may not have been getting enough nourishment, or there may be some physical disorder. If the entire litter has failed to gain weight properly, you should very definitely consider the possibility that they haven't been able to get enough nourishment from the bitch.

At this age or shortly after, you may see your bitch vomit up some of her food for the puppies to eat. This is an action which appears disgusting to some people, but it is simply the normal path of nature—the bitch is again responding to instinct, and is providing the partially digested food in her vomitus as the puppies' first somewhat solid food. By all means, don't interfere with this. It is, if nothing else, a sign to you that the puppies are ready to begin pan-feeding along with their nursing.

The puppies' first solid food should be easy to digest and highly nourishing. An excellent formula is: evaporated milk mixed with Pablum and one or two raw egg yolks to make a gruel of porridge-like consistency. Put this formula in a shallow clean pan, make sure it is at about body temperature, and then introduce the puppies to it one at a time. To do this, take a puppy and hold him to the pan, dip your finger into the gruel and wet his nose and mouth with it. He will lick at it, and may show immediate interest in the pan. If not, just touch his nose to the surface of the gruel for a moment (don't shove his nose or face into it) and let him get the idea that the stuff is, surprisingly, good. Then leave him at the edge of the pan and proceed to indoctrinate another pup.

If one is a little laggard, he will very quickly get the idea from his litter-mates, for puppies are the most imitative and greedy creatures you are ever likely to come across. If only one of the litter gets the clue, the others will follow in short order and you will have more difficulty holding them back than getting them to eat. The first feedings, while they are learning to lap efficiently, are going to be messy affairs, what with splashing and stomping about in the gruel, and more of the food may end up on them than in them, but no harm comes of it, and it is sometimes hilarious to watch.

Give them this formula once on the first day you try it, and let them get the rest of their nourishment from the bitch. The second day, let them have at it twice, with nursing in between. Depending on how much milk the bitch still has available for them, and how willing she is to continue nursing them, adjust the amount and number of gruel feedings accordingly for the next several days. You will be able to tell by observation and experimentation how much she is still able to provide for them—if they all suckle at one nursing and are all full and content afterwards, she is doing well, but if they still are unhappy and seeking food when the breasts are empty, then they need a heavier emphasis on the gruel.

As the feedings progress, you can mix small amounts of cottage cheese into the formula, more egg yolks, and finally, finely chopped cooked hamburger. This diet will prepare them for full weaning, which may be anywhere from four to six weeks of age.

POST-NATAL CARE OF THE DAM

Once she has been delivered of her puppies, the female has been promoted from bitch to dam, which terminologically is not much of an improvement. When she is back from her post-whelping breath of fresh air, she will very likely be hungry, and you can feed her a bowl of good heavy meat broth, or warm milk, or even her standard solid food if she will take it. Put the bowl right into the whelping box with her so she can eat, or drink, without having to leave her pups. Have a bowl of fresh water available to her, just outside the whelping box, at all times.

You can go on feeding her in the whelping box if she seems to appreciate it and want it that way. Otherwise, put the food down right next to the box for her. She may be glad enough after a few days to get away from the puppies while she eats. However full of mother love she may be, nursing puppies are a strain on her. Pile into her as much food as she will eat, with emphasis on lean meat, milk, and calcium supplementation. Calcium gluconate or calcium lactate are about the best commercial supplements, in the recommended dosages—otherwise give dried powdered milk mixed with her food, and include milk as an available drink for her.

Still, during the early weeks of nursing, keep a close watch for eclampsia. The highest incidence is in the first two weeks after whelping, when milk demands are the greatest. The beginning symptoms are rapid breathing, anxiety, restlessness, occasional to frequent whining and whimpering. These symptoms progress to staggering, an unsteady gait, stiffness of the legs. Almost immediately after these latter symptoms, the convulsive stage begins, so if you think you see it coming on, get a vet in a great hurry.

During her nursing, particularly if she has a small litter, one or more of her nipples may be relatively ignored, and she may have a temporary problem with caked breasts. This natural condition is also likely to occur as the puppies in later days become less dependent on their dam for milk, and at weaning time. It is simply the natural beginning of the shutting off of the milk supply—the breast is somewhat swollen and slightly hardened. Veterinary opinion is fairly evenly divided on whether you should bother to massage such caked breasts. During nursing, if one or two nipples cake, and there is plenty of milk supply left over at the others for a small litter, the best course probably is not to bother. If all the breasts are needed—sometimes, when even a full-sized litter nurses only lightly on a heavily producing dam, all or nearly all of her breasts may start to cake—then massage them gently and milk them a little to relieve some of the pressure, and they will return to normal function. At weaning, when breasts cake, and even if they become slightly inflamed, the best course is to leave everything alone. The swelling and inflammation will go down in a day or two in the normal course of affairs.

Infected breasts, or mastitis, may involve one or more of the breasts. These will be readily apparent and you are not likely to confuse this condition with simple caking—in mastitis the breasts are definitely swollen, inflamed, and are usually acutely painful to the bitch. If you see or suspect such an infection, handle the breast gently. If it causes her little or no pain or discomfort, it is probably caking. But if your handling gives her acute pain, or if there is a secretion coming from the nipple that isn't obviously milk, then get veterinary help at once. Not only can this condition be dangerous to her but if a puppy is allowed to suckle at an infected breast, he may very easily die.

During the first couple of weeks of nursing, it is a good idea to keep some sort of light on in the whelping room for the bitch at night. It will help her get around at night, and help her keep an eye on the puppies and keep from stepping on them—and it won't bother the puppies at all, because of their still-closed eyes. A good arrangement is a gooseneck lamp turned to the ceiling with a dim bulb in it, to provide some reflected light without glare. Such an arrangement is by no means vitally necessary, but it is one of the small things you can do to make life easier for her.

In early nursing, in the course of cleaning her puppies and licking them and nuzzling them to aid their urination and defecation, you may notice that the dam, in the process, licks up the urine and feces. This is an entirely natural process, and you should make no attempt to interfere with it. It is in fact quite likely that she is conserving minerals, including calcium, by this ingestion of the puppies' eliminations, as well as obeying natural instinctive commands to keep the puppies and their area clean. It will not lead to coprophagy after she is finished whelping, as the bitch loses all interest in such activity as soon as the pups are independent of her.

In fact, her instinctive drives to clean and lick the puppies can be put to good use if for any reason she has not resumed eating well once whelping is completed. Take raw or slightly cooked hamburger and put little balls of the meat on the puppies—she will lick these off and in the process will be fooled into getting some good nourishment into her.

As nursing goes on, continue giving the bitch as much to eat as she wants, as she needs all the nourishment she can get until the puppies are weaned. Then cut the food down to her normal level, even if she seems unhappy about it, and encourage her to take more exercise than she has been getting, until she returns to normal feeding and activity. It is easy for a bitch to get into the habit of overeating and lazing about—

the owners of many pet bitches sympathetically encourage the "little mother" and as a result the bitch becomes obese and shortens her life. Whelping and nursing, noble though they may be, aren't all that grand, and once they are over she should return to her normal life, and her normal weight, feeding and exercise.

ORPHAN PUPPIES

Greater love hath no owner than to raise a litter of orphan puppies— it is a full-time job, requiring attention, patience and devotion, but if you can do it successfully, there are few more rewarding tasks. An orphan litter may be only figuratively so, for although they are ordinarily orphaned by the death of the bitch in whelping or early in nursing, there are cases in which the bitch simply refuses to mother her puppies or in fact have anything at all to do with them beyond getting them born. Whatever the cause, prepare yourself for at least two weeks of unremitting work, for you are going to supply all of the mothering and care, artificially, that a dam would give the pups normally.

If it is at all possible to put the pups onto a foster mother, by all means do so. There might be a bitch somewhere in the neighborhood who has had a very tiny litter, or most of whose pups have been born dead. Breed makes no difference—the purest bred puppies can nurse quite happily on a totally mongrel dam and grow up healthy and strapping. If you are able to find a foster mother, you can persuade her that the pups belong to her if you smear them with a little of her milk, or vaginal secretions, so that they smell right to her. Introduce them cautiously, but once she has accepted them, she will nurse and care for them as if they were her own.

You are not likely to find a foster mother, however, and so the job of taking care of the pups will devolve onto you. The first order of business, assuming that the pups have been initially cleaned up and are warm and breathing, is food. There are commercial bitch-milk formulas available almost everywhere, and these are the best possible items to use for the feeding of the pups during the first two weeks. Goat's milk is also a good substitute to use, but ordinary cow's milk does not serve well unless it is used as the basis for the formula below. You can make quite a good substitute by mixing one and a half pints of whole milk with one half pint of heavy cream for the basic formula, adding one egg yolk, one-quarter ounce of white bone meal and a quarter teaspoonful of an all-purpose liquid vitamin supplement. Do *not* add sugar of milk or any other sweetening or lactose product, as natural bitch's milk is low in this factor, and an overdose of lactose or other sugars in formula is one of the causes of diarrhea in puppies.

Mix the whole formula together thoroughly, and be sure that the egg yolk is thoroughly mixed in, for there is a tendency for the egg to clog a nipple if it isn't thoroughly mixed in. Refrigerate the formula, warming as much as you need for each use. The proper temperature of nursing milk is, obviously, body temperature, and in the dog this means about 102°. You may be able to estimate it with your fingertip, but it is a good idea, the first time or two, until you learn what the proper temperature feels like, to check the formula's temperature with an ordinary clinical thermometer, thoroughly washed before you stick it into the milk. The formula's temperature can vary a few degrees to one side or the other of 102°, but if it is more than a few degrees higher or lower it will inhibit the suckling of the pups, and rob them of nourishment. As you will begin to see, raising orphan puppies is no casual job.

Depending on the size of the puppies, you may be able to use a small-size baby nipple and feeding bottle, or you may have to get a doll's bottle, with its smaller nipple, at a dime store. In either case, take a sterile pin (hold the pin in a match flame for a few seconds) and be sure that there is a clear milk hole and an airway in each nipple. Then sterilize the nipples in boiling water, let them cool and dry. Put a nipple on a bottle of formula, pick up a puppy, put the nipple in his mouth, and let him work at it. If he seems to be working without getting anything, recheck the milk hole and the airway of the nipple, and if both are clear, return to the nursing.

The sign that a puppy has had enough is when he stops suckling, or when bubbles of milk appear at his mouth, indicating that he simply can't pack any more in. It is a good idea to have several bottles and nipples on hand, so that you can take care of a number of pups in quick order. In fact, as you get better at it, you will find that you can hold a bottle in each hand, with the attached puppy lying on the floor, and thus shorten each total feeding by half. After the feeding is finished, clean both the bottles and the nipples well, and keep the nipples in a pan or glass of clean water to keep them clean until time for the next feeding.

With very tiny pups who are too small even for a doll nipple, you may have to feed via eye-dropper for the first few days until they get a little bigger. This can be a ticklish business and is, of course, considerably time-consuming. It requires constant dipping into the formula supply and then—and this is important—drop-by-drop feeding. It isn't sufficient to put the end of the dropper into the puppy's mouth and then squeeze—this way he is very likely to get more into his mouth than he can control, and will aspirate some of it into his lungs. Result: pneumonia. Therefore, if you use the dropper method, drop only one drop at a time into his mouth. It takes a while this way, but don't hurry it. It could be fatal.

After the feeding, each puppy must be burped, just like a human baby, to eliminate the air he has swallowed with the milk. Take the puppy in your hand and jiggle him gently, patting him very lightly on the back to get him to burp. About one good healthy burp from each puppy will take care of it.

Each puppy should be fed as quickly as possible after birth, and with a bellyful can then wait quite happily for four or five hours. But from then on they must be fed at four-hour intervals, night and day, for the first week. It is impossible to give an exact formula for the amount of milk they will take at each feeding, but a rough estimate is one cubic centimeter of milk for each ounce of puppy. Thus a 10-ounce puppy would take about 10 c.c.'s per feeding, or about one-third of an ounce (an ounce equals 30 c.c.). For a table of conversions of ounces, c.c.'s and other measures, see Chapter V, but for the moment a handy figure is one cup equaling about 120 c.c. of liquid, so you should have at least a cup of formula ready to feed eight 15-ounce puppies. This is of course approximate, but will give you some guide as to how much formula you should prepare, and how much you will need over the course of nursing.

Next, you will have to take care of their elimination for them. This is something the dam does with her licking and tumbling the puppies. A new-born pup is normally unable to urinate or defecate by himself, and requires the help you will have to give. Therefore, after each feeding, take a small wad of soft cotton, moistened with warm water, and rub each puppy gently along the abdomen and around the anus. This will stimulate him to void, and then he must be cleaned up. Do the massaging away from the puppies' sleeping quarters, so you won't have to clean that up so much. After the massaging and elimination, be particularly careful to wipe all the urine off the abdomen and hindquarters, for if it remains it is likely to result in urine burns of the skin. This sort of treatment you may have to keep up for four or five days, until you see that they have learned to eliminate by themselves. But even after that, continue cleaning them regularly, particularly of urine, for the danger of urine burns continues until they are able to stand.

Next, there is the problem of warmth, and possibly separation. The litter box can be any sort of small box (considerably smaller than the whelping box) and should be floored with many layers of newspaper for easy cleaning. It *must* be kept at a temperature of between 85° and 90° during the first week of their lives. This can be accomplished by an electric heater placed at the proper distance, or by a strong electric light (not a spot-light or anything of that type) shaded or otherwise guarded so that there is no danger of their touching it—the light itself won't bother them. But check the temperature of the box with a good-quality household thermometer. Don't guess, for the right temperature is vital to them.

Some authorities advise separation of orphan puppies, because of the pups' tendency to suckle on anything and everything near them—if they suckle on each others' genitals it could be quite harmful. This, however, may be predicated on insufficient nourishment—if orphan pups are constantly hungry, then they will definitely try to suckle on anything at hand, but if they are well and frequently fed, this shouldn't cause you very much trouble. In any case, separation robs the pups of their ability to warm each other by huddling together, and of whatever instinctive deep gratification they are able to get from this. If, however, you do observe that they are trying to suckle on each other continually, and for some reason increasing the feeding doesn't solve it, you can separate them by making small partitions for the box, of corrugated cardboard or thin plywood—but use this only when you can't be around to keep an eye on them. Puppies should be together.

Diarrhea may hit any or all of the pups during their first days. The most common cause of diarrhea is overfeeding, and it should be checked as soon as possible by cutting down on the food. If the entire litter seems loose, then cut down on all of them. But if only one is, or two, then identify them somehow and cut down only them. Cut down feeding by about one quarter until the stool becomes firm. If a day or two of this reduced feeding doesn't solve the diarrhea problem, get the affected pup or pups to a vet for his attention—never, never try to give a tiny puppy anything yourself for diarrhea.

After the puppies are one week old, you can reduce the temperature of the litter box to 80° and begin widening the interval of their feeding. Cut down gradually until at the end of two weeks you are feeding them every six hours, on the same formula. By this time they will have learned to urinate and defecate by themselves—but some are slower or faster learners, so keep track of which is which, and treat each individually.

At two weeks of age, you should begin thinking about distemper protection. As orphan pups may not have been able to acquire any initial protection in the colostrum of the dam's milk, they may be almost totally open to infection. You should restrict visitors to orphan puppies to the absolute minimum, and try to make it a rule that dog-owning friends stay strictly away, as distemper can be carried by humans. Also, of course, never allow any dog to come near these newborns. Because they have no colostral protection, pups of two weeks of age can sometimes be given vaccine distemper shots, or at the very least they should then be started on puppy serum to give them protection until they are older and have vaccine shots. Consult your veterinarian on the proper procedures in this case, and get them some kind of distemper protection as early as possible.

At about the end of the second week, you should begin making serious attempts to wean orphan pups. It may be rushing them a little, but it won't harm them, and it will take a great load off of you. Start them on gruel as a substitute for bottle-feeding, and promote them to finely ground cooked hamburger within a few days.

WEANING

Weaning of puppies, in most cases, can be accomplished at anywhere from four to six weeks. Once they are on pan feeding and have been getting increasingly thicker gruel, simply begin offering them whatever you are going to want to feed them as older puppies. Canned food, dry food or meat (finely chopped and cooked) is placed in front of them in their community dish, and soon they will heave to and eat lustily. At this point the puppies will be growing like rockets, so give them as much to eat as they can get into them. Let them all eat from one community bowl, for competition sparks their appetites. Watch out, though, for any runt or weakling who is being consistently shoved aside and isn't getting his fair share of the available food. It's no good trying to interfere in the community feeding to establish the runt's rights—you'll have to take him aside for his own supplemental feedings, or perhaps separate him completely from the rest and keep him on his own feeding schedule.

How much additional liquid these newly weaned puppies will need depends on what you are feeding them as their weaning food. If it is canned dog food or meat, they will be getting a great deal of liquid in the foods, both of which are about 70% water. If they are beginning on moistened dry foods, it is a good idea to have a pan of milk available to them at feeding time, and a pan of water in their area for drinking whenever they feel the need of it.

General "shotgun" vitamin and mineral supplementation of the puppies' food is very definitely recommended, no matter what you are giving them. Add a canine dietary supplement in the recommended quantities to what they're feeding on, or mix in a few drops of liquid vitamin supplement. Be particularly sure that the explosively growing pups of the larger breeds have plenty of calcium and Vitamin D, to avoid rickets.

At about the age of three weeks is the time to think of anti-distemper puppy serum, to hold even colostrally protected pups until they can have their vaccine shots—unless, of course, you have nomographically determined a proper early age for early vaccine shots. And look into the possibility of worming them at this age—they might just not need it, but the chances are excellent that they do. Do not, however, attempt to worm puppies with commercial worm preparations, no matter what the label says—this is a situation in which you should only use a specifically prescribed worm preparation from the vet, and only if the presence of worms has been confirmed.

When the puppies are about four weeks old, provided the weather is good, take them outdoors to play in the sun. Sunlight and fresh air will do them a world of good. Also, at about this time, you can begin allowing relatively unrestricted visits from the outside world, for the puppies are sturdy enough by now that a moderate amount of handling and playing won't bother them a bit, and in fact will help them form social relationships with the human race. One caution, though—be sure that children understand that puppies aren't toys, to be banged about or played with to the point of exhaustion on the part of the puppies. Even adults sometimes need a little chiding on this point.

INFORMATION FOR NEW OWNERS

Before long, your puppies will be going to new owners, and you should have a medical record of the pups, in writing, to give to each new owner as he takes a pup. Include in this record the dates of any wormings that may have been done, the drugs used (for the information of a new veterinarian who may take over their care), and the results of worming. Also include, very precisely, any shots the pups have had, with exact dates that puppy distemper serum was given, so that this protection can be completed. If the pups are placed after their vaccine distemper shots, include this information, along with the type of protection they received, again so that another vet taking over their care will know exactly what has been done.

Further records are not necessary, but new owners will appreciate as complete a pedigree as you can give them, along with such minor details as the birth weight of the puppy, and anything else you happen to think of, including, if you have your scale handy, the pup's exact weight on the day of transfer of ownership, so that the new owner can keep accurate track of weight if he or she wants to.

It is a good idea, too, to give complete *written* instructions on feeding, which the new owners can follow for at least the first few days, your own phone number in case of sudden emergencies, and the name and phone number of your veterinarian or a recommended vet in the area where the new pup will live. You may not remember how confused you were when you got your first puppy, but you can help a new owner considerably if you include, with the pup, written instructions and data.

MENTAL DEVELOPMENT OF PUPPIES

In recent years, some fascinating and basic experimental work has been done with puppies at the Hamilton Station of the Jackson Memorial Laboratory, on Mount Desert Island, Maine. Behavior students there have raised dozens of litters of puppies under widely varying and carefully controlled circumstances, have worked with learning patterns and training, and have made some significant discoveries about very precise periods in the lives of all puppies, regardless of breed.

The first period is from birth to 21 days. During this time a puppy cannot learn anything—for most of this time his eyes are still closed, and for all or nearly all of the time his ears do not work, nor does his nose. The puppy is a relatively mindless creature, needing only warmth and food. So with your own litter, don't worry much about anything beyond their physical well-being, which of course you should concern yourself about considerably.

The second period begins exactly on the 21st day of life, with a precision, from dog to dog, that at first astonished the experimenters and finally simply came to be accepted as almost unvarying fact. On that 21st day, all the pup's senses begin to work, and his nervous system seems to hook up into a working unit, all of a sudden. The week following this, until the 28th day, is probably the most vital in the mental and psychological development of the puppy—he is first aware that there is a world outside himself, that there are other individuals in it. He needs all the security he can get during this week so that he learns that the world is an okay place to be. This is one of the reasons weaning is best put off until after the fourth week. If the puppies have their dam, they should not be separated from her any more than is absolutely necessary during this period, nor should they be separated from their litter-mates, for in this one week the puppy gets his first ideas as to what and who he is, learns the security of his mother, and learns that he is a dog, forming social relationships with other dogs (his litter-mates). If it is an orphan litter, you should give the pups as much attention, care and affection as you can during this week, to give them a life-long sense of security. To the inexperienced, it may seem impossible that what happens in this one week can be so vitally important, but this recent and precise research fits in exactly with the informal experience of many professional breeders—so abide by it if you are raising a litter.

After the 28th day the next period begins, that of beginning exploration of the world outside the litter and beyond the dam. The pups can be weaned now without causing permanent psychological damage. During this period, the puppies began to establish their real social relationships with their litter-mates, and begin play-fighting to establish dominance orders within the litter. A puppy in this period can learn very simple things—to recognize his owner's voice, toys and the most basic of commands—if they are taught with kindness and without punishment. The patterns of behavior he begins to learn now are the basis for all his future learning, and if he learns right, and that people are good, and that there is nothing to fear in the world, he has every chance of turning out to be a magnificent dog. But it must be remembered, and remembered well, that because this *is* such an intensely susceptible and impressionable time, the puppy must not be subject to harsh disciplines and restraints. He can be taught simple behavior by encouragement only, and what he learns during this period will stick deeper in his mind than anything he learns later in life.

During this period, each puppy of the litter should be played with separately for a little time each day. This teaches the puppy the dignity of being an individual, and permanently imprints on his mind the relationship between him and humans. A puppy left alone with his litter during this period will become just a dog among other dogs, and all later efforts may do little to change him. One of the experiments done at Hamilton Station was the raising of a litter of Beagle puppies in a fenced-off acre field, without any contact with humans, until the age of sixteen weeks. When they were taken out of the field, it was found that the puppies were totally wild, that they would not respond to training or humans, that they did not identify people as friends but as enemies to be feared. Keep this experiment in mind, and never just leave a growing litter down in the cellar to shift for themselves except for feeding time. This is when they can and should learn about people.

The fourth period begins with the 49th day, at the end of seven weeks. During this period true learning begins, and a puppy can be taught such simple commands as Sit, Come, Heel and Fetch, again gently and with understanding. There should still be no restraints or punishments for commands disobeyed or misobeyed; the puppy should simply be shown that there are things to learn, and that he can learn them, and that learning brings praise and is fun.

Puppies who have remained with their litters will have developed normal socialization with other dogs by this time, and if they have been played with by humans, they will also have developed social relationships with humans in general. Now, however, begins the greater awareness of humans as individuals, and the puppy during this period begins to form the deepest attachment for individuals. As a result, this is an excellent time for a puppy to go to a new owner. But be a bit careful if you have any concern for the future of puppies you sell or give away at this age. If you have been good to them up to this time, they will have a good attitude towards humans, but they can still be ruined by careless treatment at this age. It is all well and good for a young puppy to go to a new owner at a time like this when he can form the strongest attachments, but this assumes intelligent and understanding new owners. If they fully understand how impressionable he still is, and how important the first few weeks in his new home will be, then seven to eight weeks is the best time they can get him. But if they think a puppy is something to be put on a chain or shut up in the cellar, then all of his early learning with them will be the wrong kind, all of your careful preparation will have gone to waste, and he will develop into just another hound, worthless to anybody.

Therefore, place puppies in homes you know or believe to be good at seven to eight weeks, if possible. For more doubtful placings, hold onto the puppies until they are about three months old—they will thus lose a little of their ability to form very strong affectionate bonds in the new home (although there will still be plenty left), but they will also lose much of their susceptibility to ruination through bad handling. For a home where they will have indifferent handling, it is far better that they come in at this age—in the end they will turn out to be better dogs, and their owners will be happier with them.

For any puppy or puppies you plan to keep for yourself, or for later placement, treat the seventh through the twelfth weeks as periods of further learning, in which the puppy establishes more and more his own individuality. He can learn even more during this period, as indicated earlier. Save any restrictions or punishments for later.

The final period begins with the fourth month of life, after about the 84th day. Here the puppy begins to cut loose finally from the litter and from the figurative apron strings. He will venture farther out into the world, and try new things just to see how everything goes. He may become deliberately provocative, and here restrictions and mild punishments can begin, for it is important at this time that the puppy learn that there are definite rules in the world, and that he has to abide by them. Still, however, keep the punishments mild, and always be consistent and understanding about the way you handle him.

If you follow these precepts, and try to be sure that any early-placed puppies are in homes where these precepts will be followed, it is very likely that the puppies will turn into dogs whose natures and behavior and abilities far exceed anything you might have thought possible. Dogs are not "just dogs" and puppies are not "just puppies," things of little or no sense and sensibility. Once that 21st day has passed, they are marvelously responsive and receptive organisms, and they will become what you make them, and only what you make them. It's well worth the trouble to make them right.

CHAPTER VIII

THE OLDER DOG

Fʀᴏᴍ the age of six years onwards, most dogs can be considered as moving into the classification of "old." This age does not by any means indicate that the dog is infirm, or will be for several years to come. In American and foreign police departments which have dog squads, it is not unusual to find a dog eight, nine or even ten years old still putting in a full day of strenuous work on the beat with his handler. Guide dogs and sheepherding dogs often work to this age, and past it. Breeds and individuals vary widely in their reaction to age—even as there are vigorous and active humans in their eighties, and others who are elderly and fading by the age of sixty. The range is even wider in dogs, some of whom are genuinely old and feeble by the age of eight or nine, with others still playful and puppyish at twelve or thirteen.

The major implications of aging in the dog are strikingly similar to those in the human. Physically, there is a slow and inevitable loss of tone throughout the entire body—the muscles become weaker, the organs no longer function at peak efficiency, the body is less adaptable to change and stress, its resistance to disease, infection and injury slowly drops as age increases. There is often graying at the muzzle as a sign of age in many dogs, although dogs do not, fortunately, become bald as humans do.

Mentally, the old dog becomes more and more a creature of habit, depending on long-established patterns of behavior, familiar places and people, familiar foods. Even a very peaceable and accommodating dog may become irritable towards strangers, although the really old dog usually seems to realize his age-induced ineffectiveness and restricts himself to grumbling and complaining.

Old age, however, is no bar to pleasurable enjoyment of life for a dog, barring specific infirmities, up to the day his body simply gives up and stops running of its own accord. He will simply enjoy life at a slower pace, and if he is well cared for, may never feel any more pains of aging than the inevitably increasing stiffness and lack of energy that are age itself. To compensate for his physical deterioration, the old dog has the absolute security of his household and your increasing love and attention as you see him growing older—these mean a great deal to him.

In this light, if you get a new puppy as a hedge against the day the old dog dies, be very careful about the distribution of your affection. True, a new puppy needs love and care, but it is vitally important to the older dog that none be taken away from him. Much as you may realize this, it is easy to think that, oh well, the old boy is a member of the family after all, and he really doesn't need so much fuss made over him. He does, for after having enjoyed your exclusive attention and affection for so many years, he may bitterly resent the intrusion of a new puppy, and he may go into a mental decline which can actually result in his earlier death. So don't disturb his feeding, sleeping or exercise habits because of the pup, and above all, never let him think that he is any the less loved because of the new acquisition.

FEEDING

The major factor to remember in feeding is that the older dog will become increasingly disturbed by sudden or radical changes in his feeding and diet. Even as slight a change as a new feeding bowl may upset him to the point where he will refuse food for days—someone other than his master preparing and serving the food may also throw him off. And of course, any sudden changes in the food itself will disturb him.

If your dog has been getting an adequate diet for all his life, there will ordinarily be no reason to change it as he grows older. He will probably eat less, but this involves no change. The only reasons for specific dietary changes are obvious signs of infirmities, or drastic lessening of good bodily appearance—dry and shaggy coat, severe loss of weight. All older dogs begin to lose the sheen and smoothness of the coat, and may become thinner and more bony, but marked changes should not be written off as simply the effects of old age, but should be regarded as possible signs of problems. In such cases there may be specific internal degenerations or illnesses which require change or supplementation of the diet, and only your veterinarian can prescribe these for him to suit the individual case. If you do have to change the diet, or introduce new supplements, do it very slowly and gradually so he will adapt himself without upset.

Older dogs are usually considered poor risks by the operators of boarding kennels. The change of circumstances may upset the older dog so much that he will literally grieve himself to death, and the change of food will also upset him to the point where he may simply refuse to eat while in the kennel. Therefore, if it is absolutely essential that he be left in a kennel, make a particular effort in this case to supply his regular food to the kennel, and make arrangements that he be fed only that. Of course, if the old dog has been going to one kennel regularly during his life, he will accept it as a normal part of living, and will probably think nothing at all of going during your annual vacation or whenever.

Constipation can be a problem of the old dog, and if this occurs, may be solved by changing his feeding schedule from once a day to two or even three smaller meals during the day. His digestive system is no longer able to handle the full load once a day as it used to, but will be able to handle the same daily amount if given in smaller meals. This recommendation does not violate the above advice about not changing his routines, for if it is done gradually he will come to accept it, and it is more important that the problem of constipation be solved.

If he has any tendency at all to become overweight, very definitely cut down his food to the point where he is simply maintaining himself at a good normal weight, not thin but without excess fat. Extra fat in the older body is one of the surest roads to early death. Here again, make the adjustment gradually—don't just suddenly cut his food down to whatever level you think proper. It is no cruelty to even the oldest and most pampered dog to cut down his food to keep his weight in line for optimum health and longevity—it is in fact a kindness, for not only will he live longer, but he will feel better and be able to move around more easily on his weaker muscles with all that fat off him. If he has become accustomed during his life to tid-bits and snacks, there is no reason to stop them, unless they are contributing to an overweight problem.

You should have an abundant supply of fresh water always available—his consumption will very likely go up as his age increases. One of the most chronic infirmities of age is diminished kidney function, which requires a greater intake of fluid. To a certain point this is considered normal, but beyond this, drastically increased water intake and urination may indicate chronic nephritis, discussed later in this chapter.

EXERCISE AND REST

Although he will have slowed down considerably, there is no reason to treat the older dog like an invalid. A certain amount of exercise is highly beneficial, for it will help maintain his muscle tone, stir his lagging appetite and help keep his excretory functions in order. On the other hand, don't urge him to excessive running or prolonged work. If he is very nearly prostrated after some activity, then it is dangerous for him and should not be continued at that intensity. Dogs in their infinite variety respond differently, some wanting nothing more than to loaf around as age advances on them. Some others, particularly those who have led active lives in, say, hunting with their masters, will be as eager as ever to go out and spend a day in the woods. With some such older dogs it seems almost a matter of pride to do as well as when they were younger, but in general they should be gently restrained, or allowed to work a little and believe they're doing as well as ever.

Be a little more careful about letting him take long walks in the cold and snow, and in the rain, and about letting him stay too long in the direct sun or in any heat. His bodily temperature regulating mechanisms have begun to lose their efficiency, too, and a snowy romp that would only have exhilirated him a few years ago may give him a severe chill now. Dry him off thoroughly when he comes in, and persuade him to sit quietly and rest awhile if he comes in from a walk in hot weather.

He will rest and sleep noticeably more as he gets older, and he may get grumpier about being disturbed by noises and people, but humor him. You'll get that way a little yourself before long.

GROOMING

It is more important now than ever that he be groomed regularly. The skin has lost some of its resiliency, and older dogs may have considerably lowered resistance to skin infections and parasites. An infestation of the major parasites that would only have caused minor annoyance and scratching in younger days may now cause severe reaction and inflammations. There is no need to bathe him less often or more often (except to control parasites) than when he was younger. Be only a little more careful about drying him after a bath, so that he doesn't get a chill.

The toenails can cause trouble, because now that he gets less exercise, they will tend to grow longer and perhaps require more frequent clipping. By this time, though, he will be a hardened veteran of such procedures, and may in fact welcome the extra attention that nail clipping brings him.

TEETH

Although dogs of all ages are relatively immune to cavities, the teeth do wear away through years of hard use, and almost all old dogs will begin to have tooth troubles. The biting surfaces of the teeth wear down, and if your dog has been chewing on bones, rocks or other hard items during his youth, they will be well worn. It is unusual for the wear to penetrate to the pulp of the tooth, and so there is rarely complication.

Calculus is very often a problem, particularly on the canine teeth and the premolars just behind them. Unless this is removed with some regularity, it will pentetrate down to irritate the gums, and will result in chronic inflammation and possible infections.

Broken and loose teeth should of course be extracted by a vet, and it is a good idea to check the dog's mouth occasionally for such conditions. If several teeth have to come out, or have come out by themselves (this is not uncommon with short-nosed breeds, who may lose some of the front teeth spontaneously), it doesn't mean that the dog has to go on a liquid diet. He should, however, be restricted to relatively soft foods, which means that biscuits and unsoaked kibbles are out as dietary items. Otherwise, even a totally toothless old dog can live quite a happy and satisfactory life—he doesn't need his teeth for fighting any more, and if he doesn't have to chew his food, all will be well.

INFIRMITIES

Chronic or acute otitis is a common problem of older dogs—such infections of the ear are more common in those dogs with hanging ear flaps which tend to retain dirt and moisture within the ear itself. You may notice it first if your dog begins to stand or sit with his head leaning even slightly to one side—not cocked intelligently in the well-known "listening at attention" pose, but simply holding the head consistently at an angle. There is also evidence of pain and disturbance in one or both ears, as evidenced by continual rubbing or scratching which terminates in self-inflicted pain as the claws hit sensitive areas. On close inspection you may find that either ear is reddened towards the canal, and that there is grayish to yellowish material exuding from the canal in small quantities. If you find this sort of symptom, don't attempt to treat it yourself or clean out the canal, but take the dog to a vet—amateur attempts at treating otitis almost always cause more trouble than relief, both directly and due to the fact that they put off competent professional treatment.

With or without a history of otitis, hearing difficulties and final deafness or near-deafness often afflict dogs, particularly those over the age of ten. If a venterinarian's examination shows no treatable infection of the ear, or blockages by wax or other physical factors, there is, of course, nothing you can do about deafness and impaired hearing from the treatment angle. You can make life easier for your dog, however, if you keep his diminished hearing in mind and try not to startle him by coming up behind him. If you suddenly touch him from the rear when he hasn't heard you approach, he may be really upset about it—it sometimes seems that the older dog is ashamed of not having heard you come. Additionally, remember that a deaf or near-deaf dog can no longer hear such sounds as may have been warning him of danger in the past— particularly automobiles, if he is accustomed to playing or lying in driveways, or crossing roads or streets.

Remember that a dog lives in an entirely different world. He has no way of communicating or receiving concepts, and if he is going deaf he cannot realize that it is something which is happening to him—he will believe simply that the sounds of the world are getting quieter. It is important, for dogs depend on their hearing a great deal, and when it goes they may still be depending subconsciously on it. If cars have always made a noise, there is no reason that they shouldn't still, as far as he is concerned. If you have ever swum in the surf, you will know how you develop an almost unconscious dependence on hearing big waves coming—if this were suddenly lost to you, you might be looking in another direction and really get swamped. Much the same can happen to a dog with automobiles or other dangers which ordinarily advertise themselves to him by noise.

Blindness or partial loss of sight is the most debilitating impairment of all, and is not at all uncommon in older dogs. If yours is a house pet, he may be almost completely blind before you notice it, for after a lifetime of getting used to the placement of the furniture, and his standard routes on the street when walking with you on leash, he may be able to get around quite well through habit plus hearing and smell. You may, in fact, first notice failing sight if you rearrange the furniture, and he bumps into a chair or other object placed in an unfamiliar spot. There is little constructive advice that can be given in such cases, other than what your own common sense would tell you, such as being careful about rearrangements of furniture until he has a chance to get used to the new situation, and increased caution about heights.

You may notice tiny growths from the edge of the eyelids, which cause irritation and eye-watering if in contact with the eye itself. If such growths do cause local irritations, your vet can usually take them off quite easily, and they should be removed.

Chronic nephritis, or kidney malfunction, has been estimated as occurring in as high as 80% of all dogs over eight years of age. There are two versions of nephritis. The one called non-uremic involves little more than allowing the dog access to as much water as he wants to drink, elimination of too salty and spicy foods from his diet, and more attention to his status as an old dog: avoidance of major surgery and anaesthesia, less exposure to extremes of cold and heat, prevention of constipation. Non-uremic nephritis is characterized by high thirst and the resultant larger amounts of urine, which tends to be pale yellow or even clear and watery.

The uremic version of nephritis is the dangerous one, and the symptoms of this type are apathy, depression, gradual loss of weight to the point of emaciation, arching of the back, stiff gait, and sometimes vomiting and a breath that smells either simply bad, or vaguely like ammonia. Such symptoms should lead you to an immediate visit to your vet, who can make a positive diagnosis, and attempt treatment. At best, at the present stage of knowledge of nephritis, treatment may swing the condition over to the non-uremic form, and the dog may live quite comfortably with the extra care needed for this lesser condition.

Incontinence, or gradual loss of control over retention of urine, may be a problem of some older dogs, either male or female. It is most often associated with chronic nephritis, for the increased drinking and resultant larger quantities of urine put a greater strain on the retentive muscles of the bladder, and these muscles are weakened by age. In such cases very little can be done about it except to give the older dog more frequent opportunities to go outside to relieve himself. It may reach the point where the old dog is forced to urinate during the night, no matter how well housebroken he was in younger days. If there is no way he can be allowed free access to the outside, such as a swinging panel in the door of a non-urban house, it might be well to set up a system of putting papers in a box in the kitchen for the old dog. He will hate to break his house-training, but bladder pressures can overcome the strongest will and training, and if he is given papers in a box and allowed to use them in emergencies, it will make it easier for him, and of course for you.

Dribbling which occurs in spayed bitches as they get older is one of the few incontinent conditions which can be aided—sometimes this can be controlled or at least lessened by shots of hormones, and this possibility should be discussed with your vet.

Chronic severe constipation can often afflict the old dog, simply through impaired function of the intestines and abdominal muscles. If your dog has been unable to defecate, or does so only with straining and difficulty, resulting in very hard stools, try giving him a dose of Milk of Magnesia (about one teaspoonful per 10 pounds of dog). If this does not bring relief within 12 to 18 hours, suspect internal disorders and have him examined. And *do not* dose him with laxatives or cathartics intended for humans! Some of them can kill him.

In the older male, even after only six years of age, constipation is often the result of enlargement of the prostate gland. This organ, enlarged, presses against the wall of the rectum and causes a physical barrier to passage of the feces. Continual straining in such cases can cause hernia— this is one of the reasons a severe case of constipation unrelieved after two doses of milk of magnesia should receive veterinary attention. The vet may be able to correct it by administration of hormones, or in extreme cases by castration, which causes the prostate to atrophy.

The most common problem of the older unspayed female is tumor or cyst of the mammary glands. Any lump or swelling in the bitch's breasts, particularly in the rear two pair, should be looked at by a veterinarian. He may be able to control the situation by hormone injections, but in severer cases he may have to remove the growth surgically. If at the time of surgical removal (or even hormone injections) he suggests spaying the bitch, don't be surprised. Spaying will often bring cysts and tumors under complete control, and the older bitch will be able to live out a healthy life. By this time there will certainly be no question of breeding her, or worries about unbalancing her hormonal system to her detriment.

DEATH AND EUTHANASIA

When the inevitable happens, through simple old age, as a result of heart failure or as the terminal phase of any disease or condition, it most frequently occurs at night, in sleep, when the body is at its lowest ebb. You will simply find your dog in the morning, dead without pain or suffering, his good life with you over. If it happens during the day when you are with him, you may be warned by several deep, gasping breaths at intervals of several seconds—this does not indicate that there is any pain, but is simply the failing body's last automatic attempts to keep air coming into the tired lungs. It is perfectly natural.

In such cases, grim though the precaution seems at a time like this, put some newspapers or preferably an old sheet or blanket under him as soon as possible after death, for when death occurs, the tone of all the muscles relaxes, and urine or feces that are contained at the moment of death will be released. If you use a sheet or blanket, put it not only under him but over him, for this precaution is not so much a sanitary one as preservation of his dignity in death. The sheet or blanket, too, will be there to carry the body in when you remove it for burial or other disposal.

Euthanasia is the most difficult subject of all. In the absence of any specific and painful infirmities, the old dog can be the best of all companions and may enjoy his life now even more than when he was a puppy. But if he is in constant pain from some chronic condition, or crippled, or so arthritic that he cannot even walk or walks only with difficulty, it is by far the kinder thing to have him put away humanely by your vet. It is well to realize at this point that because of his inability to communicate in abstract terms, the dog has no conception of the future, or of death. He cannot anticipate days to come, and thus cannot "miss" having lived longer.

The usually recommended method of euthanasia is by injection of an overdose of barbiturates into the bloodstream. With this method, the veterinarian simply injects about twice as much anaesthetic as would have been necessary to put the dog to sleep temporarily for an operation. The dog simply does that—goes to sleep without any pain or realization, and then dies in his sleep. Do not think the vet is heartless or cruel if he asks you to sign a statement that you have authorized the euthanasia— many vets will ask this as legal protection. You will probably want to be present when the anaesthetic is administered, and it is the rare vet indeed who will not allow it. It is the last thing you can do for your dog—to allow him to go into his final sleep in your arms or by your side.

There are occasional cases in which a dog is suffering from some chronic or recurrent serious disease which allows home nursing. When the case is one in which recovery is problematical, but in which you are trying to nurse him through, there may be episodes of such severe pain that you will want to have prior arrangement with your vet as to the administration of barbiturate pills yourself. Ask the vet to give or prescribe the necessary pills, and have a thorough understanding with him as to the circumstances which warrant their administration. He may only give you enough to assure unconsciousness, with instructions to bring the dog in as soon as possible for professional administration of euthanasia if it is warranted by examination. Go along with him on whatever he recommends.

*   *   *   *   *

The death of a beloved dog is a sad note on which to end this book, but this is the natural course and end of all affairs, of man or dog. This book has been written in the hope that your dog's life will have been full, active and healthy, and that at the end he will have left you with memories of good days only.

At the death of his own favorite dog in 1808, Lord Byron wrote one of the simplest and most moving tributes ever given, inscribed on a monument by the dog's grave:

> Near this spot are deposited the remains of one who possessed Beauty without Vanity, Strength without Insolence, Courage without Ferocity, and all the Virtues of Man, without his Vices. This Praise, which would be unmeaning Flattery if inscribed over human ashes, is but a just tribute to the Memory of Boatswain, a Dog.

INDEX